AF845136

Tourism Diplomacy

Tourism Diplomacy: Insights from Economic, Environmental, and Socio-Cultural Perspectives

BY

MAHMUT DEMIR

Isparta University of Applied Sciences, Türkiye

AND

ŞIRVAN ŞEN DEMIR

Süleyman Demirel University, Türkiye

emerald PUBLISHING

United Kingdom – North America – Japan – India – Malaysia – China

Emerald Publishing Limited
Emerald Publishing, Floor 5, Northspring, 21-23 Wellington Street, Leeds LS1 4DL

First edition 2025

Copyright © 2025 Mahmut Demir and Şirvan Şen Demir.
Published under exclusive licence by Emerald Publishing Limited.

Reprints and permissions service
Contact: www.copyright.com

No part of this book may be reproduced, stored in a retrieval system, transmitted in any form or by any means electronic, mechanical, photocopying, recording or otherwise without either the prior written permission of the publisher or a licence permitting restricted copying issued in the UK by The Copyright Licensing Agency and in the USA by The Copyright Clearance Center. Any opinions expressed in the chapters are those of the authors. Whilst Emerald makes every effort to ensure the quality and accuracy of its content, Emerald makes no representation implied or otherwise, as to the chapters' suitability and application and disclaims any warranties, express or implied, to their use.

British Library Cataloguing in Publication Data
A catalogue record for this book is available from the British Library

ISBN: 978-1-83708-677-1 (Print)
ISBN: 978-1-83708-676-4 (Online)
ISBN: 978-1-83708-678-8 (Epub)

Printed and bound by CPI Group (UK) Ltd, Croydon, CR0 4YY

INVESTOR IN PEOPLE

Contents

List of Figures

Chapter 7

Chapter 8

Chapter 9

Chapter 10

About the Authors

Mahmut Demir, PhD, is a Senior Professor at the Tourism Faculty at Isparta University of Applied Sciences. He received his PhD in Tourism Management at Dokuz Eylül University in 2009 and served from 1997 as a Lecturer, Associate Professor, and Full Professor in Tourism and Travel Management at different universities such as Muğla University, Süleyman Demirel University, and Isparta University of Applied Sciences in Türkiye. He was also a Postdoc Researcher at Sheffield University in 2011 in the United Kingdom. His main research interests are tourism, travel and hospitality management, digital transformation, and innovation in tourism. His books published include *Enhancing Higher Education and Research With OpenAI Models*. IGI Global (2024), *Revolutionizing the Service Industry With OpenAI Models*. IGI Global (2024), *Handbook of Research on the Impacts and Implications of COVID-19 on the Tourism Industry*. IGI-Global (2021), *Travel Agency and Tour Operator: Principles and Management* (2017), *General Tourism: Concepts and Evaluation with Different Dimensions* (2017), *Innovation Management Principles and Examples in Hotel Businesses* (2015), and *Human Resources Management and Employee Turnover* (2002).

Şirvan Şen Demir, PhD, is a Senior Professor at the Tourism Management Department of the Faculty of Economics and Administrative Sciences at Süleyman Demirel University. She received his PhD in Tourism Management at Dokuz Eylül University in 2010 and served from 1999 as a Lecturer, Associate Professor, and Full Professor in Tourism and Hospitality Management at Muğla University and Süleyman Demirel University in Türkiye. Her main research interests are tourism and hospitality management, consumer behavior, and gastronomy and culinary arts. Her books published include *Enhancing Higher Education and Research With OpenAI Models*. IGI Global (2024), *Being a Woman in Working Life Through the Perspective of Female Academics* (2021), *General Tourism: Concepts and Evaluation with Different Dimensions* (2017), *Innovation Management Principles and Examples in Hotel Businesses* (2015), *Consumer Behavior* (2015), and *Public Relations and Communication in Tourism Businesses* (2011).

Preface

The intricate and multifaceted relationship between tourism and diplomacy represents a cornerstone of modern international relations, offering a profound lens through which nations, organizations, and communities engage globally. Beyond its economic significance, tourism is a profound mechanism for fostering dialogue, mutual understanding, and cooperation among nations. In an era defined by rapid technological advancements, shifting geopolitical environments, and an ever-deepening commitment to sustainable development, the notion of tourism diplomacy transcends its traditional boundaries, emerging as a dynamic instrument of soft power, cultural exchange, and economic strategy.

This book, encompassing 10 meticulously crafted chapters, delves into the depths of tourism diplomacy, addressing its theoretical foundations, practical applications, and the myriad challenges it faces in an interconnected world. The growing recognition of tourism diplomacy as a strategic field is grounded in its capacity to transcend traditional boundaries, creating spaces where nations, communities, and individuals engage in meaningful exchange. Each chapter brings to light the diverse dimensions of tourism as a diplomatic tool, highlighting its ability to foster mutual understanding, promote national identity, and build bridges across cultural and political divides. The topics explored within these pages provide both scholars and practitioners with invaluable insights into the evolving nature of tourism diplomacy and its potential to shape the future of international cooperation.

The opening chapter explores tourism diplomacy's definition, scope, and conceptual framework. It examines its evolution, tracing the interplay between national governments, international organizations, private sector stakeholders, and nongovernmental entities. As tourism becomes increasingly intertwined with cultural representation and identity, this chapter underscores its role in fostering bilateral relations, amplifying soft power through technology and media, and addressing geopolitical instability and sustainability concerns. This foundational discussion contextualizes the subject and paves the way for subsequent chapters. As explored in Chapter 2, soft power is at the heart of tourism diplomacy. This chapter delves into how tourism shapes global perceptions and strengthens national brands. From promoting cultural heritage and gastronomy to using digital tools, tourism emerges as a formidable soft power asset. Aligning tourism initiatives with national branding goals underscores the importance of crafting a coherent narrative that resonates across borders. At the same time, the challenges of managing perception amid crises highlight the complexity of this endeavor.

As detailed in Chapter 3, governments play a pivotal role in harnessing tourism as a diplomatic tool. Through strategic policies, investments, and diplomatic missions, governments influence the trajectory of tourism diplomacy. This chapter examines the contributions of tourism ministries, embassies, and consulates in promoting national images, fostering tourism cooperation, and addressing health and safety concerns. By emphasizing the interplay between policy and practice, this chapter provides a comprehensive understanding of the governmental dimensions of tourism diplomacy. As Chapter 4 highlights, partnerships form the backbone of effective tourism diplomacy. Whether through government-to-government collaborations, public–private partnerships, or community-based initiatives, diverse stakeholders' collective effort drives tourism diplomacy's success. This chapter offers insights into innovative models such as technology-driven partnerships and corporate social responsibility (CSR) initiatives, showcasing how collaborative approaches can enhance tourism's impact on global cooperation.

Chapter 5 delves into the cultural dimensions of tourism diplomacy, emphasizing its role in promoting cultural values, fostering intercultural dialogue, and facilitating exchange. Tourism emerges as a vehicle for tolerance, social cohesion, and the development of global citizens, while cultural heritage and culinary experiences are powerful tools for building bridges. The ethical considerations surrounding these initiatives remind us of the need for sensitivity and inclusivity in preserving and sharing cultural identities. Chapter 6 focuses on the strategic alignment of tourism with international branding. It explores how destinations, cities, tour operators, hotel chains, and airlines contribute to national and regional branding efforts. By leveraging cultural heritage, natural attractions, and strategic alliances, tourism diplomacy enhances global competitiveness and creates compelling narratives that captivate international audiences. Case studies illustrate the tangible impact of branding strategies, offering inspiration for practitioners and policymakers alike.

Chapter 7 discusses how tourism diplomacy's resilience is tested in times of crisis. This chapter examines tourism's role in addressing and overcoming global challenges, from economic recovery and environmental restoration to health crises and postconflict reconstruction. Examples of postpandemic recovery and peacebuilding initiatives underscore tourism's capacity to unite communities, rebuild economies, and foster international solidarity. This chapter serves as a testament to tourism diplomacy's adaptability and transformative power in adversity. Chapter 8 highlights the transformative impact of technology on tourism diplomacy. Digital platforms, virtual reality, artificial intelligence, and blockchain revolutionize how nations engage with global audiences. By enabling personalized and culturally sensitive experiences, these tools expand the reach of tourism diplomacy and enhance its effectiveness. However, this chapter also acknowledges the challenges of digital transformation, emphasizing the importance of ethical and sustainable innovation in navigating the complexities of the digital world.

As explored in Chapter 9, sustainability lies at the core of modern tourism diplomacy. This chapter addresses the critical issues of climate change, biodiversity conservation, pollution management, and water resource protection.

Tourism diplomacy contributes to environmental stewardship and preserving natural and cultural heritage through strategic initiatives and global cooperation. The emphasis on transboundary pollution and collaborative solutions underscores the interconnected nature of these challenges and the need for collective action. The final chapter bridges theory and practice, offering a holistic view of tourism diplomacy's objectives, strategies, and real-world applications. This chapter provides a road map for leveraging tourism for soft power, cultural exchange, economic impact, and environmental conservation by examining examples from countries, international organizations, and crisis scenarios. The forward-looking perspective on challenges and future directions ensures that this chapter serves as both a summation and a call to action.

Tourism diplomacy is a beacon of hope, offering pathways for collaboration, understanding, and shared prosperity. By synthesizing theoretical insights with practical applications, the chapters in this book illuminate tourism's transformative potential in shaping a more interconnected, harmonious, and sustainable world. For scholars, this book serves as a comprehensive resource for understanding the evolving dynamics of tourism diplomacy. For practitioners, it offers actionable strategies to harness tourism's power in advancing diplomatic objectives. And for policymakers, it provides a framework for integrating tourism into broader national and international agendas. As we navigate an increasingly complex global landscape, may this book inspire innovative approaches to tourism diplomacy and foster a renewed commitment to building bridges across cultures, nations, and communities. Let this be a testament to tourism's enduring power as a force for human good, a catalyst for peace, prosperity, and global unity.

Mahmut Demir and Şirvan Şen Demir

Chapter 1

Introduction to Tourism Diplomacy

Abstract

Tourism diplomacy has become essential for fostering international relations, cultural exchange, and economic collaboration. Rooted in a rich historical context, its evolution spans from the early practices of cultural interaction and the Grand Tours of the 17th to 19th centuries to its strategic use during the Cold War and its adaptation to the dynamics of globalization in the post-Cold War era. Modern tourism diplomacy reflects a sophisticated interplay of actors and strategies, leveraging technological advancements and media to enhance its reach and influence. Key stakeholders in tourism diplomacy include national governments, international organizations, private sector entities, and nongovernmental organizations. Each brings unique strengths to promote cultural understanding and economic benefits. Tourism serves as a platform for representing national values and identity, projecting soft power, and enhancing bilateral and multilateral relationships. Its economic aspect further underscores its potential to strengthen diplomatic ties and encourage cooperation on a global scale. Despite its considerable opportunities, tourism diplomacy faces challenges such as geopolitical tensions, environmental degradation, over-tourism, cultural erosion, and infrastructure limitations. Addressing these challenges requires innovative, sustainable approaches to ensure tourism remains an effective medium for building bridges between nations and cultures. By exploring its historical foundations, critical actors, opportunities, and challenges, the discussion underscores the transformative role of tourism diplomacy in shaping contemporary global relations and advancing sustainable international collaboration.

Keywords: Tourism diplomacy; cultural representation; soft power in tourism; globalization and tourism; sustainability in tourism diplomacy

Tourism Diplomacy, 1–20

Copyright © 2025 Mahmut Demir and Şirvan Şen Demir
Published under exclusive licence by Emerald Publishing Limited

doi:10.1108/978-1-83708-676-420251001

1. Introduction

Tourism has long been recognized as more than just an economic activity; it is a platform for cultural exchange, a tool for fostering international relationships, and a means of strengthening a nation's soft power. The concept of tourism diplomacy builds on this potential, positioning tourism as a strategic component in the global arena. It is not merely about attracting visitors but also about shaping perceptions, promoting cultural understanding, and advancing economic and political objectives. Tourism diplomacy reflects the interplay between culture, economics, and politics, demonstrating how tourism can serve as a vehicle for diplomacy and cooperation.

The evolution of tourism diplomacy spans centuries, beginning with the early examples of cultural and diplomatic exchanges through travel. The rise of the Grand Tours in the 17th to 19th centuries marked a significant shift, as elites engaged in travel for leisure, cultural enrichment, and political networking. In the 20th century, tourism became a structured industry intertwined with political ideologies during periods such as the Cold War, where it was employed to foster ideological alliances. The post-Cold War era and the onset of globalization have further expanded the scope of tourism diplomacy, with modern practices integrating technology, sustainability, and inclusivity. Today, tourism diplomacy operates as a critical component of international relations, adapting to the challenges and opportunities of an interconnected world.

The effectiveness of tourism diplomacy depends heavily on the actors involved. National governments often play a central role in designing policies and initiatives to promote cultural exchange and strengthen bilateral and multilateral relations. International organizations, such as the United Nations World Tourism Organization (UNWTO), provide frameworks for collaboration and sustainable practices. The private sector, including travel agencies, airlines, and hospitality businesses, acts as a bridge between policy and practice, while nongovernmental organizations (NGOs) advocate for ethical and inclusive tourism initiatives. Together, these actors form a complex network that drives tourism diplomacy forward.

One of the most compelling aspects of tourism diplomacy lies in its ability to create opportunities for cultural representation and economic development. Tourism allows nations to showcase their cultural heritage, traditions, and values, fostering mutual understanding and respect among diverse populations. It also serves as a powerful economic driver, enhancing a country's soft power by demonstrating its stability, innovation, and hospitality. Additionally, tourism can amplify diplomatic efforts through technology and media, enabling countries to project their narratives to global audiences and engage in more effective cultural diplomacy.

Despite its potential, tourism diplomacy faces significant challenges. Geopolitical tensions, environmental concerns, and over-tourism risks substantially hinder its success. The delicate balance between preserving cultural authenticity and catering to international markets often leads to cultural erosion, while inadequate infrastructure can hinder a destination's ability to meet growing demand. Addressing these issues requires a comprehensive approach prioritizing sustainability, inclusivity, and innovation in tourism practices.

Tourism diplomacy intersects cultural exchange, economic advancement, and international relations. It offers a unique opportunity to build bridges between nations, foster mutual respect, and address shared global challenges. As the world becomes increasingly interconnected, tourism's strategic role in diplomacy will only grow, necessitating a deeper understanding of its evolution, critical actors, and the opportunities and challenges it presents. This chapter explores these dimensions, laying the groundwork for a more integrated and impactful approach to tourism diplomacy in the 21st century.

2. Conceptual Framework of Tourism Diplomacy

Tourism diplomacy is the process by which governments, international organizations, and private entities use tourism as a diplomatic instrument to promote goodwill, improve bilateral and multilateral relationships, and enhance a nation's image globally (Demir & Alper, 2021). Unlike traditional diplomacy, which involves political negotiations and state-to-state interactions, tourism diplomacy leverages the movement of people, cultural interactions, and economic exchanges within the tourism industry to build bridges between nations. By welcoming tourists, promoting their culture abroad, and collaborating with other countries on tourism initiatives, nations engage in diplomacy in a less formal, more inclusive way.

The scope of tourism diplomacy is broad and encompasses various dimensions, such as economic, cultural, political, environmental, and crisis diplomacy (Demir, 2024):

Economic Diplomacy: Tourism contributes significantly to the global economy, creating jobs, fostering infrastructure development, and generating foreign exchange. By promoting tourism, countries can engage in economic diplomacy that enhances trade and investment relations.

Cultural Diplomacy: Tourism enables cultural exchange, allowing visitors to experience and understand the values, traditions, and lifestyles of other nations. Thus, tourism diplomacy acts as cultural diplomacy, promoting mutual respect and intercultural dialogue.

Political Diplomacy: Tourism diplomacy can also play a role in political relations. Countries often use tourism to strengthen political alliances, resolve conflicts, or showcase their stability and openness to the world. Major international events like the Olympics or World Expos serve as platforms for nations to engage diplomatically through tourism.

Environmental Diplomacy: Tourism diplomacy increasingly addresses global challenges like climate change and sustainable development. Countries can lead environmental diplomacy efforts and contribute to global environmental goals by promoting eco-friendly and sustainable tourism practices.

Crisis Diplomacy: During crises such as pandemics, natural disasters, or geopolitical tensions, tourism diplomacy can be a vital tool for recovery and international solidarity. Collaborative efforts in rebuilding the tourism industry can foster resilience and restore diplomatic ties.

The conceptual framework of tourism diplomacy revolves around its role as a soft power instrument (Li, 2019). Tourism acts as a vehicle for soft power, influencing perceptions and fostering positive international relationships. Nye's (1990) concept of soft power, which focuses on the ability to attract and co-opt rather than coerce, is central to tourism diplomacy. Countries can enhance their global standing and influence by promoting a positive national image through tourism. The actors involved in tourism diplomacy include governments, international organizations like the UNWTO, NGOs, and private sector stakeholders such as tour operators and hotel chains. Each plays a role in shaping tourism policies and initiatives that contribute to diplomatic efforts.

3. The Evolution of Tourism Diplomacy

Tourism diplomacy has grown in importance with the rise of globalization and the interconnectedness of societies. Traditionally, diplomacy was seen as a practice limited to political and economic negotiations. However, in recent decades, tourism has emerged as a powerful means of diplomacy, fostering people-to-people connections, enhancing cultural understanding, and promoting mutual respect. Tourism diplomacy, as a concept, refers to the strategic use of tourism as a tool for fostering diplomatic relations between nations (Baranowski et al., 2019; Zhu et al., 2022). It includes both formal and informal mechanisms where tourism acts as a conduit for international cooperation, cultural exchange, economic development, and soft power enhancement (Pedersen & Stanoeva, 2024; Zhu et al., 2022). Over time, tourism diplomacy has evolved significantly, shaped by historical, political, economic, and technological changes (Fig. 1).

Fig. 1. The Evolution of Tourism Diplomacy.

3.1 Early Beginnings of Tourism Diplomacy

The origins of tourism diplomacy can be traced back to ancient civilizations, where travel was a privileged activity for trade, knowledge exchange, and cultural contact (Demir, 2017). For instance, athletes, scholars, and merchants traveled extensively in ancient Greece and Rome, facilitating the early forms of diplomatic engagement. These travels were not yet categorized as tourism in the modern sense, but they laid the foundation for cross-cultural exchanges that form the backbone of tourism diplomacy today. In medieval times, pilgrimage played a significant role in tourism and diplomacy. Pilgrims traveling to religious sites created interaction networks across borders, which fostered peace and cooperation (Jalalpour & Shojaeifar, 2014; Winter, 2016). The pilgrimage routes, such as the Camino de Santiago in Spain or the Hajj to Mecca, became early examples of how tourism could promote diplomacy, albeit within a religious context.

3.2 The Rise of Grand Tours (17th–19th Century)

Tourism diplomacy began to take shape more formally in the 17th century, during the era of the Grand Tour (Baranowski et al., 2019; Jalalpour & Shojaeifar, 2014). Wealthy young Europeans, mainly from Britain, embarked on extended European journeys to gain cultural exposure and enhance their education. The Grand Tour fostered cultural diplomacy by exposing future leaders, scholars, and statesmen to different cultures, arts, and political systems (Demir, 2017). During this period, the groundwork was laid for tourism to be viewed as a tool for diplomacy and mutual understanding between nations. Simultaneously, international exhibitions and expositions emerged as platforms for nations to display their industrial, scientific, and cultural achievements. These events, such as the Great Exhibition of 1851 in London, showcased progress and symbolized unity (Becker, 2016). These promoted peace through economic and cultural collaboration. With the advent of railways and steamships, these exhibitions also marked the beginnings of organized mass tourism, making travel more accessible and fostering a sense of global community.

3.3 Tourism Diplomacy in the 20th Century

The 20th century has marked a significant turning point in the evolution of tourism diplomacy. Following the devastation of World War I and II, there was a global recognition of the need for international cooperation to prevent future conflicts (Fan, 2010; Pack, 2006). Tourism emerged as a tool to foster peace and rebuild relations between nations. Establishing the UNWTO in 1975 was a significant milestone, institutionalizing tourism as a critical element of international diplomacy.

3.4 Cold War and Tourism Diplomacy

During the Cold War, tourism played a subtle but essential role in diplomacy, particularly in cultural exchange between the Eastern and Western blocs (Herrera & Pérez-Tapia, 2024; Pedersen & Stanoeva, 2024). While political tensions were high, tourism provided soft power for both sides. People-to-people diplomacy through travel and cultural exchange programs helped to bridge the ideological divide, with international fairs and events serving as neutral grounds for cooperation and dialogue. The Moscow International Film Festival and other cultural festivals were instrumental in maintaining diplomatic contact during this period. At the same time, sports tourism became an essential element of diplomacy, with events like the Olympic Games and FIFA World Cup as platforms for nations to project their image, values, and aspirations on the global stage. The 1980 Moscow Olympics and the 1984 Los Angeles Olympics, both marred by boycotts, also highlighted the intersections of tourism, sports, and international relations.

3.5 Post-Cold War Era and Globalization

The end of the Cold War in the early 1990s, combined with rapid globalization, saw a new wave of tourism diplomacy. With the fall of ideological barriers and the rise of market economies, tourism became a significant contributor to international economic diplomacy. Countries began actively promoting themselves as tourist destinations, viewing tourism as a means to build their national image, attract investment, and foster goodwill (Baranowski et al., 2019; Yang, 2019). International fairs, exhibitions, and cultural events gained even more prominence during this time (Demir & Dalgıç, 2022). Expo 2000 in Hannover, for example, showcased global cooperation in environmental and technological innovations. Similarly, international gastronomy competitions like Bocuse d'Or and sports tournaments such as the Rugby World Cup became platforms for nations to engage diplomatically while promoting their cultural heritage. Cultural festivals, such as the Edinburgh and Cannes Film Festivals, became powerful diplomatic tools, attracting visitors and participants worldwide. These events stimulated tourism and enhanced cultural understanding and international collaboration (Demir & Dalgıç, 2022; Suntikul, 2019).

3.6 Modern-Day Tourism Diplomacy

In the 21st century, tourism diplomacy has evolved into a multifaceted tool for fostering international relations. Globalization and digital transformation have enhanced countries' interconnectedness, enabling tourism to play a more prominent role in diplomacy. Key areas of modern tourism diplomacy include cultural diplomacy, sports diplomacy, gastronomy diplomacy, and sustainable tourism.

Cultural diplomacy through tourism has expanded with the rise of international cultural festivals and exchange programs (Abuan, 2021; Winter, 2016). Festivals like the Venice Biennale, the Rio Carnival, and the Coachella Valley Music and Arts Festival attract a global audience, showcasing the cultural richness of the host nations. These events serve as platforms for soft power, allowing countries to project their culture, values, and identity to the world. Tourism boards and governments have increasingly recognized the role of these festivals in enhancing bilateral relations, leading to collaborations between nations in organizing such events (Demir & Dalgıç, 2022). For example, joint cultural festivals between France, Japan, India, and the United States highlight how tourism diplomacy can foster greater cooperation and understanding between nations.

Sports tourism has also become a vital aspect of tourism diplomacy (Leight et al., 2011). Events like the Olympic Games, FIFA World Cup, and Commonwealth Games have long been used as diplomatic platforms. Host nations view these events as opportunities to enhance their global image, attract investment, and promote international peace and unity.

Gastronomy has emerged as another powerful tool for tourism diplomacy in recent years (Demir & Alper, 2021). International gastronomy competitions like Bocuse d'Or, culinary festivals like the San Sebastián Gastronomika, and food tourism experiences are vital in cultural exchange and diplomacy. Countries increasingly use their culinary heritage to promote their identity and foster international relations. Gastronomy diplomacy often transcends traditional political boundaries, allowing for deeper connections based on shared culinary experiences (Demir & Alper, 2021). For example, UNESCO's recognition of Intangible Cultural Heritage, including culinary traditions like the Mediterranean diet or Mexican cuisine, has helped countries use food for diplomatic engagement.

Sustainable tourism has become a central theme in modern tourism diplomacy (Rozanah & Ishqila, 2024; Xu et al., 2020). With global concerns over climate change, countries are increasingly using tourism to promote environmental responsibility and cooperation. Initiatives like the UNWTO's Sustainable Development Goals (SDGs) place tourism at the heart of global efforts to combat climate change, reduce poverty, and promote peace.

4. Critical Actors in Tourism Diplomacy

Tourism diplomacy operates at the intersection of various sectors, collaborating with multiple actors to promote tourism as a tool for international relations. Each actor plays a unique and vital role in shaping how tourism contributes to diplomatic efforts, including promoting cultural understanding, economic cooperation, and political alliances. The critical actors in tourism diplomacy (Fig. 2) range from national governments and international organizations to private sector stakeholders and NGOs.

4.1 National Governments

National governments are arguably the most influential actors in tourism diplomacy. Governments set the policies and frameworks governing how tourism interacts with international relations through their ministries, foreign affairs

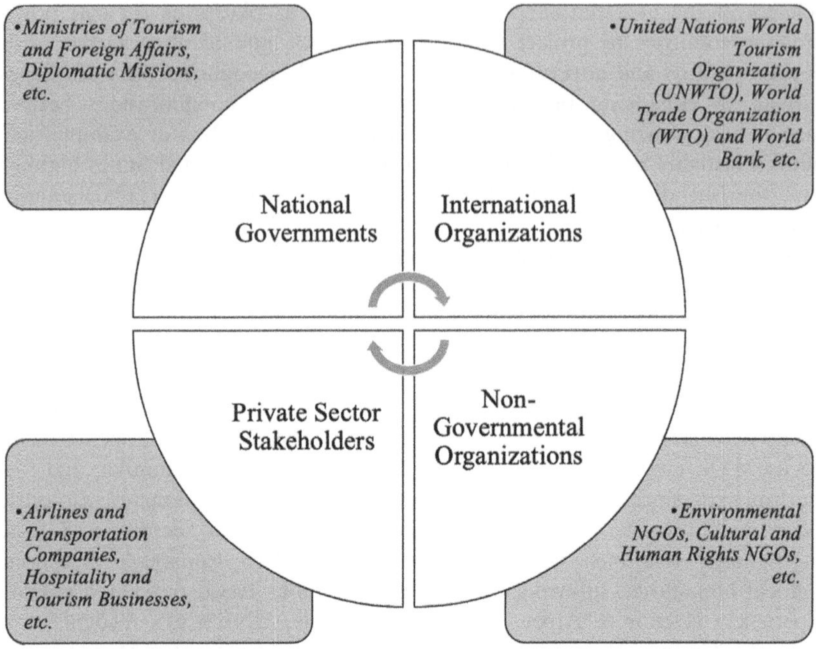

Fig. 2. The Critical Actors in Tourism Diplomacy.

departments, and diplomatic missions (Parthenis et al., 2023). Governments often view tourism as a strategic tool for promoting national interests, both economically and culturally (Zugasti, 2019). Tourism ministries are responsible for developing strategies and usually collaborate with ministries of foreign affairs to ensure that tourism aligns with broader diplomatic goals. For instance, a country might emphasize sustainable tourism to reinforce its global leadership in environmental issues or promote cultural tourism to strengthen its identity and heritage on the international stage. Countries like France, Spain, and Italy, known for their rich cultural heritages, have strategically used their tourism ministries to promote themselves as premier tourist destinations.

On the other hand, embassies and consulates are extensions of national governments abroad (Sihaloho et al., 2024) and serve as essential nodes in tourism diplomacy. They organize and support cultural events, exhibitions, and fairs that help to promote the country's tourism potential. Diplomats often engage in bilateral or multilateral negotiations to create favorable tourist conditions, such as easing visa restrictions, establishing direct flight routes, or securing tourism-related investment from foreign partners. For example, China's diplomatic missions have played a significant role in negotiating visa-free travel agreements with various countries, facilitating more accessible travel for Chinese tourists, and promoting outbound tourism as a diplomatic tool.

4.2 International Organizations

International organizations play a critical coordinating and regulatory role in tourism diplomacy (Demir, 2017). These bodies often establish global standards and frameworks that guide tourism policies across nations, ensuring that tourism remains a force for economic growth, cultural exchange, and sustainable development. The United Nations World Tourism Organization (UNWTO, 2024) is the most prominent international organization focused on tourism. It promotes tourism as a driver of sustainable development, economic growth, and cross-cultural understanding. Through its various initiatives and programs, the UNWTO encourages member states to collaborate on tourism regulation, crisis management, and environmental sustainability. For example, the organization's Global Tourism Resilience Program guides countries in rebuilding their tourism sectors following natural disasters or political crises, thereby supporting diplomatic relations.

The UNWTO also facilitates global forums and conferences where countries can share best practices, negotiate tourism-related agreements, and develop collective strategies to enhance tourism's role in international relations. By acting as a platform for dialogue, the UNWTO fosters cooperation and partnerships among its member states, thereby reinforcing tourism's diplomatic role on a global scale. While not directly tourism-focused, organizations like the World Trade Organization (WTO) and the World Bank influence tourism diplomacy through their economic development and trade initiatives (Schiavon, 2022). For instance, the WTO's agreements on trade in services have significant implications for tourism, as they affect the movement of people, goods, and services across borders. The World Bank, on the other hand, often funds tourism-related projects in developing countries, framing tourism as a tool for economic development and poverty alleviation. These initiatives contribute to diplomatic relations by promoting cooperation between donor and recipient countries, often enhancing the soft power of supporting nations.

4.3 Private Sector Stakeholders

The private sector is essential in tourism diplomacy, particularly in investment, innovation, and international collaboration (Faraji et al., 2021; Oktaviana et al., 2021). Private companies, including airlines, hotel chains, and tour operators, play a crucial role in creating and sustaining the infrastructure that supports tourism. Their activities often align with government and diplomatic efforts, especially in promoting tourism as a critical element of economic diplomacy. Airlines are pivotal in facilitating international tourism, as they connect nations and enable the movement of people across borders. Many national airlines, such as Emirates, Turkish Airlines, and Singapore Airlines, have become symbols of their countries' global reach and ambitions. These airlines often work closely with governments to promote their destinations through advertising campaigns, sponsorships, and joint marketing initiatives. National carriers also serve as diplomatic tools themselves. For instance, Qatar Airways and Emirates have been used to project their home countries' images of wealth, innovation, and global connectivity. Tour operators and airlines directly shape diplomatic relationships between countries by opening new routes and expanding tourism opportunities, often fostering closer economic ties. Major hotel chains and tour operators also contribute significantly to tourism diplomacy. Companies like Marriott, Hilton, and TUI Group operate across numerous countries, providing vital infrastructure for international tourism. These businesses engage in diplomacy by fostering relationships with local governments, investing in tourism development projects, and participating in public–private partnerships.

4.4 Nongovernmental Organizations

NGOs are increasingly crucial in tourism diplomacy, especially in promoting sustainability, human rights, and community development (Pedersen & Stanoeva, 2024; Xu et al., 2020). Environmental NGOs are critical in tourism diplomacy, as they help countries develop tourism policies that protect natural resources while fostering eco-friendly travel (Zhu et al., 2022). By advocating for responsible tourism, environmental NGOs contribute to the positive image and soft power of nations prioritizing sustainability, such as Costa Rica or Bhutan, giving the audience hope for the future of tourism. Cultural NGOs, like UNESCO, and human rights organizations also significantly impact tourism diplomacy (Suntikul, 2019; Winter, 2016). UNESCO, in particular, is instrumental in preserving and promoting cultural heritage sites globally, which enhances a country's ability to attract tourists and strengthens its cultural diplomacy. Human rights–focused NGOs ensure that tourism benefits local communities and upholds ethical standards, supporting equitable and inclusive tourism development.

5. The Importance and Opportunities of Tourism Diplomacy

Tourism diplomacy is a powerful tool for fostering international relations, cultural exchange, and economic development in an increasingly interconnected world. By leveraging tourism's unique assets, countries can not only enhance their global standing but also create a myriad of opportunities that benefit both their citizens and international communities. In tourism diplomacy, soft power plays a pivotal role as nations seek to build positive images, influence international opinion, and strengthen relationships through tourism's cultural, social, and economic exchange. Tourism has become one of the most effective channels for projecting soft power. It allows countries to showcase their culture, values, and way of life to a global audience. Unlike hard power, often associated with military or economic coercion, soft power relies on persuasion and the ability to inspire admiration (Şen, 2019). Tourism enables this by offering immersive experiences that create emotional connections between people from different countries.

5.1 Tourism as a Platform for Cultural Representation

Tourism diplomacy employs soft power; one of the most direct ways is through cultural representation (Demir & Dalgıç, 2022). Tourism allows for the exchange of cultures, ideas, and values, which can lead to greater understanding between nations. Through tourism diplomacy, countries can share their traditions, arts, languages, and lifestyles with the world, fostering intercultural dialogue and reducing conflicts. Cultural exchange is a fundamental aspect of tourism diplomacy, serving as a bridge between nations and promoting mutual understanding through shared experiences. When people travel, they not only visit new places but also engage with different cultures, traditions, and histories (Demir & Dalgıç, 2022). Tourism diplomacy harnesses this potential by promoting international cultural exchanges, which contribute to diplomatic relations, strengthen soft power, and enhance mutual respect among nations.

Governments often encourage these cultural exchanges through bilateral agreements, sister-city partnerships, or cultural events designed to unite people from other countries. Tourism diplomacy facilitates these exchanges by promoting cultural festivals, art exhibitions, and educational programs. For example, the "Visit China Year" campaigns and similar initiatives by countries like Japan and France are designed to showcase the nation's cultural heritage to international tourists. These efforts not only boost tourism revenues but also promote a deeper understanding of the host country's traditions and values, which contributes to improving diplomatic relations. Cultural exchange through tourism also is a powerful tool for promoting national identity and preserving cultural heritage. Countries use tourism diplomacy to highlight unique cultural aspects, such as historical landmarks, cuisine, art, and traditional practices, to differentiate themselves in the global tourism market.

This process is evident in countries like Italy, Mexico, and India, which emphasize their rich cultural histories as part of their tourism diplomacy strategies. Promoting UNESCO World Heritage sites, for example, not only attracts tourists but also affirms the country's commitment to preserving and sharing its cultural heritage (Suntikul, 2019; Winter, 2016). Egypt's pyramids, China's Great Wall, and Italy's ancient Roman ruins symbolize national pride and identity. By promoting such heritage, nations enhance their international standing and influence. Moreover, modern tourism diplomacy leverages festivals, exhibitions, and performances to boost soft power (Demir & Dalgıç, 2022). Programs such as cultural exchange scholarships, youth exchanges, and language courses create long-term connections between countries by allowing participants to experience each other's cultures firsthand. Multilateral organizations like the United Nations Educational, Scientific and Cultural Organization (UNESCO) are critical in facilitating these cultural exchanges. For instance, UNESCO's World Heritage programs encourage countries to collaborate on preserving cultural sites, thereby strengthening international cooperation.

5.2 Promoting Values and Identity Through Tourism

In addition to cultural expression, tourism provides an essential channel for nations to promote their values and national identity globally. Tourists visiting a country engage in its social and political environment, which can lead to a deeper understanding of that nation's core values. For instance, Scandinavian countries like Norway and Sweden use tourism to promote their commitment to sustainability, equality, and social welfare. Their clean cities, renewable energy sources, and inclusive societies are showcased as part of the tourist experience, enhancing their global image as progressive and responsible nations. Similarly, countries with strong religious or ideological identities, such as Saudi Arabia or India, use tourism as a soft power tool by promoting spiritual or religious tourism. The Hajj pilgrimage in Saudi Arabia attracts millions of Muslims annually, strengthening the country's status as a spiritual center in the Islamic world. India promotes itself as the birthplace of major religions like Hinduism, Buddhism, and Sikhism, using pilgrimage tourism to project its image as a spiritual and culturally diverse nation. Tourism diplomacy also allows countries to promote inclusivity and tolerance as part of their national identity (Baranowski et al., 2019; Suntikul, 2019). Countries like Canada and New Zealand have built their tourism industries around themes of multiculturalism and respect for indigenous peoples. These values are embedded in their tourism offerings, from indigenous-led tours to multicultural festivals. This type of tourism strengthens its soft power by presenting these nations as progressive, peaceful, and welcoming to all visitors.

5.3 The Economic Dimension of Tourism Diplomacy and Soft Power

Tourism diplomacy is not just about enhancing cultural ties but also about driving economic growth (Xu et al., 2020; Ye et al., 2020). It is crucial in advancing economic growth by fostering international cooperation, promoting investment, and facilitating the exchange of resources and knowledge across borders. More than just a driver of economic development, tourism diplomacy plays a significant role in promoting cultural understanding and appreciation. As countries strive to enhance their global presence, tourism has emerged as a vital driver of economic development, particularly for nations with rich cultural heritage, natural attractions, or a strong services sector. Countries actively engaging in tourism diplomacy tend to see increases in foreign direct investment, international partnerships, and economic collaboration (Demir & Alper, 2021; Pedersen & Stanoeva, 2024). Tourism often acts as a gateway to fostering other industries, such as real estate, retail, and education. Tourism's multiplier effect on local economies further highlights its role in diplomacy, particularly in developing countries where tourism significantly contributes to GDP.

Promoting Foreign Direct Investment (FDI) through Tourism Diplomacy: One of the critical ways tourism diplomacy stimulates economic growth is by attracting foreign direct investment (FDI) (Okafor et al., 2021). National governments often use tourism promotion campaigns, international fairs, and diplomatic missions to showcase the potential of their tourism sectors to foreign investors. By highlighting the profitability of tourism-related ventures such as resorts, transportation, and infrastructure projects, countries can draw significant investment that contributes to both short-term and long-term economic development. By leveraging tourism to highlight economic achievements, countries can enhance their soft power and influence international perceptions (Minardi et al., 2021). Countries that excel in specific industries – such as Switzerland in banking or Japan in technology – often use tourism to showcase their prowess in these fields. Countries like the United Arab Emirates and Indonesia have effectively used tourism diplomacy to attract FDI in their hospitality and infrastructure sectors. Dubai, for instance, has positioned itself as a luxury tourism destination through high-profile global events and diplomatic partnerships, drawing billions in FDI to support the construction of hotels, shopping centers, and leisure attractions.

Facilitating Trade and International Partnerships: Tourism diplomacy creates trade and international partnership opportunities by fostering connections between countries, businesses, and individuals (Minardi et al., 2021). As governments promote tourism, they create networks that open avenues for exporting goods and services, developing joint ventures, and collaborating on infrastructure projects. Countries like Singapore and Japan have successfully integrated tourism diplomacy into their broader trade and economic strategies. By hosting international events and conferences, they draw attention to their economies and industries, paving the way for bilateral and multilateral trade agreements contributing to economic growth.

Boosting Local Economies and Employment: At the local level, tourism diplomacy generates economic growth by increasing employment, supporting small businesses, and fostering regional development (Demir, 2017; Salman, 2023). As tourism expands through international diplomatic efforts, local economies benefit from increased demand for services such as accommodations, restaurants, transportation, and entertainment. Countries like Turkey, Spain, and Thailand have successfully used tourism diplomacy to support their local economies by promoting their cultural heritage, natural beauty, and unique experiences on the global stage. These countries attract millions of tourists annually, whose spending directly contributes to local businesses and drives regional economic development.

5.4 Enhancing Bilateral Relations Through Tourism

Tourism can also be a diplomatic tool for fostering bilateral relations between countries, particularly in strengthening ties between governments and their populations. Soft power is critical in these interactions, as tourism helps create goodwill and mutual understanding between nations (Şen, 2019). For instance, visa-free travel agreements or tourism partnerships between nations can signal a deepening of diplomatic ties. Such contracts often reflect the desire to build strong bilateral relationships, encouraging more frequent exchanges of people and ideas. China's Belt and Road Initiative (BRI) offers a prime example of how tourism can enhance diplomatic relations (Lee, 2020; Ye et al., 2020). As part of its BRI strategy, China has actively promoted cultural and educational exchanges through tourism, especially with Southeast Asia, Central Asia, and African countries. China strengthens its influence and soft power in partner countries by investing in tourism infrastructure and fostering tourism flows to these regions. These relationships are often reinforced through joint tourism projects, promotional campaigns, and cultural festivals highlighting Chinese culture and values.

Similarly, tourism is a strategic tool for resolving tensions or building bridges between countries with strained diplomatic relations (Demir & Alper, 2021). Sports tourism, for instance, has often played a mediating role. When South Korea hosted the 2018 Winter Olympics in Pyeongchang, athletes from North Korea participated despite the ongoing political tensions between the two nations. This engagement, though brief, contributed to diplomatic rapprochement, demonstrating how tourism, in the form of sports diplomacy, can help reduce hostilities and create opportunities for dialogue.

5.5 Technology and Media for the Amplification of Soft Power in Tourism

In the digital age, technology and media have amplified the role of soft power in tourism diplomacy (Yang, 2019; Zugasti, 2019). Social media platforms like Instagram, Facebook, and TikTok have enabled countries to project their tourism appeal instantly to global audiences. However, the influencers, travel bloggers, and digital nomads genuinely wield the power, shaping a country's image by sharing their travel experiences with millions of followers, amplifying the nation's soft power. Countries like Iceland and New Zealand have not just harnessed digital tourism campaigns; they have excelled in them, enhancing their soft power to a remarkable degree. Iceland's "Inspired by Iceland" campaign (Pálsdóttir, 2016), which uses social media influencers to promote the country's natural beauty, has attracted tourists and projected an image of environmental stewardship and adventure. Similarly, New Zealand's use of cinematic environments – notably in the "Lord of the Rings" films – has not just bolstered its soft power but also inspired others by associating the country with fantasy, wonder, and pristine nature. In this way, technology has become a critical tool for amplifying soft power in tourism diplomacy, enabling countries to reach broader and more diverse audiences than ever before.

6. Challenges in Tourism Diplomacy

Despite its positive aspects, using tourism as a diplomatic tool can present challenges. Political instability, conflicts, and environmental crises can hinder the effectiveness of tourism diplomacy (Jalalpour & Shojaeifar, 2014; Zhu et al., 2022). Overtourism and its impact on cultural heritage, ecosystems, and local communities also pose significant challenges. Furthermore, diplomatic tensions between countries can affect tourism flows, such as when governments impose travel restrictions or issue advisories (Demir, 2017). These obstacles range from geopolitical tensions and environmental concerns to over-tourism and inadequate infrastructure. Understanding these challenges is critical for effectively leveraging tourism as a diplomatic tool.

6.1 Geopolitical Tensions and Instability

One of the most significant challenges in tourism diplomacy is managing geopolitical tensions and political instability (Huang & Liu, 2024). Diplomatic relations between countries can be strained by territorial disputes, economic sanctions, or conflicts affecting tourism flows. For example, travel bans, visa restrictions, or negative travel advisories issued by governments can severely limit citizens' ability to visit certain countries, thereby hindering the exchange of cultural and economic benefits. Political instability in a tourist destination also discourages international visitors, regardless of diplomatic efforts to attract them (Demir & Alper, 2021). Countries like Egypt, which relies heavily on tourism, have faced significant drops in visitor numbers during periods of political upheaval despite their efforts in tourism diplomacy. Ensuring stable and peaceful international relations is essential for tourism diplomacy to thrive, yet it remains challenging in a world of shifting political alliances and conflicts.

6.2 Environmental and Sustainability Concerns

The environmental impact of tourism presents another challenge for tourism diplomacy, especially in an era of increasing awareness about climate change and sustainable development (Timothy & Gelbman, 2022). While tourism can promote conservation and understanding of natural and cultural heritage, it can also lead to environmental degradation if not appropriately managed. Over-tourism, deforestation, pollution, and the depletion of natural resources are significant concerns, particularly in ecologically sensitive destinations. Countries that depend on tourism often face the challenge of balancing economic growth with environmental sustainability. Tourism diplomacy initiatives may promote these destinations internationally. Still, if the influx of visitors is within the region's capacity to handle it sustainably, the negative environmental impacts can erode the assets that attract tourists.

6.3 Over-Tourism and Cultural Erosion

Over-tourism, where too many visitors overwhelm a destination, is a growing concern in popular locations like Venice, Barcelona, and Bali. The strain on local infrastructure, increased costs of living, and disruption of local communities can lead to resentment among residents. In such cases, tourism diplomacy efforts aimed at promoting these destinations can backfire if the benefits of tourism are perceived to be outweighed by its harmful effects. Over-tourism can lead to cultural erosion, where the influx of foreign visitors dilutes local traditions and practices (Baranowski et al., 2019; Pedersen & Stanoeva, 2024). Commercializing culture for tourist consumption can result in the loss of authenticity, leading to cultural heritage degradation. Countries must navigate this challenge carefully, ensuring that tourism diplomacy promotes cultural exchange without undermining the integrity of local communities and traditions.

6.4 Inadequate Infrastructure and Capacity Issues

Tourism diplomacy is most effective when countries have the necessary infrastructure to support an influx of international visitors (Abuan, 2021). However, in many developing nations, inadequate transportation systems, insufficient accommodation, and poor connectivity can hinder tourism growth, even when diplomatic efforts successfully attract tourists. For example, countries like Cambodia and Myanmar have rich cultural and historical offerings but often need help with infrastructure limitations that impact the visitor experience.

7. Conclusion

Tourism diplomacy, a key player in fostering peace, understanding, and cooperation among nations, is increasingly recognized for its role in fostering global connections, promoting cultural exchange, and stimulating economic growth. In the interconnected and dynamic world of the 21st century, nations understand that tourism is more than just a leisure industry – it is a potent diplomatic instrument capable of influencing international relations, enhancing soft power, and addressing critical global issues. The complex interplay between tourism and diplomacy highlights the sector's potential to profoundly shape the global geopolitical environment. At the heart of tourism diplomacy lies the concept of cultural exchange. Tourism enables countries to project their cultural identity and values to the world, helping them engage in meaningful interactions with foreign visitors and fostering cross-cultural understanding. This exchange promotes mutual respect and appreciation, which are the foundations of successful diplomatic relations. As people travel and experience different cultures, they become more open to diverse perspectives, reducing stereotypes and prejudices that can strain international relations. In this way, tourism serves as a bridge that connects people across borders, helping to forge stronger bonds of cooperation and friendship.

Moreover, tourism diplomacy is intricately linked to the notion of soft power. Nations that effectively use tourism to enhance their global image, promote their cultural heritage, and showcase their values can strengthen their international standing. Soft power is a subtle yet effective tool in diplomacy, allowing countries to influence others without force or coercion. Through tourism, nations can project an image of openness, inclusivity, and innovation, positively impacting their diplomatic relations with other countries. Events such as international festivals, sporting events, and cultural exhibitions serve as platforms where nations can display their achievements, engage in dialogue, and build relationships that transcend political boundaries. The economic benefits of tourism diplomacy are undeniable. Tourism, a significant driver of economic growth, significantly contributes to the GDP of many countries, especially those that rely heavily on tourism as a key industry. Through diplomatic efforts, countries can attract foreign direct investment (FDI) in their tourism sectors, facilitate trade, and create job opportunities for local populations. This economic interdependence fosters stronger diplomatic ties as countries recognize the mutual benefits that tourism can bring. In addition, tourism diplomacy opens the door to bilateral and multilateral agreements that further enhance economic cooperation between nations, leading to long-term sustainable development.

However, the practice of tourism diplomacy has its challenges. Geopolitical tensions, environmental concerns, and the pressures of over-tourism present significant obstacles to the success of tourism as a diplomatic tool. In addressing these challenges, nations must adopt sustainable tourism practices that prioritize environmental protection and local community well-being while promoting cross-border cooperation. This underscores the need for sustainable practices in tourism diplomacy. Sustainability, in particular, has become a central concern for the future of tourism diplomacy. As the world grapples with the impacts of climate change, tourism must evolve to ensure that it does not contribute to environmental harm. Nations are increasingly looking at ways to make tourism more sustainable, from adopting eco-friendly practices in the hospitality industry to promoting responsible travel that minimizes the carbon footprint. This shift toward sustainable tourism is essential not only for preserving natural resources but also for enhancing the diplomatic appeal of countries that are seen as leaders in environmental stewardship. Tourism diplomacy, in this context, can serve as a platform for promoting global cooperation on climate change and sustainability issues, further cementing its role in addressing some of the world's most pressing challenges today.

In addition to environmental sustainability, the rise of technology is also reshaping tourism diplomacy. The digital transformation of the tourism sector has opened new avenues for diplomatic engagement, allowing countries to reach global audiences more efficiently and effectively. Through digital marketing, social media, and virtual tourism experiences, nations can promote their destinations to a broader audience, engaging potential visitors worldwide. Moreover, digital tools can facilitate the creation of virtual cultural exchange programs, enabling people to engage in cross-cultural experiences without the need for physical travel. This digital shift is not just a trend but a necessity that presents both opportunities and challenges for tourism diplomacy as nations must navigate the complexities of digital privacy, cybersecurity, and the digital divide between developed and developing countries. Another critical aspect of tourism diplomacy is the role of governments and public–private partnerships in facilitating its success. Governments play a key role in creating policies and frameworks that promote tourism as a diplomatic tool, while the private sector provides the infrastructure and services necessary to sustain the industry. Collaboration between public and private entities is crucial for ensuring that tourism development aligns with both diplomatic objectives and sustainable practices. By working together, governments and businesses can create a tourism ecosystem that not only drives economic growth but also fosters positive international relations, underscoring the importance of their collaboration.

Tourism diplomacy also plays a significant role in crisis management, particularly during global challenges such as pandemics, natural disasters, and political instability. The COVID-19 pandemic, for example, highlighted the vulnerability of the tourism sector and its critical importance to many economies. In response, many nations turned to tourism diplomacy to coordinate recovery efforts, rebuild trust among travelers, and restore confidence in international travel. The ability of tourism diplomacy to facilitate cooperation and solidarity during times of crisis underscores its value as a tool for resilience and recovery in the face of global challenges. Looking to the future, the potential of tourism diplomacy is immense. Emerging trends such as space tourism, digital nomadism, and the rise of experiential travel offer new opportunities for nations to engage in diplomatic relations through tourism. As technology continues to advance, the boundaries of tourism will expand, providing innovative ways for nations to showcase their cultural heritage, strengthen their soft power, and engage with the global community. At the same time, the growing focus on sustainability and responsible tourism will not only shape but also ensure the future of tourism diplomacy as nations work together to ensure that tourism remains a force for good in the world.

Tourism diplomacy is a multifaceted and dynamic tool crucial in shaping international relations. Tourism diplomacy can create a more peaceful, interconnected, and prosperous world by promoting cultural exchange, enhancing soft power, driving economic growth, and addressing global challenges. As the worldwide tourism environment continues to evolve, nations that harness the power of tourism diplomacy will be better positioned to navigate the complexities of the international arena and foster positive relationships with the global community. The future of tourism diplomacy is bright, and its importance in global affairs will only continue to grow in the years to come.

References

Abuan, R. E. M. (2021). Cultural diplomacy of Thailand and Indonesia in the Philippines. *MJIR | Malaysian Journal of International Relations*, *9*(1), 88–104.

Baranowski, S., Covert, L. P., Gordon, B. M., Jobs, R. I., Noack, C., Rosenbaum, A. T., & Scott, B. C. (2019). Discussion: Tourism and diplomacy. *Journal of Tourism History*, *11*(1), 63–90.

Becker, E. (2016). *Overbooked: The exploding business of travel and tourism*. Simon and Schuster.

Demir, M. (2017). *Seyahat Acentacılığı ve Tur Operatörlüğü: İlkeler ve Yönetim*. Detay Yayıncılık.

Demir, M. (2024). *Genel turizm: kavramlar ve farklı boyutlarıyla değerlendirme*. Detay Yayıncılık.

Demir, M., & Alper, P. (2021). G20 summit menus as a means of gastrodiplomacy: Messages to the world via menus. *International Journal of Gastronomy and Food Science*, *25*, 1–8.

Demir, M., & Dalgıç, A. (2022). Examining gastronomy festivals as the attractiveness factor for tourism destinations: The case of Turkey. *Journal of Convention & Event Tourism*, *23*, 412–434. https://doi.org/10.1080/15470148.2022.2089797

Fan, S. P. (2010). The effects of China's tourism diplomacy and a "united front". *China: An International Journal*, *8*(02), 247–281.

Faraji, A., Khodadadi, M., Nematpour, M., Abidizadegan, S., & Yazdani, H. R. (2021). Investigating the positive role of urban tourism in creating sustainable revenue opportunities in the municipalities of large-scale cities: The case of Iran. *International Journal of Tourism Cities*, *7*(1), 177–199.

Herrera, J. L. Q., & Pérez-Tapia, G. (2024). Tourism as a driver of soft power: The case of South Korea. In J. Chica-Olmo, M. Vujičić, R. A. Castanho, U. Stankov, & E. Martinelli (Eds.), *Sustainable tourism, culture and heritage promotion: Development, management and connectivity* (pp. 221–228). Springer.

Huang, Y., & Liu, Y. (2024). A critical reflection on tourism geopolitics: Research progress and future agenda. *Tourism Geographies*, 1–17.

Jalalpour, S., & Shojaeifar, J. (2014). The tourism industry and the international relations. *World Journal of Environmental Biosciences*, *6*, 68–72.

Lee, L. T. (2020). *Chinese people's diplomacy and developmental relations with East Asia: Trends in the Xi Jinping era*. Routledge.

Leight, N., Chan, R., & Krasnodebska, M. (2011). PDiN Quarterly–Trends in public diplomacy: June, July and August 2011. *Place Branding and Public Diplomacy*, *7*, 299–315.

Li, F. (2019). Tourism diplomacy: Levels, attributes and functions. *Tourism Tribune*, *34*(3), 113–124.

Minardi, A., Afriantari, R., & Hasanah, N. U. (2021). Indonesian tourism diplomacy to India. *Indonesian Tourism Diplomacy to India*, *1*(1), 1–13.

Nye, J. S. (1990). Soft power. *Foreign policy*, 80, 153–171.

Okafor, L. E., Tan, C. M., & Khalid, U. (2021). Does panda diplomacy promote Chinese outbound tourism flows? *Journal of Hospitality and Tourism Management*, *49*, 54–64.

Oktaviana, R. F., Muhammad, A. S., Kurnianingsih, F., & Mahadiansar, M. (2021). Internal condition analysis on tourism development of Bintan Regency 2019. *Indonesian Journal of Tourism and Leisure*, *2*(1), 51–61.

Pack, S. D. (2006). Tourism and international engagement, 1945–1957. In S. D. Pack (Ed.), *Tourism and dictatorship: Europe's peaceful invasion of Franco's Spain* (pp. 39–56). Palgrave Macmillan US.

Pálsdóttir, I. H. (2016). Promoting Iceland: The shift from nature to people's power. *Place Branding and Public Diplomacy*, *12*, 210–217.

Parthenis, S., Moira, P., & Mylonopoulos, D. (2023). Blurring the lines: Governance and management in the promotion of religious and spiritual sites. In D. Bozonelos & P. Moira (Eds.), *The politics of religious tourism* (pp. 84–104). CABI.

Pedersen, S. B., & Stanoeva, E. (2024). Tourism diplomacy in cold war Europe: Symbolic gestures, cultural exchange and human rights. *Contemporary European History*, 1–17.

Rozanah, A., & Ishqila, N. A. (2024). The influence of public diplomacy in G20 2022 summit in Indonesia's post-pandemic tourism and ecotourism recovery efforts. *Journal of Social Political Sciences*, *5*(1), 45–56.

Salman, Y. (2023). Tourism and classic diplomacy: The case of strengthening Israeli–Tanzanian bilateral relations. *Tourism Review International*, *27*(2), 125–139.

Schiavon, J. A. (2022). Mexican foreign policy. In *Oxford research encyclopedia of international studies*. https://doi.org/10.1093/acrefore/9780190846626.013.684

Şen, O. (2019). Targeted soft power in Turkish new foreign policy and its impact on origins of in-bound tourists. *Journal of Tourism Theory and Research*, *5*(1), 65–74.

Sihaloho, R. A. H., Prabowo, T. B., & Pamungkas, C. (2024). China's belt and road initiative implementation maneuvers in the South Pacific region. *Nation State: Journal of International Studies*, *7*(1), 53–70.

Suntikul, W. (2019). Gastrodiplomacy in tourism. *Current Issues in Tourism*, *22*(9), 1076–1094.

Timothy, D. J., & Gelbman, A. (2022). *Routledge handbook of borders and tourism*. Taylor & Francis.

UNWTO. (2024). *UN Tourism*. https://www.unwto.org. Accessed October 14, 2024.

Winter, T. (2016). Heritage diplomacy and tourism in Asia. In C. Michael Hall & S. J. Page (Eds.), *The Routledge handbook of tourism in Asia* (pp. 45–53). Routledge.

Xu, H., Wang, K., & Song, Y. M. (2020). Chinese outbound tourism and soft power. *Journal of Policy Research in Tourism, Leisure and Events*, *12*(1), 34–49.

Yang, J. (2019). *Analysing the effects of international tourism on soft power*. University of San Diego.

Ye, F., Park, J., Li, C., & He, Y. (2020). The relationship between China-South Pacific island countries tourism and trade in the context of the belt and road initiative. *Island Studies Journal*, *15*(2), 73–92.

Zhu, J., Siriphon, A., Airey, D., & Mei-Lan, J. (2022). Chinese tourism diplomacy: A chinese–style modernity review. *Anatolia*, *33*(4), 550–563.

Zugasti, J. E. S. (2019). Casa México: Promotion, innovation and cultural diplomacy in South by Southwest (SXSW). *Revista Mexicana de Política Exterior*, (117), 85–98.

Chapter 2

Soft Power and Tourism: Global Image Management

Abstract

Tourism is vital to international relations because it is a powerful tool for shaping global perceptions and projecting soft power. By encouraging cultural exchange and enhancing national identity, tourism allows countries to create and maintain a positive global image. This process entails utilizing cultural heritage, culinary tourism, natural environments, and digital campaigns as strategic instruments for soft power diplomacy. Incorporating tourism into national branding strategies amplifies its capacity to align global perception with a country's identity and diplomatic objectives. The interplay between tourism diplomacy and international perception management highlights tourism's capacity to influence how nations are viewed globally. Countries can create lasting impressions that resonate with global audiences by hosting cultural festivals, promoting ecotourism, and showcasing gastronomic traditions. However, challenges such as geopolitical tensions, cultural misrepresentation, and sustainability concerns complicate efforts to manage perceptions effectively. Navigating these complexities requires innovative approaches that balance national interests with global expectations. Tourism also bridges national branding and soft power, positioning itself as a strategic tool to enhance bilateral and multilateral relations. Countries can amplify their influence and strengthen international partnerships by aligning tourism initiatives with broader national branding objectives. As digital technologies and virtual platforms continue to transform global communication, the future of tourism diplomacy lies in its ability to adapt to emerging trends while maintaining its foundational role in cultural and perception management.

Keywords: Soft power; global perception management; national branding; tourism diplomacy; cultural exchange

Tourism Diplomacy, 21–41

Copyright © 2025 Mahmut Demir and Şirvan Şen Demir
Published under exclusive licence by Emerald Publishing Limited

doi:10.1108/978-1-83708-676-420251002

1. Introduction

In the interconnected world of the 21st century, the ability of nations to influence global perceptions through soft power has emerged as a crucial component of international relations; unlike hard power, which relies on coercion and force, soft power leverages cultural appeal, shared values, and diplomacy to shape the preferences and attitudes of global audiences. As a dynamic and multidimensional sector, tourism has become indispensable for projecting soft power and managing a nation's global image. Through carefully curated experiences, tourism fosters cultural interaction, promotes national identity, and facilitates mutual understanding among diverse societies.

Tourism's role in global image management is deeply intertwined with its capacity to build and project national identity. By showcasing the unique cultural heritage, gastronomic traditions, natural environments, and vibrant festivals, countries craft narratives that resonate with international visitors and enhance their global standing. These cultural exchanges also serve a diplomatic function, strengthening bilateral and multilateral relationships. Geopolitical tensions, environmental concerns, cultural homogenization, and misrepresentation pose significant hurdles, demanding innovative and context-sensitive strategies.

A pivotal aspect of tourism diplomacy is its influence on international perception management. Tourism offers a platform for nations to craft and sustain a positive global image, utilizing storytelling and experiences to communicate values, strengths, and aspirations. From grand cultural exhibitions to digital tourism campaigns, the tools and strategies employed in tourism diplomacy are evolving rapidly. Yet, the effectiveness of these initiatives often hinges on the ability to navigate complex global challenges, including misinformation and the impacts of global crises.

The relationship between national branding and tourism further highlights the strategic significance of this sector. As countries increasingly incorporate tourism into their branding efforts, they aim to align their global image with long-term economic, cultural, and diplomatic objectives. When executed effectively, national branding elevates tourism's potential to bridge cultural divides and promote sustainable development. This alignment of goals underscores tourism's role not just as a facilitator of economic growth but as a bridge to understanding and collaboration.

Soft power strategies in tourism diplomacy encompass various tools, each tailored to amplify a country's cultural and natural assets. Cultural heritage sites, culinary traditions, ecotourism destinations, and cultural events are potent mediums to engage international audiences. In addition, the digital revolution has expanded the reach of tourism diplomacy, enabling countries to connect with global audiences through virtual tours, social media campaigns, and immersive technologies. These digital advancements not only democratize access to cultural experiences but also ensure that tourism remains relevant in an increasingly digitalized world.

As nations strive to project their identities and values globally, tourism diplomacy is vital for fostering cultural understanding, enhancing international cooperation, and strengthening soft power. Strategically integrating tourism into global image management efforts highlights its importance as a multidimensional tool for shaping perceptions, promoting national branding, and addressing global challenges. Exploring these themes underscores tourism's transformative potential in a world where cultural connection and mutual respect are essential for sustainable progress.

2. Soft Power and Cultural Interaction

In the modern era of diplomacy, soft power has emerged as a vital tool for countries to project influence and shape global perceptions through non-coercive means (Nye, 1990). Among the various facets of soft power, cultural interaction is one of the most effective ways for nations to foster goodwill, build relationships, and enhance their global standing. In tourism diplomacy, soft power is exercised by promoting cultural values, heritage, and national identity to attract foreign tourists and create a positive image of the country (Herrera & Pérez-Tapia, 2024). By fostering cross-border travel and cultural exchanges, tourism serves as a platform for countries to showcase their uniqueness and strengths, enhancing their global appeal.

Tourism diplomacy is crucial in promoting a nation's culture, history, and traditions to a global audience (Iwabuchi, 2018; Nye, 1990; Rehman et al., 2023). The resulting cultural exchange not only deepens understanding and appreciation of different ways of life but also serves as a potent tool for enhancing soft power. By breaking down barriers and fostering lasting connections between people of different nations, tourism diplomacy becomes essential for countries to strengthen international relationships and build a positive national identity. Cultural interaction is at the core of tourism diplomacy (Xu et al., 2020; Yang, 2019). When people travel, they engage with the destination country's culture, language, and customs. These interactions are personal experiences and crucial elements of soft power. Cultural exchange fosters empathy, breaks stereotypes, and builds trust between nations. It allows countries to project their values and ideals in a way that resonates with international audiences, thereby enhancing their soft power (Rehman et al., 2023; Şen, 2019).

Cultural interaction occurs in various forms in tourism diplomacy. For instance, heritage tourism, where visitors explore historical sites and cultural landmarks, offers a direct way for nations to showcase their cultural richness. Events such as festivals, exhibitions, and international cultural celebrations allow countries to display their traditions and artistic achievements, engaging tourists and fostering goodwill. This form of diplomacy extends beyond formal political channels, allowing countries to communicate directly with foreign populations (Wüst & Nicolai, 2023; Xu et al., 2020). For example, countries like Japan, France, and Italy have successfully used tourism to enhance their soft power by promoting their cultural heritage, cuisine, and artistic traditions. Japan's global appeal as a destination for its unique blend of traditional and modern culture, France's reputation as the center of art and fashion, and Italy's cultural legacy in architecture and cuisine are all examples of how tourism strengthens cultural interaction and soft power. These nations leverage tourism to maintain a positive global image and foster international cooperation.

3. The Role of Tourism in Global Image Management

Tourism has long been a critical driver of global interactions, offering countries an avenue to present themselves to the world. It becomes a significant tool for global image management, where countries strategically use tourism to shape perceptions, foster diplomacy, and strengthen their international presence. This intersection of tourism and diplomacy, often called "tourism diplomacy," is an essential mechanism for soft power. Tourism allows nations to promote their cultural heritage, values, and policies to enhance their global standing (Demir, 2017). As Lee et al. (2023) stated, the importance of a destination's image is universally recognized in the tourism sector.

3.1 Building National Identity Through Tourism

A country's image is deeply tied to its national identity, often constructed and communicated through tourism. When foreign tourists visit a country, they interact with its people, environments, and attractions and engage with a curated narrative of its history, values, and identity (Demir, 2017). Tourism diplomacy, in this sense, allows nations to construct and manage this narrative actively, ensuring that international visitors leave with a favorable impression. For instance, Japan has successfully managed its global image through tourism diplomacy by promoting its unique blend of ancient traditions and cutting-edge modernity (Guan & Huang, 2023). By highlighting cultural assets such as traditional tea ceremonies, samurai history, and innovative technologies, Japan positions itself as a country where the past and future coexist harmoniously (Gripentrog, 2015; Iwabuchi, 2018). This carefully curated image enhances Japan's national identity and reinforces its status as a global cultural powerhouse, which, in turn, benefits its diplomatic relations with other nations.

Tourism has a transformative power that allows countries to reframe or rehabilitate their international image (Adler-Nissen & Tsinovoi, 2019; Yang et al., 2020). Countries that have experienced political instability, economic difficulties, or negative media coverage often use tourism to reintroduce themselves to the global community. For example, Rwanda has invested heavily in tourism, promoting itself as a destination for eco-tourism and wildlife conservation, mainly through its renowned mountain gorilla trekking. This shift has helped transform Rwanda's global image from one associated with the tragic events of the 1994 genocide to a country of resilience, conservation, and innovation, improving its international reputation and strengthening diplomatic ties.

3.2 Cultural Exchange and Diplomacy Through Tourism

Tourism promotes mutual understanding and respect, which are key components of diplomacy (Bhandari, 2022; Clancy, 2011). Individuals who travel to foreign countries engage in cross-cultural interactions that foster these values. These interactions are the bedrock of tourism diplomacy, as they foster interpersonal connections that transcend national boundaries. By offering opportunities for cultural exchange, countries can create lasting bonds with foreign visitors, leading to stronger diplomatic ties and a more favorable global image.

One of the most notable examples of cultural diplomacy through tourism is China's Belt and Road Initiative (BRI), which significantly focuses on tourism and cultural exchange (Vhumbunu, 2019). Through this initiative, China invites tourists from participating countries to visit its cultural heritage sites, learn about its history, and engage with its people. Tourism diplomacy enhances China's image as a cultural and economic leader while strengthening its bilateral relations with partner countries. By promoting its rich cultural history and modern achievements, China can project a soft power influence that complements its broader geopolitical strategy. Furthermore, tourism-driven cultural exchanges often go beyond simple sightseeing. Many countries offer programs that immerse tourists in local traditions, such as cooking classes, language courses, and homestays with local families. These experiences foster a deeper understanding and appreciation of different cultures, creating lasting impressions that resonate even after tourists return home.

Tourism diplomacy is essential for countries that rely on tourism as a significant economic driver. Fostering good diplomatic relations with key tourist markets ensures a steady flow of visitors and revenue. For instance, countries in the Caribbean, which depend heavily on tourism, have actively engaged in tourism diplomacy to maintain strong ties with nations like the United States, Canada, and the United Kingdom (Demir, 2017). These diplomatic efforts are not just limited to traditional government-to-government relations but also involve public–private partnerships, such as collaborations with international airlines, hotel chains, and tour operators. By strategically managing these relationships, Caribbean nations ensure that they remain attractive destinations for tourists from these key markets, which, in turn, strengthens their global standing and economic stability.

Tourism diplomacy also addresses global challenges, such as climate change, public health crises, and international security (Becken & Scott, 2024; Scott et al., 2016). For example, during the COVID-19 pandemic, countries worldwide engaged in tourism diplomacy to coordinate travel restrictions, implement safety measures, and promote safe travel practices (Demir et al., 2020, 2021). By working together to address these challenges, countries demonstrated their commitment to international cooperation, strengthening their global image as responsible and proactive members of the international community.

3.3 Challenges in Managing Global Image Through Tourism Diplomacy

One of the key challenges in managing global image through tourism diplomacy is the need for authenticity (Demir & Alper, 2021). Tourists today are increasingly savvy and seek genuine, immersive experiences rather than carefully constructed facades. Countries must balance promoting a positive image and offering authentic experiences that resonate with visitors. Failure to do so can lead to negative perceptions and harm a country's global reputation. Another challenge is the risk of over-tourism, which can damage the very cultural and natural assets that attract tourists in the first place (Becken & Scott, 2024; Scott et al., 2016). Countries like Thailand and Spain have struggled with the negative impacts of over-tourism, such as environmental degradation and the displacement of local communities. Managing these issues requires careful planning and collaboration between governments, local communities, and the private sector. Countries that successfully address these challenges enhance their image as responsible and sustainable tourism destinations, while those that fail risk damaging their global reputation.

4. Tourism Diplomacy and International Perception Management

Tourism diplomacy has become an influential tool in shaping how countries are perceived globally. It goes beyond the traditional roles of diplomacy, using tourism to promote a nation's image, values, and culture to the international community. In this context, international perception management refers to how countries control and influence how global audiences view them. By carefully curating the experiences that tourists have and communicating messages, countries can craft a positive and compelling international image, enhancing their soft power and diplomatic reach.

4.1 The Role of Tourism in Shaping Perception

Tourism is one of the most direct and tangible ways for people to interact with a foreign country. Unlike media portrayals, which can sometimes be skewed or incomplete, tourism offers individuals the opportunity to experience a country's culture, hospitality, and environment firsthand. The impressions that tourists form during their visit play a significant role in shaping their perception of the country, and these perceptions often influence how they discuss and portray that nation to others upon returning home (Szondi, 2008; Vhumbunu, 2019). For countries with a strong tourism sector, the impact of tourism diplomacy is especially pronounced. Nations like France, Italy, and Thailand have successfully leveraged their rich cultural heritage, historical landmarks, and natural beauty to create favorable international images (Beirman, 2020; Okafor et al., 2021). France, for example, is seen globally as a hub of culture, art, and romance, thanks in part to the millions of tourists who visit Paris and other parts of the country each year. These countries carefully manage how their tourism sectors represent their national identity, ensuring that the experiences they offer tourists are consistent with the image they wish to project on the world stage.

4.2 Crafting a National Image Through Tourism Diplomacy

Tourism diplomacy offers countries a powerful means to manage their national image. By focusing on cultural exchange and offering unique experiences that highlight a country's strengths, governments foster positive associations among international visitors (Zhang et al., 2020). Countries like Japan and South Korea have been particularly adept at using tourism diplomacy to shape their global image. Japan has promoted itself as a country that blends tradition with modernity, emphasizing its ancient temples and traditional culture alongside high-tech cities and innovative industries.

Similarly, South Korea has successfully used the global popularity of K-pop, Korean cuisine, and historical sites to attract tourists and enhance its international image (Kim, 2016; Kim et al., 2022). These countries have recognized the importance of connecting cultural products and experiences with tourism, creating a lasting impression on visitors and extending their influence beyond their borders. Moreover, national tourism campaigns, such as "Visit Malaysia" or "Incredible India," are more than marketing efforts – they are instruments of diplomacy (Hussin, 2018). These campaigns convey specific messages about the country's identity, values, and ambitions. They position the country as welcoming, culturally rich, and worth visiting while strategically highlighting elements that align with international trends and preferences. These nations manage international perceptions and strengthen their soft power by doing so.

4.3 Perception Management in the Face of Challenges

Tourism diplomacy is instrumental in helping countries manage their image during or after crises. Natural disasters, political instability, or negative media coverage can severely damage a country's international reputation. However, countries can mitigate the damage through strategic tourism initiatives and even turn perceptions around. Rwanda, for instance, is a prime example of how tourism diplomacy can rehabilitate a country's global image (Gentry, 2018). After the 1994 genocide, Rwanda faced a massive challenge in overcoming negative perceptions. However, through deliberate efforts to promote its unique wildlife and natural beauty – particularly gorilla trekking – and its commitment to environmental sustainability, Rwanda successfully rebranded itself as a premier eco-tourism destination. This remarkable transformation not only helped boost its economy but also served as an inspiring example of resilience and a forward-looking approach for other countries (Roeder, 2011).

Countries that have faced political unrest or security concerns have used tourism diplomacy to assure the world of their stability and attractiveness. Egypt, for example, has faced challenges with political instability and terrorism, which have significantly affected its tourism industry. However, through targeted campaigns and improved security measures, Egypt has restored its image as a safe and desirable destination. It has focused on its rich historical sites, such as the pyramids and ancient temples, to attract tourists and improve international perceptions (Al-Azab, 2019; Nakayama, 2022).

4.4 The Future of Tourism Diplomacy in Perception Management

As the world becomes more globalized, tourism diplomacy will continue to be a critical tool for managing international perceptions. In an age of instant communication and social media, tourists' experiences and opinions can spread quickly, influencing the views of millions worldwide. Countries that effectively engage in tourism diplomacy and manage their image in this fast-paced environment will be better positioned in global affairs (Demir & Demir, 2024). Furthermore, emerging trends like sustainable tourism, responsible travel, and digital tourism will play an increasingly important role in tourism diplomacy. Countries that align their tourism offerings with these global trends will attract more visitors and enhance their international image as forward-thinking, responsible global citizens. It's crucial for countries to recognize and adapt to these trends, as they will shape the future of tourism diplomacy and international perception management in the 21st century.

5. The Link Between National Branding and Tourism

National branding and tourism are closely interconnected, particularly in the context of tourism diplomacy. National branding refers to a country's strategic efforts to shape and promote a distinct and positive image of itself on the global stage (Tijani et al., 2024). At the same time, tourism diplomacy leverages tourism as a soft power tool to strengthen diplomatic ties and international relationships (Fig. 3).

5.1 National Branding as a Strategic Tool

National branding is a form of soft power that allows countries to shape their global image. It is built on the premise that a strong and appealing national image can enhance international relations, attract investment, and encourage tourism. A well-executed national branding strategy highlights a country's unique characteristics – such as its culture, history, values, and aspirations – projecting these elements to align with global trends and audience expectations (Therkelsen & Halkier, 2008). Many people's understanding of a country is based on either direct experience through travel or the indirect influence of tourism campaigns and the experiences shared by others (Linardaki & Aslanides, 2020). Therefore, tourists' experiences and the narratives communicated through tourism marketing and diplomatic efforts directly influence how the country is perceived globally. A thriving tourism strategy amplifies national branding by promoting a coherent, appealing image that reflects the country's identity and strengths.

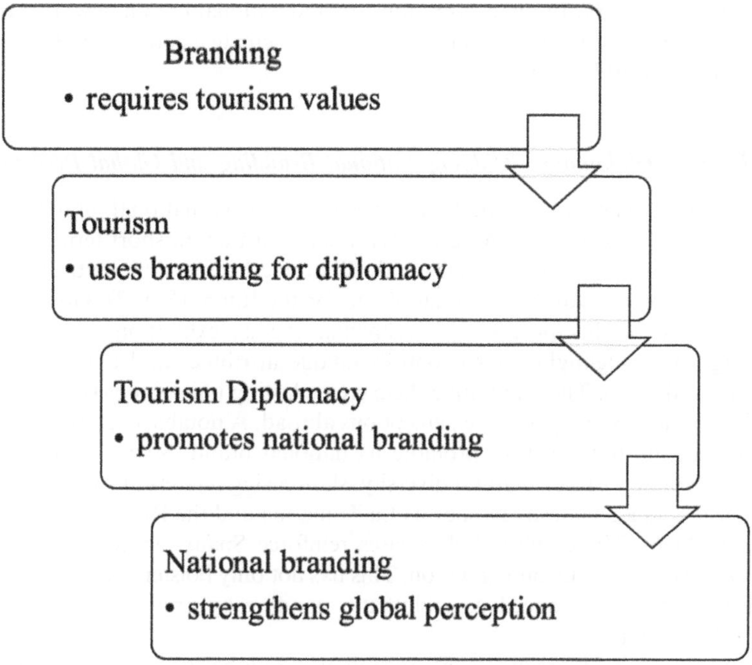

Fig. 3. Tourism Diplomacy as a Bridge Between National Branding and Global Perception.

5.2 The Role of Tourism in National Branding

Tourism is critical to communicating national identity and reinforcing national branding efforts (Demir & Tür, 2019). When a country promotes its tourist attractions, it essentially showcases what it offers. These cultural, historical, or natural attractions are imbued with the nation's values and identity and become central to the nation's brand image. For instance, countries like Italy and France are globally recognized for their cultural heritage and historical landmarks, such as the Colosseum and the Eiffel Tower, which are integral in shaping national brands (Therkelsen & Gram, 2010). The promotion of these iconic symbols not only attracts millions of tourists each year but also reinforces the perception of Italy as a cradle of civilization and France as a beacon of art and culture. The consistent projection of these images through tourism diplomacy helps solidify their place in the global consciousness, aligning the national brand with specific cultural, historical, or geographical markers.

New Zealand has successfully branded itself as a pristine and adventurous destination through its tourism campaigns, particularly by promoting its stunning natural environments featured in films like The Lord of the Rings (Ermann & Hermanik, 2018). This branding has attracted adventure tourists and environmental enthusiasts, reinforcing New Zealand's image as an eco-friendly and adventurous country. In these cases, tourism and national branding work hand in hand, each supporting and amplifying the other to create a cohesive and attractive image on the world stage.

5.3 Tourism Diplomacy: Bridging National Branding and Global Perception

Tourism diplomacy is a long-term investment where national branding and tourism converge (Demir & Alper, 2021). It's not just about short-term gains but also about building international goodwill, strengthening diplomatic relations, and promoting a favorable national image for the future (Fig. 3). Governments often engage in this process by organizing events, exhibitions, and cultural exchanges that highlight their country's unique attributes and appeal to international audiences. These initiatives help create lasting impressions of the country and its people, fostering positive perceptions abroad. A notable example is Spain's use of tourism diplomacy to promote its national brand. Spain has positioned itself as a country of rich cultural diversity, showcasing regions like Catalonia and Andalusia and iconic festivals such as La Tomatina and the Running of the Bulls (Viguer, 2016). These cultural showcases reinforce Spain's image as a vibrant, culturally rich, and welcoming nation. This has not only bolstered Spain's tourism numbers but also enhanced its diplomatic standing by promoting cultural ties with other countries.

South Korea's "Korean Wave" or Hallyu – a global phenomenon driven by Korean pop culture – has been a cornerstone of its tourism diplomacy efforts. By leveraging the popularity of K-pop, K-dramas, and Korean cuisine, South Korea has effectively used tourism to enhance its national brand, attracting international tourists eager to experience the culture firsthand (Bae et al., 2017; Kim, 2007). The success of this strategy has strengthened South Korea's global image as a modern, technologically advanced, and culturally dynamic nation, showcasing how tourism diplomacy can significantly enhance a country's soft power and international standing.

5.4 Aligning Tourism With National Branding Goals

One of the most critical aspects of tourism diplomacy is the need for a cohesive approach. It's essential that the tourism experiences and messaging are aligned with broader national branding goals. This alignment ensures that the narratives communicated through tourism reflect the values and image the country wants to project globally. For instance, a country that seeks to brand itself as an environmentally responsible nation should ensure that its tourism practices are sustainable and that eco-tourism is a prominent aspect of its international tourism campaigns (White & Kolesnicov, 2015). This cohesive approach is not just beneficial; it's necessary for achieving national branding goals.

Costa Rica provides an excellent example of this approach. The country has successfully branded itself as a leader in eco-tourism, emphasizing its commitment to sustainability and conservation (Pop et al., 2020). This national brand aligns with its tourism offerings, focusing on nature-based tourism, wildlife conservation, and sustainable practices. Costa Rica has created a powerful, positive image that resonates globally and attracts like-minded tourists by ensuring its tourism sector reflects its national branding goals. Nations like the United Arab Emirates (UAE) have utilized tourism to project a forward-thinking and innovative image (Tudor, 2022). Cities like Dubai and Abu Dhabi have positioned themselves as luxury, modernity, and cutting-edge architecture hubs. By emphasizing futuristic development, luxury tourism, and high-profile events like the Dubai Expo, the UAE has successfully branded itself as a global center of innovation and progress.

6. Soft Power Tools and Strategies for Tourism Diplomacy

Tourism diplomacy, a critical component of a country's soft power strategy, harnesses the allure of its culture, heritage, and natural resources to bolster international relations and foster goodwill (Demir & Dalgıç, 2022). Tourism, a natural source of soft power, allows for economic, social, cultural, and environmental direct interaction with a country's values and identity. This direct interaction not only promotes international cooperation but also increases a country's reputation (Fig. 4).

6.1 Cultural Heritage as a Soft Power Tool in Tourism

Cultural heritage is one of the most potent elements countries can leverage in tourism diplomacy to enhance their soft power (Suntikul, 2019). By utilizing cultural heritage through tourism, countries enable foreign visitors to experience and engage with their past and present (Lähdesmäki, 2021; Winter, 2016).

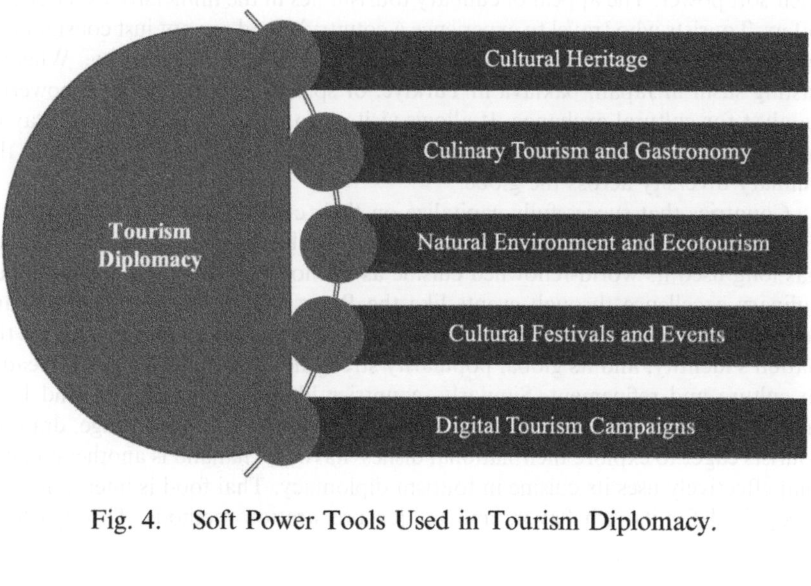

Fig. 4. Soft Power Tools Used in Tourism Diplomacy.

Cultural heritage tourism is particularly effective because it taps into the growing global interest in authentic experiences (Platts et al., 2023; Singh & Rana, 2021). Travelers increasingly seek meaningful connections with the places they visit, longing to understand the cultural and historical context behind what they see. This interaction provides countries with a direct channel to project their values, showcase their achievements, and foster a sense of respect for their cultural contributions to world history. For instance, countries like Egypt, Greece, and Italy attract millions of visitors yearly to their ancient monuments and historical landmarks, using these sites to communicate their rich histories and promote a positive national identity.

Beyond economic benefits, cultural heritage also strengthens diplomatic ties by cultivating a shared interest in preservation (Wiktor-Mach, 2019; Winter, 2016). International organizations like UNESCO recognize and protect World Heritage Sites, drawing global attention to a country's cultural treasures. This shared responsibility for safeguarding heritage encourages international cooperation and collaboration. By promoting their cultural heritage, nations establish themselves as guardians of global history, bolstering their soft power and diplomatic influence on the world stage.

6.2 Culinary Tourism and Gastronomy as Soft Power in Diplomacy

Culinary tourism, or gastronomy tourism, is a leisure activity and a strategic soft power tool that countries can use to enhance their diplomatic efforts. As a universal language, food transcends borders; a country's cuisine often serves as an ambassador for its culture (Demir & Alper, 2021). By promoting their unique culinary traditions through tourism, nations can forge solid cultural connections and project a positive image on the international stage, significantly enhancing their soft power. The appeal of culinary tourism lies in the immersive experience it offers. Tourists who travel to experience a country's food are not just consuming a meal but engaging with that nation's culture, history, and identity. Whether tasting sushi in Japan, baklava in Türkiye, or spices in India, food is a powerful catalyst for cultural exchange. It allows visitors to understand a nation's way of life and promotes dialogue, encouraging travelers to explore and appreciate the culinary diversity across the globe.

Countries that successfully capitalize on their culinary traditions significantly enhance their soft power (Cabral et al., 2024; Zreik, 2023). For example, France has long used its world-renowned cuisine as a smooth power tool, promoting its culinary excellence through events like the Bocuse d'Or, international culinary schools, and Michelin-starred restaurants. French cuisine is closely tied to the nation's identity, and its global popularity strengthens France's image as a leader in culture and refinement. Similarly, countries like Mexico and Thailand have used their unique cuisines to enhance their visibility on the world stage, drawing tourists eager to explore their national dishes' flavors. Thailand is another country that effectively uses its cuisine in tourism diplomacy. Thai food is internationally recognized for its rich flavors and unique preparation methods. Through food festivals, cooking classes, and culinary tours, Thailand has successfully branded itself as a destination for food enthusiasts. The global popularity of Thai cuisine helps foster positive perceptions of the country, reinforcing its soft power.

In addition to promoting national identity, culinary tourism fosters international cooperation. Countries often collaborate on food festivals, culinary tours, and exchange programs, bringing chefs and food experts together to share knowledge and expertise (Demir & Dalgıç, 2022). This kind of cultural diplomacy strengthens bilateral ties and encourages the exchange of ideas between nations. Furthermore, the global popularity of a country's cuisine leads to economic and diplomatic benefits, as food exports and culinary tourism generate revenue and foster goodwill (Hussin, 2018; Zreik, 2023). Nations can project an image of hospitality, creativity, and cultural pride through gastronomy, enhancing their soft power. By sharing their culinary traditions with the world, countries can create lasting impressions and build cultural bridges that extend beyond the dining table, contributing to a more favorable perception of their national brand.

6.3 Natural Environment and Ecotourism as Soft Power in Diplomacy

The natural environment and ecotourism offer another powerful avenue through which countries can exercise soft power in tourism diplomacy (Negassa, 2024). A country's natural beauty, biodiversity, and commitment to environmental sustainability can significantly enhance its global image, positioning it as a responsible and attractive destination. Ecotourism, in particular, has gained popularity in recent years as travelers become more environmentally conscious and seek destinations that promote sustainability and conservation.

Countries rich in natural resources, such as rainforests, mountains, beaches, and wildlife reserves, leverage these assets to attract tourists and promote environmental stewardship. This boosts tourism revenue and enhances the country's conservation and sustainable development leader reputation. For example, Costa Rica has successfully positioned itself as a global leader in ecotourism, promoting its lush rainforests, biodiversity, and commitment to renewable energy. The country's green tourism initiatives have not only drawn millions of eco-conscious travelers but also strengthened its soft power by showcasing its environmental leadership on the global stage. Ecotourism also fosters international cooperation in environmental preservation (Negassa, 2024; Yang & Lin, 2022). Many countries collaborate on transnational conservation projects, such as wildlife corridors and protected marine areas, to ensure the sustainability of their natural resources (Henry & Mostafanezhad, 2019; Hohl, 2013). This shared responsibility for protecting the planet's biodiversity creates opportunities for diplomatic dialogue and collaboration. By promoting ecotourism, countries highlight their contributions to global environmental efforts, thus enhancing their international standing and soft power influence.

Furthermore, ecotourism serves as a platform for cultural diplomacy by promoting indigenous cultures and traditional knowledge related to environmental stewardship (Rozanah & Ishqila, 2024; Sahoo et al., 2024). In many regions, local communities play a key role in conserving natural resources and maintaining biodiversity. Ecotourism initiatives involving these communities provide economic benefits, preserve their cultural heritage, and promote cross-cultural understanding. Visitors who participate in eco-tours often engage with local guides and communities, gaining insights into traditional ways of life and environmental practices. This exchange fosters mutual respect and appreciation, further strengthening the soft power potential of ecotourism. Ecotourism also offers a unique opportunity to blend environmental and cultural diplomacy, creating lasting bonds between nations and contributing to a more harmonious global community.

6.4 Cultural Festivals and Events as Soft Power Tools in Tourism

Cultural festivals and international events represent an effective soft power mechanism in tourism diplomacy (Abuan, 2021; Grincheva, 2024). These gatherings showcase a country's artistic, musical, and cultural achievements, offering a unique platform for nations to present themselves to a global audience. Festivals allow countries to highlight their traditions, folklore, and contemporary culture, attracting international visitors and fostering cultural exchange (Demir & Dalgıç, 2022).

By hosting large-scale international cultural events, nations can project their identity and values, creating a favorable image that resonates globally. For example, the Rio Carnival in Brazil is not only a celebration of local music and dance but also a key element of Brazil's soft power strategy. The festival draws millions of tourists each year, offering a vivid representation of Brazilian culture and hospitality. The Olympic Games, for instance, are a powerful soft power tool. Nations that hosted the Olympics, such as China in 2008 or Brazil in 2016, used the platform to project their modernity, capability, and global relevance. Similarly, international film festivals like Cannes and Venice provide a stage for countries to showcase their creative industries, attracting global attention and reinforcing their cultural influence.

Some researchers (e.g., Grincheva, 2013; Hjorthén, 2021; Pedersen & Stanoeva, 2024) state that cultural festivals and events foster diplomatic relations by encouraging collaboration between countries. Many international festivals feature participants worldwide, creating cultural exchange and dialogue opportunities. For instance, events like the Edinburgh International Festival and the Dubai Expo bring together artists, performers, and creators from diverse cultural backgrounds, promoting cross-border collaboration and understanding. These events serve as a form of cultural diplomacy, allowing countries to engage in "soft" international relations through the arts. Festivals often celebrate diversity and inclusivity, promoting values that resonate with global audiences (Grincheva, 2024; Zugasti, 2019). Countries that position themselves as hubs for cultural creativity and diversity can significantly enhance their soft power. For example, the Notting Hill Carnival in London celebrates multiculturalism, attracting tourists worldwide and projecting an image of openness and inclusivity.

Such festivals not only promote tourism but also send a message about a country's values and societal norms (Demir & Alper, 2021).

These events, in addition to fostering cultural exchange, play a significant role in economic development. Festivals generate substantial revenue by attracting tourists and stimulating related industries such as hospitality, transportation, and retail. Combined with the cultural and diplomatic benefits, this economic impact underscores the strategic importance of festivals in enhancing a nation's soft power (Isar, 2020; Shannon, 2024). Furthermore, festivals can serve as potent symbols of a nation's cultural identity, drawing international attention year after year and solidifying a country's reputation as an artistic leader.

6.5 Digital Tourism Campaigns and Virtual Diplomacy

In today's digital age, virtual tourism and digital diplomacy have also become powerful soft power strategies in tourism diplomacy. Countries increasingly use digital platforms to promote their culture, heritage, and tourism destinations, reaching global audiences without physical travel (Demir & Demir, 2024). Virtual reality (VR) and augmented reality (AR) experiences, in particular, allow potential tourists to explore destinations and cultural landmarks from the comfort of their homes. For example, during the COVID-19 pandemic, many countries turned to virtual tourism to maintain their visibility on the global stage. Museums, cultural landmarks, and natural wonders were made accessible through virtual tours, keeping international interest alive even when travel was restricted. Digital diplomacy allows countries to continue engaging with global audiences, enhancing their soft power by maintaining cultural relevance and visibility. Moreover, social media platforms are increasingly used in tourism diplomacy to project a positive image of a country. Countries like Australia and New Zealand have invested heavily in social media campaigns that promote their natural beauty, wildlife, and outdoor experiences. As stated by some researchers (e.g., Bennett & Iaquinto, 2023; Hjorthén, 2021; Saha & Raghuvanshi, 2025), these digital campaigns reach millions of potential tourists worldwide, contributing to the countries' soft power by creating a sense of connection and desire to visit.

7. Conclusion

The intersection of soft power and tourism, particularly in global image management, highlights tourism's unique and significant role in shaping global perceptions. As explored throughout this chapter, tourism is a powerful tool for cultural interaction, national branding, and perception management, influencing how countries are viewed internationally. Strategies that leverage tourism for diplomatic purposes are diverse, from promoting cultural heritage to utilizing modern digital platforms. All of these contribute to a country's ability to project a positive global image.

At the core of soft power is the ability to foster cultural interaction, and tourism is one of the most effective vehicles for this. Through tourism, nations can showcase their cultural diversity and heritage, offering both tourists and locals opportunities to engage in meaningful exchanges. These interactions not only help visitors gain a deeper understanding of the host country's values and traditions but also serve as a foundation for diplomatic ties. By encouraging cultural exchange, tourism becomes a bridge for dialogue, mutual respect, and cooperation between nations, all essential elements of soft power.

Tourism's role in managing global perceptions of a country is multi-faceted. It begins with building national identity through tourism, where iconic landmarks, cultural heritage sites, and traditions are emphasized to create an internationally resonated distinct image. When effectively branded through tourism, national identity allows countries to assert their uniqueness globally. Moreover, tourism diplomacy facilitates cultural exchange and international diplomacy. Festivals, art exhibitions, and other cultural events attract tourists and serve as platforms for international cooperation. This cultural diplomacy enhances a nation's soft power by promoting understanding and goodwill, strengthening diplomatic relationships. However, managing a global image through tourism diplomacy presents challenges. Negative stereotypes, crises, or mismanagement of tourism resources can harm a country's reputation. Nations must approach tourism with a clear and adaptive strategy for maintaining a positive image, even in the face of difficulties.

Tourism plays a significant role in shaping international perceptions. Through tourism diplomacy, countries can craft and promote an image that aligns with their strategic interests, influencing how the international community perceives them. This involves a careful balancing act – using tourism to highlight cultural strengths and successes while addressing environmental sustainability, political instability, or negative media portrayals. Effective perception management requires flexibility and resilience. Countries that successfully manage their image through tourism diplomacy often excel in turning challenges into opportunities. For instance, nations that have faced crises like natural disasters or political unrest have utilized tourism to demonstrate their recovery and resilience, reshaping global perceptions. The future of tourism diplomacy in perception management will likely involve more sophisticated approaches, particularly as digital tools and virtual tourism grow in prominence. Countries must adapt to changing global dynamics and use tourism to maintain their influence, fostering an image of openness, innovation, and cultural richness.

The link between national branding and tourism is undeniable, as tourism is often the first direct interaction many individuals have with a country. The experiences and narratives that tourists carry with them upon returning home contribute to the nation's overall brand. Whether through cultural festivals, natural attractions, or culinary tourism, the experiences a country offers to its visitors are key elements of its national brand. Tourism diplomacy acts as a bridge between national branding and global perception. A country's ability to align its tourism strategies with its broader national branding goals ensures consistency in its message to the world. For example, countries that emphasize eco-tourism as part of their national brand not only attract environmentally conscious travelers but also promote a global image of environmental stewardship. Aligning tourism with national branding goals requires a coordinated effort between governments, tourism boards, and the private sector. Countries that are successful in this alignment can build strong, positive associations with their national identity, enhancing their soft power and global standing.

Cultural heritage is one of the most potent soft power tools in tourism. By preserving and promoting historical landmarks, art, and traditions, nations can appeal to the global community's interest in culture and history, enhancing their diplomatic influence. Culinary tourism and gastronomy are also highly effective in soft power diplomacy. Food is a universal language, and countries that promote their unique cuisines create memorable experiences that leave lasting impressions on visitors. Culinary tourism helps establish a connection with a nation's cultural identity, fostering goodwill and interest in deeper engagement.

Ecotourism, focusing on sustainability and natural beauty, is another critical soft power tool. Nations that emphasize ecotourism not only attract environmentally conscious travelers but also position themselves as leaders in global environmental preservation efforts. This aligns with broader global concerns about climate change and sustainability, enhancing a country's international reputation. Cultural festivals and events serve as vibrant platforms for nations to engage with the world diplomatically. These events not only allow countries to showcase their creativity, traditions, and contemporary innovations but also foster international collaboration and dialogue, making the global community feel more connected and engaged.

Finally, as a soft power strategy, tourism diplomacy is increasingly important in shaping how nations are perceived globally. Digital tourism campaigns and virtual diplomacy have emerged as innovative soft power strategies. As technology evolves, virtual reality tours, social media campaigns, and online cultural exchanges allow nations to reach broader audiences, offering immersive experiences that shape global perceptions without requiring physical travel. These digital tools are particularly valuable in maintaining international visibility and engagement during times of crisis, such as the COVID-19 pandemic, providing reassurance about the resilience of tourism diplomacy.

References

Abuan, R. E. M. (2021). Cultural diplomacy of Thailand and Indonesia in the Philippines. *MJIR| Malaysian Journal of International Relations*, *9*(1), 88–104.

Adler-Nissen, R., & Tsinovoi, A. (2019). International misrecognition: The politics of humour and national identity in Israel's public diplomacy. *European Journal of International Relations*, *25*(1), 3–29.

Al-Azab, M. R. (2019). A future vision to promote intra-regional tourism between Egypt and Africa. *Minia Journal of Tourism and Hospitality Research*, *7*(1), 1–22.

Bae, E. S., Chang, M., Park, E. S., & Kim, D. C. (2017). The effect of Hallyu on tourism in Korea. *Journal of Open Innovation: Technology, Market, and Complexity*, *3*(4), 1–12.

Becken, S., & Scott, D. (2024). Tourism and climate change stocktake: A call to action. *Journal of Sustainable Tourism*, *32*(9), 2018–2038.
Beirman, D. (2020). *Restoring tourism destinations in crisis: A strategic marketing approach*. Routledge.
Bennett, M. M., & Iaquinto, B. L. (2023). The geopolitics of China's arctic tourism resources. *Territory, Politics, Governance*, *11*(7), 1281–1302.
Bhandari, K. (2022). Tourism and commercial nationalism. *Annals of Tourism Research*, *95*, 1–13.
Cabral, Ó., Lavrador, L., Orduna, P., & Moreira, R. (2024). From the kitchen to the embassy: A rapid review of gastronomic approaches in diplomacy. *Place Branding and Public Diplomacy*, 1–13.
Clancy, M. (2011). Re-presenting Ireland: Tourism, branding and national identity in Ireland. *Journal of International Relations and Development*, *14*, 281–308.
Demir, M. (2017). *Seyahat Acentacılığı ve Tur Operatörlüğü: İlkeler ve Yönetim*. Detay Yayıncılık.
Demir, M., & Alper, P. (2021). G20 summit menus as a means of gastrodiplomacy: Messages to the world via menus. *International Journal of Gastronomy and Food Science*, *25*, 1–8. https://doi.org/10.1016/j.ijgfs.2021.100368
Demir, M., & Dalgıç, A. (2022). Examining gastronomy festivals as the attractiveness factor for tourism destinations: The case of Turkey. *Journal of Convention & Event Tourism*, *23*, 412–434. https://doi.org/10.1080/15470148.2022.2089797
Demir, M., Demir, Ş. Ş., Dalgıç, A., & Ergen, F. D. (2021). Impact of COVID-19 pandemic on the tourism industry: An evaluation from the hotel managers' perspective. *Journal of Tourism Theory and Research*, *7*(1), 44–57. https://doi.org/10.24288/jttr.857610
Demir, M., & Demir, Ş. Ş. (2024). Digital technologies and applications in tourist guidance: The dilemma between adopting innovations and career concerns. *Journal of Human Resources in Hospitality & Tourism*, 1–25.
Demir, M., Günaydın, Y., & Demir, Ş. Ş. (2020). Koronavirüs (Covid-19) salgınının Türkiye'de turizm üzerindeki öncülleri, etkileri ve sonuçlarının değerlendirilmesi. *International Journal of Social Sciences and Education Research*, *6*(1), 80–107.
Demir, Ş. Ş., & Tür, E. (2019). Otel logosu ne söyler? Tüketiciler ne algılar? *Journal of Tourism Theory and Research*, *5*(1), 51–64.
Ermann, U., & Hermanik, K. J. (2018). *Branding the nation, the place, the product*. Routledge.
Gentry, J. A. (2018). The instrumental use of norms in war: Impact on strategies and strategic outcomes. *Comparative Strategy*, *37*(1), 35–48.
Grincheva, N. (2013). Cultural diplomacy 2.0: Challenges and opportunities in museum international practices. *Museum & Society*, *11*(1), 39–49.
Grincheva, N. (2024). The past and future of cultural diplomacy. *International Journal of Cultural Policy*, *30*(2), 172–191.
Gripentrog, J. (2015). Power and culture: Japan's cultural diplomacy in the United States, 1934–1940. *Pacific Historical Review*, *84*(4), 478–516.
Guan, H., & Huang, Y. (2023). Analysis of Japan's public diplomacy toward China. *Open Journal of Political Science*, *13*(4), 414–437.
Henry, J., & Mostafanezhad, M. (2019). The geopolitics of volunteer tourism. In D. J. Timothy (Ed.), *Handbook of globalisation and tourism* (pp. 295–304). Edward Elgar Publishing.

Herrera, J. L. Q., & Pérez-Tapia, G. (2024). Tourism as a driver of soft power: The case of South Korea. In J. Chica-Olmo, M. Vujičić, R. A. Castanho, U. Stankov, & E. Martinelli (Eds.), *Sustainable tourism, culture and heritage promotion: Development, management and connectivity* (pp. 221–230). Springer.

Hjorthén, A. (2021). Old world homecomings: Campaigns of ancestral tourism and cultural diplomacy, 1945–66. *Journal of Contemporary History*, *56*(4), 1147–1170.

Hohl, A. (2013). Ecotourism as an instrument to conserve biodiversity. In C. A. Tisdell (Ed.), *Handbook of tourism economics: Analysis, new applications and case studies* (pp. 813–843). World Scientific Publishing Co. Pte. Ltd.

Hussin, H. (2018). Gastronomy, tourism, and the soft power of Malaysia. *Sage Open*, *8*(4), 1–11.

Isar, Y. R. (2020). Cultural diplomacy: India does it differently. *Cultural Diplomacy and International Cultural Relations*, *I*, 47–58.

Iwabuchi, K. (2018). Pop-culture diplomacy in Japan: Soft power, nation branding and the question of 'international cultural exchange. In L. Ang, Y. Isar, & P. Mar (Eds.), *Cultural diplomacy: Beyond the national interest?* (pp. 65–78). Routledge.

Kim, J. (2007). Why does Hallyu matter? The significance of the Korean wave in South Korea. *Critical Studies in Television*, *2*(2), 47–59.

Kim, H. S. (2016). The Korean wave as soft power public diplomacy. In N. Chitty, L. Ji, G. D. Rawnsley, & G. Hayden (Eds.), *The Routledge handbook of soft power* (pp. 434–444). Routledge.

Kim, J. H., Kim, K. J., Park, B. T., & Choi, H. J. (2022). The phenomenon and development of K-Pop: The relationship between success factors of K-Pop and the national image, social network service citizenship behavior, and tourist behavioral intention. *Sustainability*, *14*(6), 3200.

Lähdesmäki, T. (2021). Heritage diplomacy discourses in the EU: Notions on cultural diplomacy, cultural heritage, and intercultural dialogue among EU officials and heritage practitioners. *Ethnologia Europaea*, *51*(2), 48–71.

Lee, E., Chung, N., & Koo, C. (2023). Exploring touristic experiences on destination image modification. *Tourism Management Perspectives*, *47*, 1–14.

Linardaki, C., & Aslanides, A. (2020). From poem and song to cultural diplomacy: Challenges and opportunities for place branding and tourism promotion. *Place Branding and Public Diplomacy*, *16*(4), 304–315.

Nakayama, B. J. (2022). Information vs the cyberspace domain. *Journal of Cyber Policy*, *7*(2), 213–229.

Negassa, S. B. (2024). Tourism diplomacy: Fostering economic development through global connectivity. In A. B. Basnur (Ed.), *Tourism: For global connectivity and economic development* (pp. 68–75). Paramedia Komunikatama.

Nye, J. S. (1990). Soft power. *Foreign Policy*, 80, 153–171.

Okafor, L. E., Tan, C. M., & Khalid, U. (2021). Does panda diplomacy promote Chinese outbound tourism flows? *Journal of Hospitality and Tourism Management*, *49*, 54–64.

Pedersen, S. B., & Stanoeva, E. (2024). Tourism diplomacy in cold war Europe: Symbolic gestures, cultural exchange and human rights. *Contemporary European History*, 1–17.

Platts, E. J., Keifer, H. L., & Samuels, K. L. (2023). Carbon footprints of travel to world heritage sites: Communicating climate to potential tourists through a consumption-based life-cycle assessment. *Journal of Heritage Tourism*, *18*(4), 407–426.

Pop, N. A., Baba, C. A., Anysz, R. N., & Tohanean, D. (2020). National branding strategy and its effects on business and tourism. *Proceedings of the International Conference on Business Excellence*, *14*(1), 1005–1013.

Rehman, H. U., Warraich, S. K., & Kharl, S. H. (2023). The rise of India's soft power in the post-cold war era and its regional ramifications, with an emphasis on Pakistan. *Annals of Human and Social Sciences*, *4*(3), 36–47.

Roeder, L. W. (2011). Diplomatic theory and practice. In *Diplomacy, funding and animal welfare* (pp. 1–101).

Rozanah, A., & Ishqila, N. A. (2024). The influence of public diplomacy in G20 2022 summit in Indonesia's post-pandemic tourism and ecotourism recovery efforts. *Journal of Social Political Sciences*, *5*(1), 45–56.

Saha, R., & Raghuvanshi, L. (2025). Intercultural communication in tourism during COVID-19 pandemic: Analyzing audience appeal of indian tourism campaign through social media. In S. S. Ghosh, D. Roy, T. Putatunda, & N. Ray (Eds.), *Language and cross-cultural communication in travel and tourism* (pp. 49–67). Apple Academic Press.

Sahoo, M., Mohanty, P. P., Kaushik, S., Islam, M. K., & Rourt, L. (2024). Ecotourism or ecological concerns? Tracing the impact of economic policy uncertainty and natural resources on tourism-driven ecological footprints. *Environmental Science and Pollution Research*, 1–17.

Scott, D., Hall, C. M., & Gössling, S. (2016). A report on the Paris Climate Change Agreement and its implications for tourism: Why we will always have Paris. *Journal of Sustainable Tourism*, *24*(7), 933–948.

Şen, O. (2019). Targeted soft power in Turkish new foreign policy and its impact on origins of in-bound tourists. *Journal of Tourism Theory and Research*, *5*(1), 65–74.

Shannon, J. H. (2024). Melodies heard and unheard: The promise and limits of cultural diplomacy through music. In M. R. Lopes da Cunha, J. Shannon, S. M. Sørensen, & V. Danielson (Eds.), *Music and cultural diplomacy in the Middle East: Geopolitical re-configurations for the 21st century* (pp. 71–92). Springer International Publishing.

Singh, R. P., & Rana, P. S. (2021). Cultural diplomacy in India: Dispersal, heritage representation, contestation, and development. In O. Niglio and E. Y. J. Lee (Eds.). *Transcultural diplomacy and international law in heritage conservation: A dialogue between ethics, law, and culture* (pp. 231–256). Springer Nature Pte Ltd.

Suntikul, W. (2019). Gastrodiplomacy in tourism. *Current Issues in Tourism*, *22*(9), 1076–1094.

Szondi, G. (2008). Central and Eastern European public diplomacy: A transitional perspective on national reputation management. In N. Snow & P. M. Taylor (Eds.), *Routledge handbook of public diplomacy* (pp. 312–333). Routledge.

Therkelsen, A., & Gram, M. (2010). Branding Europe–between nations, regions and continents. *Scandinavian Journal of Hospitality and Tourism*, *10*(2), 107–128.

Therkelsen, A., & Halkier, H. (2008). Contemplating place branding umbrellas. The case of coordinated national tourism and business promotion in Denmark. *Scandinavian Journal of Hospitality and Tourism*, *8*(2), 159–175.

Tijani, A., Majeed, M., Ofori, K. S., & Abubakari, A. (2024). Country branding research: A decade's systematic review. *Cogent Business & Management*, *11*(1), 1–10.

Tudor, A. C. (2022). From London to Dubai-171 years of national branding through world expos (1851–2022). *Europolity-Continuity and Change in European Governance, 16*(1), 129–152.

Vhumbunu, C. H. (2019). Conceptualizing China's belt and road initiative public diplomacy towards Africa. *African Journal of Democracy and Governance, 6*(1), 162–194.

Viguer, B. A. (2016). *Spain-culture smart!: The essential guide to customs and culture*. Bravo Limited.

White, C., & Kolesnicov, I. (2015). Nation branding in a transitional democracy: The role of corporate diplomacy in promoting national identity. *Place Branding and Public Diplomacy, 11*, 324–337.

Wiktor-Mach, D. (2019). Cultural heritage and development: UNESCO's new paradigm in a changing geopolitical context. *Third World Quarterly, 40*(9), 1593–1612.

Winter, T. (2016). Heritage diplomacy and tourism in Asia. In C. M. Hall & S. J. Page (Eds.), *The Routledge Handbook of Tourism in Asia* (pp. 45–53). Routledge.

Wüst, A., & Nicolai, K. (2023). Cultural diplomacy and the reconfiguration of soft power: Evidence from Morocco. *Mediterranean Politics, 28*(4), 554–579.

Xu, H., Wang, K., & Song, Y. M. (2020). Chinese outbound tourism and soft power. *Journal of Policy Research in Tourism, Leisure and Events, 12*(1), 34–49.

Yang, J. (2019). *Analysing the effects of international tourism on soft power*. University of San Diego.

Yang, I. C. M., French, J. A., Lee, C., & Watabe, M. (2020). The symbolism of international tourism in national identity. *Annals of Tourism Research, 83*, 1–16.

Yang, D., & Lin, C. A. (2022). Are pandas effective ambassadors for promoting wildlife conservation and international diplomacy? *Sustainability, 14*(18), 11383.

Zhang, J., Adhikari, D., Fahmy, S., & Kang, S. (2020). Exploring the impacts of national image, service quality, and perceived value on international tourist behaviors: A Nepali case. *Journal of Vacation Marketing, 26*(4), 473–488.

Zreik, M. (2023). Stirring up soft power: The role of Chinese Cuisine in China's cultural diplomacy. In K. Kankaew (Ed.), *Global perspectives on soft power management in business* (pp. 292–306). IGI Global.

Zugasti, J. E. S. (2019). Casa México: Promotion, innovation and cultural diplomacy in South by Southwest (SXSW). *Revista Mexicana de Política Exterior*, (117), 85–98.

Chapter 3

The Role of the Governments in Tourism Diplomacy

Abstract

Governments play a pivotal role in shaping tourism diplomacy, employing strategic policies, investments, and diplomatic missions to strengthen international ties and foster economic growth. By facilitating visa and customs procedures, establishing bilateral tourism agreements, and implementing health and safety measures, state policies leverage tourism as a diplomatic tool to enhance cross-border cooperation. Strategic government initiatives aimed at protecting cultural heritage and attracting foreign investment further underscore the importance of tourism as a driver of international collaboration. These projects bolster tourism infrastructure and superstructure and amplify a nation's ability to project its cultural identity and values globally. Diplomatic missions, including embassies and consulates, serve as critical actors in tourism promotion, facilitating partnerships and enhancing collaboration through diplomatic channels. Engagements with international organizations and global campaigns spearheaded by national tourism boards illustrate how governments use public diplomacy to influence international perceptions and stimulate tourism. Tourism ministries, as facilitators of national branding, organize events, launch promotional campaigns, and work to establish a cohesive image of their countries, demonstrating the multifaceted role of tourism in fostering mutual understanding. However, challenges persist. From geopolitical tensions and insufficient infrastructure to the complexities of international cooperation, governments must navigate various obstacles to implement tourism diplomacy initiatives effectively. By addressing these challenges through innovative strategies and sustained international engagement, governments can maximize tourism's potential as a diplomatic and economic tool. This section highlights the significance of governmental actions in advancing tourism diplomacy and their broader implications for global relations.

Tourism Diplomacy, 43–67

Copyright © 2025 Mahmut Demir and Şirvan Şen Demir

Published under exclusive licence by Emerald Publishing Limited
doi:10.1108/978-1-83708-676-420251003

Keywords: Tourism diplomacy; government policies; diplomatic missions; cultural heritage protection; public diplomacy in tourism

1. Introduction

Tourism diplomacy has become an essential element of international relations, with governments playing a critical role in shaping how tourism contributes to a nation's global standing. Using tourism as a soft power, governments can influence international perceptions, build diplomatic ties, and enhance national branding. In this regard, government policies, investments, and strategic actions are key to maximizing tourism's potential in diplomacy (Carbone, 2017; Salman, 2023). The impact of government policies on tourism diplomacy is profound (Manfredi-Sánchez, 2022; Xu et al., 2020). Regulations, visa policies, and international agreements can either facilitate or hinder the flow of tourists. Governments can significantly enhance their country's appeal as a tourism destination through strategic policymaking, fostering cross-cultural exchanges, and strengthening international relationships.

Furthermore, government investments in tourism infrastructure, marketing, and cultural preservation support diplomatic efforts. These investments signal a commitment to tourism as a diplomatic tool and create opportunities for deeper engagement with the global community. Diplomatic missions, such as embassies and consulates, significantly promote tourism abroad (Oliver, 2016; Rana, 2013). These missions often collaborate with tourism ministries and other governmental bodies to organize events, campaigns, and promotional activities that showcase a country's tourism offerings. This active promotion of tourism as part of diplomatic relations not only contributes to economic growth but also fosters cultural diplomacy and international cooperation.

Government policies that support tourism in international relations are a crucial aspect of tourism diplomacy. By fostering an environment conducive to tourism growth, governments can significantly enhance their country's attractiveness to tourists while promoting diplomatic initiatives (Çokişler & Çokişler, 2023; Faucher, 2016). These policies, including incentives for international tourism partnerships, fostering exchange programs, and promoting sustainable tourism practices, play a key role in shaping a country's tourism diplomacy. Tourism ministries are pivotal in advancing a country's diplomatic goals and bridging the tourism industry and diplomatic efforts, often leading public diplomacy initiatives (Haq & Medhekar, 2019; Jamieson & Nadkarni, 2009). These ministries use tourism as a platform to showcase a country's culture, history, and values to the world. By coordinating tourism promotion activities, implementing supportive policies, and representing the nation on the international stage, tourism ministries significantly contribute to a country's diplomatic goals through tourism (Fig. 5).

2. The Effect of Government Policies on Tourism Diplomacy

Governments increasingly recognize the strategic importance of tourism not just as a sector of economic significance but also as a diplomatic instrument that can

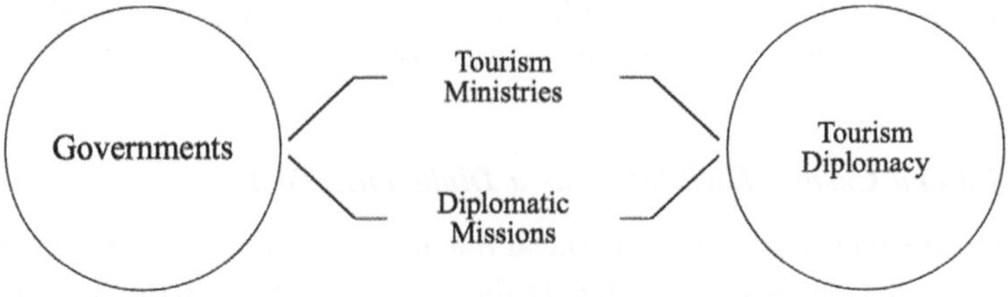

Fig. 5. Governments in Tourism Diplomacy.

build bridges between nations. Through tourism diplomacy, countries enhance their global image, strengthen bilateral ties, and contribute to creating a more interconnected world. The various government policies that shape the tourism environments are central to this process, including visa facilitation, strategic partnerships, and health and safety protocols (Fig. 6). These policies are critical in creating a favorable environment for international tourism while addressing the challenges of balancing security, economic interests, and diplomatic goals. The facilitation of visas and customs procedures, for instance, not only encourages travel but also reflects a nation's openness to engagement with the international community. Strategic partnerships and bilateral agreements between countries

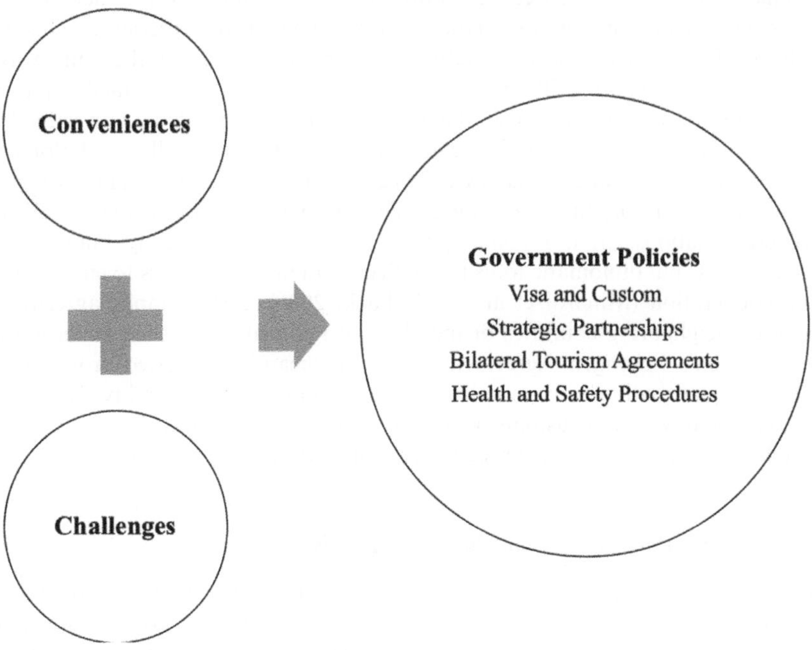

Fig. 6. Government Policies on Tourism Diplomacy.

enhance tourism flows and strengthen diplomatic ties. At the same time, state policies are essential in overcoming security concerns and global crises.

2.1 Visa and Custom Facilitation as a Diplomatic Tool

Visa and customs policies play a crucial role in tourism diplomacy by acting as a bridge between countries, encouraging tourism flows, and fostering international relationships (Minardi et al., 2021; Wang et al., 2019). Visa facilitation, or easing visa regulations, is one of the most effective ways for governments to promote tourism. Governments significantly increase inbound tourists by simplifying visa procedures, reducing costs, or even introducing visa exemptions for certain countries (Pack, 2006). This, in turn, strengthens diplomatic ties, creates opportunities for cultural exchange, and enhances mutual understanding between nations. For instance, countries that have adopted e-visas or visa-on-arrival policies have seen notable increases in tourist arrivals. These measures streamline the process for tourists, making it easier and more convenient to visit a country, thereby positioning tourism as a tool for diplomacy.

Custom facilitation, similarly, is an essential aspect of enhancing tourism by simplifying procedures at entry points such as airports and border crossings (Wang et al., 2019; Ye et al., 2020). Efficient customs processes not only contribute to the overall visitor experience but also reduce wait times and complexities, fostering goodwill. For instance, countries that adopt international standards for customs procedures allow for duty-free imports and facilitate the movement of personal goods encourage a smoother travel experience. This not only benefits tourists but also strengthens the diplomatic image of the country as a welcoming destination. By emphasizing the role of customs facilitation in enhancing the visitor experience, the audience will feel considered and valued.

Visa and customs facilitation can also be used strategically in diplomatic negotiations. Governments may extend visa-free travel to certain countries as part of broader trade or diplomatic agreements, signaling goodwill and enhancing bilateral relations. In this context, visa policies are not merely bureaucratic requirements but diplomatic tools that reflect a country's openness to engagement and cooperation (Minardi et al., 2021; Pack, 2006). For example, agreements between neighboring countries or members of regional blocs, such as the European Union's Schengen Agreement, have significantly facilitated cross-border tourism, contributing to economic integration and regional stability. By stressing the role of visa and customs policies as diplomatic tools, the audience will feel enlightened and aware of their significance in international relations.

2.2 Strategic Partnerships and Bilateral Tourism Agreements

Strategic partnerships and bilateral tourism agreements are the main components of tourism diplomacy, allowing countries to collaborate to boost tourism flows and enhance diplomatic relations (Cheer & Herrschner, 2018; Su et al., 2022). These partnerships typically involve governments, tourism boards, and other key stakeholders working together to promote tourism between two countries, often through joint marketing initiatives, shared infrastructure investments, and coordinated tourism policies. These agreements go beyond economic interests and significantly contribute to cultural exchange and mutual understanding between nations, strengthening diplomatic ties (Dharmawan et al., 2024).

Bilateral tourism agreements are often the result of high-level diplomatic negotiations, where tourism is viewed as a sector that can foster cooperation between countries (Quer, 2021; Salman, 2023). These agreements can include visa relaxation policies, direct flight connections, and mutual promotion of each other's tourism destinations. For example, countries that enter into Open Skies Agreements, which allow for unrestricted air travel between them, often experience a significant increase in tourism. Such agreements reduce barriers to entry, making travel more accessible and appealing, and serve as a diplomatic tool to enhance relations. They can also encourage investment in tourism infrastructure, such as hotels, resorts, and cultural centers, that benefit both countries.

Strategic partnerships in tourism can also encompass collaboration on large-scale events, such as international expos or sporting events, which draw global audiences (Demir & Dalgıç, 2022). Co-hosting such events provides a platform for countries to not only display their tourism potential but also to bolster diplomatic relations. A prime example is the FIFA World Cup, which has been co-hosted by multiple countries, enhancing their tourism industries and diplomatic standing in the global arena.

Tourism agreements often extend to sustainable tourism practices, where countries collaborate on preserving natural and cultural heritage while promoting responsible tourism (Salman, 2023; Su et al., 2022). This involves sharing best practices for environmental conservation, promoting eco-tourism, and developing policies that ensure the long-term sustainability of tourist destinations (Cheer & Herrschner, 2018; Quer, 2021). Through these efforts, countries can align their tourism goals with broader diplomatic objectives, such as promoting environmental awareness and global cooperation on climate change.

2.3 Facilitating Health and Safety Procedures Through Tourism Diplomacy

Facilitating health and safety procedures is increasingly becoming a core aspect of tourism diplomacy, particularly in the wake of global health crises like the COVID-19 pandemic (Demir et al., 2020). Governments recognize that a strong focus on health and safety can restore confidence in international travel and enhance their diplomatic relations by demonstrating a commitment to protecting tourists. Tourism diplomacy in this context involves collaboration between countries to establish uniform health protocols, share best practices, and ensure that health measures are respected across borders (Demir et al., 2021; Kelman et al., 2020).

One of the critical ways that governments facilitate health and safety procedures through tourism diplomacy is by establishing bilateral or multilateral agreements on health standards for travelers (Labonté et al., 2018). For example, during the COVID-19 pandemic, many countries developed health corridors or "travel bubbles," allowing for the safe movement of travelers between nations with low infection rates. These agreements often included coordinated testing protocols, quarantine regulations, and health certification requirements, which helped restart international tourism while ensuring the safety of tourists and local populations. Such initiatives not only restarted international tourism but also underscored the pivotal and significant role of tourism diplomacy in addressing global health challenges, as they required close cooperation between governments, health organizations, and the private sector.

Health and safety procedures in tourism also protect tourists from other risks, such as natural disasters, terrorism, and crime (Demir et al., 2021; Kelman et al., 2020). Governments can use tourism diplomacy to work together on risk mitigation strategies, such as early warning systems for natural disasters, international security protocols for tourist sites, and the sharing of intelligence on potential threats. By facilitating cooperation in these areas, tourism diplomacy contributes to creating a safer environment for tourists, which is essential for the long-term growth of the tourism sector.

Moreover, facilitating health and safety procedures through tourism diplomacy often involves collaboration with international organizations, such as the World Health Organization (WHO) and the United Nations World Tourism Organization (UNWTO) (Kelman et al., 2020; Labonté et al., 2018). These organizations play a crucial and informative role in guiding best practices for health and safety in tourism, helping governments to align their policies with international standards. For instance, the UNWTO's guidelines for the safe reopening of tourism have been adopted by many countries, helping to ensure that tourism can resume safely while minimizing the risk of COVID-19 transmission. Through such collaborations, tourism diplomacy plays a vital role in maintaining global health security and ensuring the sustainability of the tourism sector.

2.4 Challenges in Supporting Tourism Through State Policies

While state policies play a vital role in supporting tourism, governments often face several challenges (Fig. 6) in aligning these policies with the goals of tourism diplomacy (Fayard, 2024; Joppe et al., 2024). One of the main challenges is balancing national security concerns with the facilitation of tourism. Visa policies, for example, must ensure the safety and security of citizens while also being flexible enough to encourage tourism. Striking this balance is difficult, as overly restrictive policies can deter potential tourists, while overly lenient policies may pose security risks.

Another challenge in supporting tourism through state policies is managing the impact of tourism on local communities and environments (Joppe et al., 2024; Ormerod & Wood, 2021). While tourism can be a significant driver of economic growth, it can also lead to over-tourism, environmental degradation, and the displacement of local populations if not appropriately managed. Governments need to develop policies that promote sustainable tourism, balancing the needs of tourists with the preservation of cultural heritage and natural resources. This requires collaboration between governmental departments, such as those responsible for tourism, the environment, and cultural affairs, and engagement with local communities and the private sector.

Economic inequality between nations also presents a challenge in supporting tourism diplomacy. Developing countries may lack the infrastructure, financial resources, and expertise to benefit from tourism fully. In these cases, state policies need to focus on building capacity and fostering international partnerships that can support the development of the tourism sector (Fayard, 2024; Sorzano & Miller, 2018). This may include investments in transportation infrastructure, training programs for tourism professionals, and the creation of incentives for foreign investment in tourism projects. Importantly, international aid and development agencies can play a significant role in helping countries develop their tourism industries in a way that is sustainable and beneficial to local communities. Their involvement underscores the potential for global collaboration and assistance in supporting tourism.

Global crises, such as pandemics, natural disasters, and political instability, pose significant challenges to supporting tourism through state policies (Demir et al., 2021). The COVID-19 pandemic, for example, led to unprecedented travel restrictions and a collapse in international tourism, forcing governments to rethink their tourism policies. In response, many governments introduced policies aimed at supporting the recovery of the tourism industry, such as financial aid for tourism businesses, promotional campaigns to attract domestic tourists, and the development of health and safety protocols for travelers (Joppe et al., 2024; Ormerod & Wood, 2021). However, these policies must be carefully designed to ensure that they are not just responsive but also flexible and resilient enough to respond to future crises. The need for adaptability and flexibility in policy design is urgent and cannot be overstated.

3. Government Tourism Investments and Diplomatic Strategies

In tourism diplomacy, government investments play a pivotal role in advancing a nation's diplomatic and economic objectives. By investing in the tourism sector, governments stimulate economic growth and promote their countries as attractive destinations, thereby enhancing international relations (Şen, 2019). These investments are often strategically aligned with diplomatic efforts to promote cultural exchange, foster international cooperation, and attract foreign direct investment (FDI) in tourism infrastructure. Governments utilize tourism diplomacy to achieve several key objectives, including protecting cultural heritage, attracting foreign investment, and developing tourism infrastructure and superstructure. These efforts are not solely about enhancing a country's tourism appeal but also aim to strengthen international ties and position the nation as a global player. At the same time, diplomatic strategies focused on attracting foreign investment to help build the necessary infrastructure and superstructure to boost tourism.

3.1 Government Projects for the Protection of Cultural Heritage

One of the most significant ways governments can leverage tourism diplomacy is through projects to protect and promote cultural heritage. These initiatives, which include preserving historical sites, traditional customs, and intangible cultural elements, serve a dual purpose. They not only safeguard national identity and history but also act as a platform for international engagement through tourism. By investing in these projects, governments enhance their country's attractiveness to tourists and strengthen cultural diplomacy (Cameron, 2015; Folmer et al., 2016; Winter, 2016). For example, countries like Italy, Greece, and Egypt have invested heavily in restoring and promoting their ancient sites. These projects attract global tourists while reinforcing their historical significance on the world stage. Such efforts contribute to diplomatic relations by showcasing the country's commitment to preserving shared human history, thus fostering goodwill among international partners.

Governments frequently collaborate with international organizations such as UNESCO, the World Tourism Organization (UNWTO), or foreign governments to secure funding, expertise, and international support for heritage conservation projects. These partnerships further enhance diplomatic ties as countries promote and protect global heritage (García, 2024; Singh & Rana, 2021). For example, international efforts to restore the Great Wall of China or the temples of Angkor Wat have involved cross-border collaboration, improving these sites and strengthening diplomatic relationships between the involved countries.

Another aspect of tourism diplomacy gaining prominence is preserving intangible cultural heritage (Lähdesmäki, 2021; Özlem, 2019; Singh & Rana, 2021; Winter, 2016). Governments increasingly focus on safeguarding traditional music, dance, and craftsmanship. Initiatives like cultural festivals, international exhibitions, and traditional arts performances are crucial in promoting cultural exchange and dialogue. These projects not only invite foreign tourists to experience the country's heritage firsthand but also reinforce a country's soft power. These efforts support both tourism and diplomatic objectives by shaping a positive global image and attracting cultural tourists.

3.2 Diplomatic Strategies for Attracting Foreign Investment in Tourism

Governments employ diplomatic tools and techniques to entice foreign investors to fund tourism-related projects, stimulating economic growth, job creation, and the development of crucial infrastructure (Bouzanis, 2009; Kristensen, 2020). These diplomatic strategies often include negotiating investment agreements, creating favorable regulatory environments, and promoting public–private partnerships (Okano-Heijmans, 2012; Wang et al., 2023). One common diplomatic strategy involves signing bilateral or multilateral investment treaties (BITs and MITs) that provide legal protections and incentives for foreign investors. These agreements typically offer guarantees against expropriation, fair treatment clauses, and mechanisms for dispute resolution, which reduce the risks associated with foreign investment. Governments can attract international capital into their tourism sectors by providing a stable and predictable investment environment (Okafor et al., 2021; Quer, 2024). For example, countries in the Caribbean, such as the Dominican Republic and Jamaica, have successfully attracted FDI through BITs, promoting the development of luxury resorts and tourism infrastructure.

Governments also leverage diplomatic missions and trade delegations to attract foreign tourism investment. These high-level diplomatic visits often involve meetings with potential investors, providing governments a platform to showcase investment opportunities in their tourism sectors. These missions are a vital part of tourism diplomacy, as they enable governments to build personal relationships with key foreign investors, address their concerns, and highlight the country's competitive advantages (Kristensen, 2020; Wang et al., 2023). Another significant diplomatic strategy involves offering tax incentives, reduced regulatory barriers, and special economic zones (SEZs) designed explicitly for tourism development (Quer, 2024; Wang et al., 2023). These measures make a country more attractive to foreign investors, who may seek lower operating costs or more accessible access to critical markets. Countries like the United Arab Emirates and Indonesia have successfully implemented SEZs to attract major international hotel chains, resort developers, and other tourism-related businesses. By using tourism diplomacy to offer favorable investment conditions, governments can create a competitive edge in the global tourism market.

3.3 Attracting Tourism Infrastructure Investments Through Tourism Diplomacy

Tourism infrastructure refers to the physical and organizational structures the tourism industry needs to function, including transportation systems, accommodation, utilities, and communication networks (Demir & Demir, 2024). Through tourism diplomacy, governments seek to secure international investments that help develop or improve airports, roads, ports, and public transportation systems, which are essential for facilitating the movement of tourists and enhancing the overall visitor experience (Grudtsyn, 2024; Thirumaran et al., 2021). One of the most proactive ways governments attract infrastructure investments is by positioning their country as a strategic hub for international travel. This is particularly relevant for countries that serve as transit points between regions, such as the Gulf States. These countries have attracted massive investments in airport infrastructure and airline partnerships through tourism diplomacy. For instance, Dubai's tourism strategy has been closely linked to developing its world-class airport and expanding Emirates Airlines, which have helped transform the city into a global tourism and business hub. These developments were made possible through diplomatic efforts, including bilateral aviation agreements, international marketing campaigns, and foreign investment partnerships.

Governments collaborate with foreign investors and private companies to finance and build essential infrastructure in this highly effective model (Thirumaran et al., 2021; Van Noort, 2021). These partnerships often emerge from diplomatic engagements, where governments negotiate mutually beneficial terms for both the state and private investors. Governments may provide incentives such as tax breaks, long-term leases, or land grants to encourage foreign companies to invest in infrastructure projects to enhance the country's tourism potential. Another diplomatic strategy for attracting tourism infrastructure investments involves using international development banks and multilateral financial institutions (Winter, 2016; Zhang et al., 2020). Governments can leverage their diplomatic relationships with organizations such as the World Bank, the International Monetary Fund (IMF), and regional development banks to secure financing for large-scale infrastructure projects. These institutions often provide low-interest loans or grants for projects that improve transportation networks, water systems, and energy supplies, which are critical to tourism development. Countries in Southeast Asia, such as Vietnam and Cambodia, have used such funding to improve their tourism infrastructure, making their destinations more accessible and appealing to international tourists.

3.4 Attracting Tourism Superstructure Investments Through Tourism Diplomacy

Tourism superstructure refers to the facilities and services directly related to tourism, such as hotels, resorts, restaurants, entertainment venues, and cultural centers (Demir, 2017). Attracting investments in these areas is crucial for a country's ability to offer high-quality tourism experiences that can compete on a global scale. Governments use tourism diplomacy to attract foreign investors to develop tourism superstructure by promoting investment opportunities, creating favorable conditions for development, and showcasing their countries as attractive destinations for luxury tourism, cultural tourism, and eco-tourism. Some countries have attracted international hotel chains, amusement parks, and luxury resorts through diplomatic efforts, contributing significantly to tourism revenue. This success is a testament to the role of governments in ensuring the stability and growth of the local tourism industry (Abuan, 2021; Dermawan et al., 2022).

Governments also use diplomatic tools to secure foreign investment in superstructure by negotiating joint ventures with international companies. Foreign investors collaborate with local businesses or the government in these joint ventures to develop tourism-related facilities. Such partnerships often come with the added benefit of knowledge transfer, where foreign expertise in hospitality management, marketing, and service quality enhances the local tourism industry's standards (Alipour & Kilic, 2005; Dermawan et al., 2022). For example, African and Caribbean countries have successfully attracted foreign investors to develop eco-lodges and sustainable resorts, promoting environmental conservation while offering tourists unique experiences. Moreover, governments use tourism diplomacy to create specialized tourism zones that attract foreign investment in the superstructure.

3.5 Diplomatic Missions and Tourism Promotion Activities

Governments leverage tourism diplomacy through diplomatic missions, such as embassies and consulates (Bouzanis, 2009; Kobierecka & Kobierecki, 2024). These institutions serve as vital channels for promoting tourism, fostering international cooperation, and facilitating relationships between nations. Diplomatic missions not only represent their country's interests abroad but also play a central role in attracting tourists, showcasing cultural heritage, and creating an inviting image of their homeland. This role is not just a duty but a source of pride and responsibility for these missions. Tourism promotion through diplomatic missions involves various activities, from organizing cultural events to negotiating bilateral tourism agreements. Embassies and consulates often collaborate with local tourism boards, international organizations, and private sector stakeholders to market their country as a desirable tourist destination. These missions engage in public diplomacy efforts to promote soft power by facilitating cultural exchange and dialogue through tourism. However, diplomatic tourism promotion has challenges, including navigating complex international relations, adapting to local market conditions, and competing with other nations for tourist attention. These challenges underscore the need for strategic solutions in this field.

3.6 The Role of Embassies and Consulates in Tourism Promotion

Embassies and consulates are pivotal in promoting tourism as part of their broader diplomatic mandate (Boromisa & RadityaLežaić, 2014; Fernández, 2019). As official representatives of their governments abroad, these diplomatic institutions are not only responsible for fostering positive relationships with host countries but also for creating a sense of connection and understanding. They present their nation in the best possible light, highlighting their home country's cultural, historical, and recreational attractions. In doing so, embassies and consulates are vital links between foreign travelers and the destination, encouraging international tourism while supporting the local tourism industry.

Embassies often organize and host cultural events, exhibitions, and festivals to showcase their country's unique cultural heritage, art, cuisine, and traditions (Lee & Ruël, 2012; Rana, 2013). Tourism events promote tourism and enhance the host country's understanding and appreciation of the nation being represented. These events contribute to the country's soft power by fostering cultural diplomacy and attracting tourists intrigued by the experiences showcased. In addition to cultural events, consulates play a critical role in providing practical assistance to potential tourists. They offer visa services, distribute tourism brochures and guides, and give information on travel requirements, accommodations, and attractions. Consulates also serve as contact points for tourism boards and travel agencies, ensuring that foreign visitors receive accurate and up-to-date information about the country. For example, the Italian consulate in New York works closely with Italian tourism authorities to provide American tourists with detailed information about travel to Italy, including tips on cultural etiquette, transportation, and sightseeing.

Moreover, diplomatic missions use targeted marketing campaigns to attract specific tourist demographics. Depending on the country's strengths and tourism objectives, these campaigns are designed to appeal to adventure travelers, history buffs, or luxury tourists. Many embassies collaborate with local media, travel bloggers, and influencers to promote tourism through social media campaigns and digital marketing efforts (Fernández, 2019; Pack, 2006). By leveraging modern marketing tools, embassies and consulates can reach a broader audience and promote tourism in ways that not only resonate with contemporary travelers but also intrigue them, sparking their interest in the country's unique offerings.

3.7 Facilitating Tourism Cooperation Through Diplomatic Channels

Diplomatic missions facilitate tourism cooperation between countries through formal and informal channels. One of their essential functions is establishing and maintaining bilateral and multilateral agreements that encourage tourism exchange. These agreements often involve simplifying visa requirements, improving transportation links, and fostering partnerships between tourism industries. Bilateral tourism agreements negotiated through diplomatic channels are common tools to promote tourism cooperation (Cheng, 2015; Xu et al., 2020). These agreements typically include provisions that encourage mutual tourism promotion, joint marketing campaigns, and the development of tourism infrastructure. More importantly, they foster mutual understanding and empathy. For instance, the China-ASEAN Tourism Cooperation Agreement, facilitated through diplomatic channels, promotes cultural and tourism exchange between China and ASEAN member countries. This agreement has increased tourist flows between these nations, strengthened their economic ties, and fostered mutual understanding through tourism. In addition to formal agreements, diplomatic missions are key in organizing joint tourism initiatives, such as tourism fairs, roadshows, and travel trade missions. These initiatives allow diplomatic missions to engage directly with tourism professionals and promote their countries as top destinations for international travelers (Dai et al., 2017; Kim et al., 2016).

Diplomatic missions also play a crucial role in enhancing the quality and competitiveness of the tourism sector (Qiu et al., 2015; Xu et al., 2020). They do this by promoting the exchange of knowledge and best practices between countries. Embassies and consulates often act as conduits for tourism professionals to learn from one another through training programs, workshops, or internships. Such exchanges help enhance the quality and competitiveness of the tourism sector by allowing countries to learn from each other's successes and challenges (Dai et al., 2017; Qiu et al., 2015). For example, through diplomatic efforts, countries in Latin America have established tourism cooperation programs with Spain to enhance their capabilities in heritage tourism and hospitality management. Through their diplomatic efforts, embassies and consulates contribute to building stronger international relationships and promoting sustainable tourism development. Encouraging collaboration between governments and tourism stakeholders creates an environment where tourism can flourish, benefiting both the sending and receiving countries.

3.8 Tourism Promotion in Collaboration With International Organizations

International organizations play a significant role in shaping global tourism trends, and diplomatic missions often collaborate with these entities to promote their countries as tourist destinations. Organizations like the UNWTO, UNESCO, and the International Civil Aviation Organization (ICAO) provide frameworks for tourism development, sustainable practices, and cultural heritage preservation, all vital for successful tourism diplomacy (Fig. 7). Diplomatic missions engage with these organizations to enhance their tourism promotion efforts and ensure their country is aligned with international tourism standards and practices (Demir, 2017).

Collaboration with organizations like UNWTO (2024) is a key strategy for diplomatic missions to leverage global tourism initiatives and gain visibility on the international stage. Through these partnerships, countries can participate in global campaigns, such as World Tourism Day, which raises awareness of

Fig. 7. International Organizations for Tourism Diplomacy.

tourism's economic and social importance. By aligning their tourism promotion activities with international campaigns, embassies can significantly boost their country's profile as a desirable tourist destination. For example, Morocco's diplomatic missions have actively collaborated with UNWTO to promote sustainable tourism, increasing international recognition of Morocco's eco-tourism offerings.

Diplomatic missions significantly promote their country's World Heritage Sites, often working closely with UNESCO (2024). These cultural and natural landmarks are significant draws for international tourists, and being included on the World Heritage List elevates a country's status in the global tourism market. For instance, in collaboration with UNESCO, Italy has worked extensively through its diplomatic channels to promote its World Heritage Sites, such as the Colosseum and the Leaning Tower of Pisa.

The ICAO is another key partner in promoting tourism, particularly air travel and accessibility. Diplomatic missions collaborate with the ICAO (2024) to ensure that their country's airports and aviation policies align with international standards, making it easier for tourists to travel to their destination. Countries with well-developed aviation infrastructure, like Singapore and the United Arab Emirates, have successfully used their diplomatic channels to engage with the ICAO, increasing tourist arrivals through enhanced air connectivity.

3.9 Challenges in Tourism Promotion Through Diplomatic Missions

While diplomatic missions are essential in promoting tourism, they face several challenges that can hinder their effectiveness. One of the primary challenges is the political climate between the sending and receiving countries. Diplomatic tensions or conflicts can negatively impact tourism promotion efforts, as potential travelers may perceive a destination as unsafe or unwelcoming (Bouzanis, 2009; Kharel, 2023). For example, strained relations between countries can result in travel advisories, discouraging tourism and creating barriers to effective promotion through diplomatic channels.

Another significant challenge is the fierce competition for tourist attention in the increasingly crowded global tourism market. Diplomatic missions must continually innovate and adapt their promotional strategies to stand out among the many countries vying for tourists. This demands significant resources and expertise, which may not always be readily available to all diplomatic missions, especially those from smaller or less-developed nations (Mark, 2010; Spies, 2019). The pressure to compete with established tourism powerhouses like France, Spain, and the United States can make it difficult for emerging destinations to attract the attention they need to grow their tourism sectors. Limited financial and human resources often constrain embassies' and consulates' ability to engage in tourism promotion activities fully. This can lead to a lack of dedicated personnel or funding for tourism-related events, marketing campaigns, and collaborations with local tourism boards. In some cases, diplomatic missions may struggle to balance tourism promotion with other diplomatic priorities, such as trade relations, security issues, or political negotiations (Sulaiman & Wilson, 2018; Tessema & Haile, 2022).

Cultural differences and local market conditions also challenge effective tourism promotion through diplomatic missions (Kharel, 2023; Wigley, 2015). Understanding potential tourists' preferences, behaviors, and motivations in different regions requires a deep understanding of local cultures and trends. Diplomatic missions must tailor their promotional efforts to suit the tastes and interests of the local population, which can be challenging in diverse and complex markets. For example, promoting adventure tourism in Japan may require different strategies than in the United States, and diplomatic missions must be able to adapt their approach accordingly. The rise of digital platforms and social media has revolutionized tourism promotion, and diplomatic missions must keep pace with these changes. Traditional methods of tourism promotion, such as brochures and travel fairs, are increasingly being replaced by digital marketing campaigns and influencer partnerships. Diplomatic missions may face challenges in adopting these new tools and technologies, particularly if they lack the expertise or resources to engage effectively with online platforms (Demir, 2017).

4. The Role of Tourism Ministries as a Tool for Public Diplomacy

Tourism has become essential for nations to engage in public diplomacy in the globalized world. Tourism diplomacy involves using tourism to enhance a country's soft power, build international relationships, and promote cultural exchange. The tourism ministries are at the core of these efforts and collaborate closely with national tourism boards, embassies, consulates, and international organizations. This collaborative approach is critical to promoting their countries as attractive tourist destinations and fostering a sense of unity and shared purpose. Tourism ministries facilitate public diplomacy by organizing global promotional campaigns, hosting events, and coordinating international tourism initiatives (Avraham, 2018; Rosendorf & Rosendorf, 2014). However, tourism ministries face several challenges in their public diplomacy efforts, including political instability, financial constraints, and competition in the global tourism market (Rosendorf & Rosendorf, 2014; Strömbom, 2019).

4.1 Tourism Ministries as Facilitators of National Image

Tourism ministries are critical in shaping and promoting a nation's image abroad. By carefully crafting tourism strategies and public diplomacy initiatives, these ministries serve as key facilitators in how international audiences perceive their country (Abraham, 2024; Stachowiak et al., 2024). Tourism not only presents a positive image that aligns with a country's cultural values, historical heritage, and modern advancements but also brings significant economic benefits. The tourism ministry is often responsible for designing marketing campaigns and policies highlighting these aspects, ensuring their nation stands out as an appealing destination for tourists (Demir, 2017). A significant aspect of this responsibility is to ensure that the image promoted internationally aligns with the country's diplomatic goals. For instance, nations like Türkiye have heavily promoted their cultural traditions, environments, and hospitality through campaigns run by their tourism ministries, all of which contribute to positioning the country as a peaceful and welcoming destination. This positive national image boosts the country's reputation, facilitating smoother diplomatic relations and encouraging international cooperation.

Tourism ministries often focus on key themes or symbols that resonate with global tourists, such as a country's natural wonders, cultural landmarks, or even a unique aspect of its society, such as gastronomy or art. For example, Italy's tourism ministry promotes the country's world-renowned art, culture, and food, which not only draws tourists but also reinforces the image of Italy as a nation rich in history and culture. The benefits of this are twofold: while tourism numbers increase, the country also strengthens its position as a cultural and diplomatic leader on the global stage (Mansfeld, 2006; Stachowiak et al., 2024). Tourism ministries also balance preserving cultural integrity and appealing to modern tourism trends in promoting national image (Hazbun, 2006; Lamnadi, 2010). Some countries, like Bhutan, have implemented strict tourism policies to maintain cultural authenticity while promoting their image as sustainable, eco-conscious destinations. Bhutan's tourism ministry limits the number of tourists annually and requires visitors to follow eco-friendly guidelines, thus supporting the country's diplomatic stance on environmental conservation and responsible tourism. Through carefully designed public diplomacy efforts, tourism ministries are architects of a nation's international image.

4.2 National Tourism Boards and Global Promotion Campaigns

National tourism boards, often operating under the guidance of tourism ministries, are instrumental in launching global promotion campaigns that support a country's tourism diplomacy objectives (Baalbaki & Zizka, 2024; Senbeto et al., 2024). These boards function as specialized agencies responsible for marketing and promoting tourism domestically and internationally. By organizing targeted campaigns, collaborating with the private sector, and participating in international tourism fairs, national tourism boards work to elevate their country's profile on the global stage.

One of the most impactful tools in global promotion campaigns is branding. National tourism boards create distinct branding strategies that capture their country's essence, whether through slogans, logos, or visual imagery (Demir & Tür, 2019). For instance, "Incredible India" has been a remarkably successful global branding campaign designed by India's tourism board to showcase the country's diverse environments, culture, and spirituality. The campaign has not only attracted millions of tourists but has also enhanced India's soft power by promoting its rich heritage and modern aspirations.

These global promotion campaigns are often launched in collaboration with international tourism organizations and other key stakeholders in the travel industry, such as airlines, hotel chains, and tour operators (Blázquez-Resino et al., 2024; Moilanen & Rainisto, 2009). National tourism boards frequently participate in global trade shows like ITB Berlin or the World Travel Market in London, where they network with industry professionals, tour operators, and journalists to promote their country as a desirable destination. Through these events, countries can showcase their tourism offerings and build partnerships that increase tourist arrivals and strengthen diplomatic ties.

Tourism boards leverage modern marketing tools like social media, influencer partnerships, and online advertising to reach a broader and more diverse audience. Social media campaigns, for example, have become vital to tourism promotion, allowing national tourism boards to engage with potential tourists directly and in real-time. Countries like Australia have embraced social media platforms to run campaigns like "Tourism Australia's 100 Jobs" that engage audiences worldwide, offering immersive content highlighting Australia's unique experiences.

Tourism boards also significantly shape perceptions of their destinations (Baalbaki & Zizka, 2024; Pack, 2010). They develop partnerships with international media outlets to promote their destinations through documentaries, travel shows, and feature articles. By working with global media, they can tell compelling stories that appeal to potential tourists and shape perceptions of their country. For example, the New Zealand Tourism Board has effectively used film to promote tourism, capitalizing on the success of the "Lord of the Rings" film series filmed in New Zealand. The country's stunning environments became synonymous with Middle-earth, significantly boosting New Zealand's tourism numbers and reinforcing its image as a land of natural beauty.

4.3 Tourism Diplomacy Through Events Held by Tourism Ministries

Tourism ministries often organize large-scale events, conferences, and cultural festivals as part of their tourism diplomacy efforts (Demir & Dalgıç, 2022). These events serve as platforms for promoting tourism, fostering international collaboration, and enhancing a country's soft power. By hosting international events, tourism ministries provide opportunities for cultural exchange, showcase their nation's strengths, and position their country as a leader in the global tourism industry. One of the most prominent examples of tourism diplomacy through events is hosting world expos, which allow countries to showcase their technological innovations, cultural heritage, and tourism potential (Demir & Dalgıç, 2022; Kobierecka & Kobierecki, 2024). Dubai's Expo 2020, organized in part by the UAE's Ministry of Tourism, was a prime example of how a nation can use a global event to boost tourism while also advancing its diplomatic agenda. The expo attracted millions of international visitors, fostering cultural exchange and promoting the UAE as a forward-thinking and innovative nation. In addition to direct tourism benefits, the event created a platform for the UAE to engage with global leaders and strengthen its diplomatic relationships.

Cultural festivals organized by tourism ministries also play a key role in tourism diplomacy. These festivals, whether focused on music, food, film, or art, offer a way for countries to engage with international audiences on a cultural level, fostering mutual understanding and appreciation (Kobierecka & Kobierecki, 2024; Ormerod & Wood, 2021). For example, Spain's tourism ministry has used events like the annual "San Fermín" festival in Pamplona and "La Tomatina" in Buñol to attract international tourists while showcasing the country's rich cultural traditions. These festivals boost tourism and reinforce Spain's image as a country with vibrant cultural offerings. Conferences and summits hosted by tourism ministries, such as the World Tourism Conference or regional tourism forums, are also vital to tourism diplomacy. These events bring together global tourism leaders, policymakers, and stakeholders to discuss issues ranging from sustainable tourism to economic development (Demir, 2017). Tourism ministries hosting such events position their countries as thought leaders in the global tourism industry while fostering international cooperation and knowledge exchange. For example, the World Travel & Tourism Council (WTTC) Global Summit, often hosted by a country's tourism ministry, serves as a platform for high-level discussions on tourism's impact on the global economy, providing diplomatic engagement and promotion opportunities.

4.4 Challenges Faced by Tourism Ministries in Public Diplomacy

Despite tourism ministries' crucial role in public diplomacy, they face several challenges that can hinder their effectiveness. One of the most significant challenges is the unpredictable nature of international relations (Barker, 2010; Gordon, 2024). Diplomatic tensions, political instability, or even conflicts can negatively affect tourism promotion efforts, making it difficult for tourism ministries to attract foreign visitors or build international partnerships. For instance, political disputes between nations often lead to travel advisories, discouraging potential tourists and complicating tourism diplomacy efforts. Another challenge is the increasingly competitive nature of the global tourism market. Tourism ministries must constantly innovate to differentiate their countries from other destinations and stand out in a crowded field. With many countries investing heavily in tourism promotion, tourism ministries face the pressure of maintaining a distinct and attractive national image while competing with other nations for a share of the global tourism market (Miño, 2023; Shanks, 2009). Countries like the Maldives, for example, are known for their luxury resorts and pristine beaches but must continuously enhance their offerings to remain competitive against other tropical destinations.

Financial constraints also pose a significant challenge for tourism ministries in developing nations. Effective tourism diplomacy requires substantial investment in marketing campaigns, international events, and infrastructure (Gordon, 2024; Miño, 2023). However, many tourism ministries operate with limited budgets, which can restrict their ability to launch large-scale promotional campaigns or participate in global tourism events. This is particularly problematic for countries that rely heavily on tourism for economic growth but lack adequate financial resources to promote their destinations. Moreover, tourism ministries often face challenges aligning their public diplomacy efforts with their governments' broader foreign policy goals (Barker, 2010; Shanks, 2009). While tourism diplomacy aims to promote a positive national image and attract foreign visitors, it may sometimes conflict with other diplomatic priorities, such as trade policies or security concerns. Balancing tourism promotion with other diplomatic objectives requires careful coordination between tourism ministries and foreign affairs departments.

5. Conclusions

The role of governments in tourism diplomacy has evolved into a multifaceted framework that influences international relations, national identity, and economic development. In today's interconnected world, government involvement in tourism extends beyond mere promotional efforts, positioning itself as a strategic diplomatic instrument. This chapter has explored the depth and diversity of governmental actions in tourism diplomacy, highlighting its influence through policy, infrastructure investment, diplomatic representation, and public diplomacy mechanisms. Together, these efforts underscore the importance of tourism diplomacy as a tool for advancing national interests, enhancing cross-cultural exchange, and fostering economic growth.

The effectiveness of tourism diplomacy is often shaped by government policies that enhance travel accessibility and visitor engagement. Policies surrounding visa facilitation and customs processes are essential for building welcoming environments for international travelers. When countries streamline these processes, they project an image of openness and accessibility, strengthening international ties. However, executing these policies can be complex, involving negotiations, security considerations, and regional cooperation. Strategic partnerships and bilateral tourism agreements further illustrate the power of diplomacy in tourism, where nations collaborate to share resources, exchange best practices, and boost visitor flows in mutually beneficial ways. Nevertheless, governments also face challenges, as aligning tourism growth with national policy objectives can sometimes conflict with environmental, social, or security considerations. Maintaining a balance between these objectives requires a well-thought-out approach, where tourism diplomacy is continuously fine-tuned to respond to evolving global dynamics.

Government investments in tourism reveal a commitment to economic growth, cultural preservation, and international collaboration. Projects aimed at safeguarding cultural heritage are essential in this regard, as they protect a nation's history while promoting its unique attractions. Such initiatives contribute to an appealing tourism profile and foster international goodwill, primarily when cultural preservation is conducted in collaboration with foreign stakeholders or organizations. Additionally, tourism diplomacy opens channels for attracting foreign investment into the tourism sector, from infrastructure to superstructure projects. These investments are crucial for creating a tourism environment that meets international standards and appeals to diverse visitor demographics. However, diplomatic efforts to attract these investments require governments to communicate stability, reliability, and economic potential effectively. Ultimately, well-coordinated government strategies in tourism diplomacy serve as magnets for international investors and underscore a country's readiness to participate in the global tourism market.

Diplomatic missions, particularly embassies and consulates, are critical in promoting tourism. Embassies offer practical support to potential travelers and actively engage in promotional activities to enhance a nation's appeal abroad. The efforts made through these channels underscore tourism's role in cultural diplomacy, where promoting travel also fosters understanding and respect between different cultures. Collaborations with international organizations enable nations to participate in global tourism initiatives, lending credibility and visibility to their tourism sector internationally. However, diplomatic missions face obstacles, as they must navigate political tensions, cultural differences, and budget limitations hindering tourism promotion. By addressing these challenges with tact and adaptability, diplomatic missions can enhance tourism promotion activities, emphasizing the benefits of travel and exchange as a bridge between societies.

Tourism ministries play an instrumental role in shaping a country's international image through targeted public diplomacy efforts. By launching global campaigns, developing national tourism boards, and hosting events, these ministries create a narrative around the nation's identity and values, which can appeal to international tourists and contribute to a positive global reputation. Events hosted by tourism ministries serve not only as platforms for tourism promotion but also as venues for international engagement, where nations showcase their culture, values, and hospitality. Despite these advantages, tourism ministries also confront challenges, such as aligning promotional strategies with shifting public diplomacy goals and addressing the complexities of competing in a dynamic global market. Ensuring these campaigns resonate with international audiences requires adaptability, innovative thinking, and a commitment to presenting an authentic and inclusive national image.

References

Abraham, V. (2024). Consumer animosity in tourism research: A horizon 2050 paper. *Tourism Review*, 1–11. https://doi.org/10.1108/TR-10-2023-0741

Abuan, R. E. M. (2021). Cultural diplomacy of Thailand and Indonesia in the Philippines. *MJIR| Malaysian Journal of International Relations*, *9*(1), 88–104.

Alipour, H., & Kilic, H. (2005). An institutional appraisal of tourism development and planning: The case of the Turkish Republic of North Cyprus (TRNC). *Tourism Management*, *26*(1), 79–94.

Avraham, E. (2018). Image repair strategies adopted by MENA national tourism boards during and following crises. In D. Timothy (Ed.), *Routledge handbook on tourism in the Middle East and North Africa* (pp. 241–256). Routledge.

Baalbaki, J., & Zizka, L. (2024). Egyptian crises and destination brand image: The resurrection of the mummy. *Current Issues in Tourism*, *27*(6), 887–905.

Barker, F. (2010). Maximizing the migration policy buck: Uniting temporary labor, development and foreign policy goals in New Zealand. *Policy and Society*, *29*(4), 321–331.

Blázquez-Resino, J. J., Martínez-Ruiz, M. P., & Muro Rodríguez, A. I. (2024). Spain is different! An analysis of the promotion strategies in the tourism industry in Spain. *Journal of Historical Research in Marketing*, *16*(1), 25–47.

Boromisa, A. M., & Raditya Ležaić, A. (2014). Croatian commercial diplomacy–stepping stone toward economic recovery? *International Journal of Diplomacy and Economy*, *2*(3), 172–184.

Bouzanis, J. (2009). The economic face of public diplomacy: International business promotion and tourism. In E. H. Potter (Ed.), *Branding Canada: Projecting Canada's soft power through public diplomacy* (pp. 173–193). McGill-Queen's University Press.

Cameron, C. (2015). UNESCO and cultural heritage: Unexpected consequences. *A Companion to Heritage Studies*, 322–336.

Carbone, F. (2017). International tourism and cultural diplomacy: A new conceptual approach towards global mutual understanding and peace through tourism. *Tourism: An International Interdisciplinary Journal*, *65*(1), 61–74.

Cheer, J. M., & Herrschner, I. (2018). Cinematic diplomacy and the exotic other in the film Tanna: Implications for bilateral relations and tourism. *International Journal of Tourism Anthropology*, *6*(3), 201–218.

Cheng, Y. (2015). Do national policies contribute to regional cross-border integration?: The case of the program of cooperation between Northeast China and Russia's Far East and Eastern Siberia (2009–2018). In J. Huang & A. Korolev (Eds.), *International cooperation in the development of Russia's Far East and Siberia* (pp. 202–228). Palgrave Macmillan UK.

Çokişler, D. E., & Çokişler, N. (2023). A conceptual overview of the relationship between tourism and peace in terms of international relations theories. *Current Issues in Tourism*, *26*(5), 708–717.

Dai, B., Jiang, Y., Yang, L., & Ma, Y. (2017). China's outbound tourism–Stages, policies and choices. *Tourism Management*, *58*, 253–258.

Demir, M. (2017). *Genel Turizm: Kavramlar ve Farklı Boyutlarıyla Değerlendirme*. Detay Yayıncılık.

Demir, M., & Dalgıç, A. (2022). Examining gastronomy festivals as the attractiveness factor for tourism destinations: The case of Turkey. *Journal of Convention & Event Tourism*, *23*, 412–434. https://doi.org/10.1080/15470148.2022.2089797

Demir, M., & Demir, Ş.Ş. (2024). Is the global technological outage a caution for the service industries? Evidence from the tourism industry. *Current Issues in Tourism*, 1–21. https://doi.org/10.1080/13683500.2024.2408581

Demir, M., Demir, Ş. Ş., Dalgıç, A., & Ergen, F. D. (2021). Impact of COVID-19 pandemic on the tourism industry: An evaluation from the hotel managers' perspective. *Journal of Tourism Theory and Research*, *7*(1), 44–57. https://doi.org/10.24288/jttr.857610

Demir, M., Günaydın, Y., & Demir, Ş. Ş. (2020). Koronavirüs (Covid-19) salgınının Türkiye'de turizm üzerindeki öncülleri, etkileri ve sonuçlarının değerlendirilmesi. *International Journal of Social Sciences and Education Research*, *6*(1), 80–107.

Demir, Ş. Ş., & Tür, E. (2019). Otel logosu ne söyler? Tüketiciler ne algılar? *Journal of Tourism Theory and Research*, *5*(1), 51–64.

Dermawan, W., Darmawan, I., Mustofa, M. U., & Djuyandi, Y. (2022). Paradiplomacy practices in Indonesia: Comparative analysis of Aceh-Quebec. *Politics & Policy*, *50*(2), 363–379.

Dharmawan, D., Amiruddin, A., Ekasari, S., Asry, W., & Munizu, M. (2024). Analysis of the influence of bilateral relations among countries, foreign policy and tourism regulations on the competitiveness of local tourism in Indonesia. *Innovative: Journal of Social Science Research*, *4*(3), 13701–13709.

Faucher, C. (2016). Cultural diplomacy and international cultural relations in twentieth-century Europe. *Contemporary European History*, *25*(2), 373–385.

Fayard, G. (2024). The geopolitics of outbound travel: Theorizing outgoing tourism as state strategy. *Environment and Planning C: Politics and Space*, *42*(5), 881–900.

Fernández, I. C. (2019). Tourism diplomacy council. *Revista Mexicana de Política Exterior*, *117*, 23–35.

Folmer, A., Revier, H., & Cupido, T. (2016). Sustainable tourism development and the world heritage status of the Wadden Sea: The case of Terschelling. *Research in Hospitality Management*, *6*(1), 45–50.

García, P. (2024). Diplomatic heritage: The involvement of the world monuments fund in the Sacred Valley of the Incas, Cuzco, Peru 1. In G. Bozoğlu, G. Campbell, L. Smith, & C. Whitehead (Eds.), *The Routledge international handbook of heritage and politics* (pp. 552–567). Routledge.

Gordon, R. (2024). Concepts and strategies required to develop the professional integration of travel and tourism. In B. Prideaux & D. Beirman (Eds.), *Handbook on crisis and disaster management in tourism* (pp. 280–294). Edward Elgar Publishing.

Grudtsyn, N. A. (2024). The impact of global and regional challenges on the decrease in tourist flows. *Geography, Environment, Sustainability*, *17*(3), 47–63.

Haq, F., & Medhekar, A. (2019). Is spiritual tourism a peace vehicle for social transformation and economic prosperity in India and Pakistan? In A.-M. Nedelea & M.-O. Nedelea (Eds.), *Marketing peace for social transformation and global prosperity* (pp. 189–211). IGI Global.

Hazbun, W. (2006). Explaining the Arab Middle East tourism paradox. *The Arab World Geographer*, *9*(3), 201–214.

ICAO. (2024). *Focus: ICAO'S Strategic Objectives*. https://www.icao.int/Pages/default.aspx. Accessed 10 22, 2024.

Jamieson, W., & Nadkarni, S. (2009). A reality check of tourism's potential as a development tool. *Asia Pacific Journal of Tourism Research*, *14*(2), 111–123.

Joppe, M., Laesser, C., & Mann, S. (2024). Tourism policies reloaded: Towards a comprehensive framework. In C. Pforr, M. Pillmayer, M. Joppe, N. Scherle, & H. Pechlaner (Eds.), *Tourism policy-making in the context of contested wicked problems: Politics, paradigm shifts and transformation processes* (pp. 303–320). Emerald Publishing Limited.

Kelman, I., Sydnes, A. K., Duda, P. I., Nikitina, E., & Webersik, C. (2020). Norway-Russia disaster diplomacy for Svalbard. *Safety Science*, *130*, 1–12.

Kharel, H. (2023). The growing importance of development diplomacy. *NCWA Annual Journal*, 1–10.

Kim, S. S., Prideaux, B., & Timothy, D. (2016). Factors affecting bilateral Chinese and Japanese travel. *Annals of Tourism Research*, *61*, 80–95.

Kobierecka, A., & Kobierecki, M. M. (2024). Public diplomacy and nation branding in action: Swiss Embassy's participation in the night of museums event in Warsaw. *Place Branding and Public Diplomacy*, *20*(2), 204–217.

Kristensen, A. E. (2020). Foreign direct investment in the Chinese outbound tourism industry: The policies, participants and possibilities. *Journal of Policy Research in Tourism, Leisure and Events*, *12*(1), 8–20.

Labonté, R., Crooks, V. A., Valdés, A. C., Runnels, V., & Snyder, J. (2018). Government roles in regulating medical tourism: Evidence from Guatemala. *International Journal for Equity in Health*, *17*, 1–10.

Lähdesmäki, T. (2021). Heritage diplomacy discourses in the EU: Notions on cultural diplomacy, cultural heritage, and intercultural dialogue among EU officials and heritage practitioners. *Ethnologia Europaea*, *51*(2), 48–71.

Lamnadi, Y. (2010). The evaluation of tourism marketing model within Moroccan public policy management. *Athens Journal of Tourism*, *6*(1), 15–38.

Lee, D., & Ruël, H. (2012). Introduction: Commercial diplomacy and international business: Merging international business and international relations. In H. Ruël (Ed.), *Commercial diplomacy and international business: A conceptual and empirical exploration* (pp. xiii–xix). Emerald Group Publishing Limited.

Manfredi-Sánchez, J. L. (2022). The political economy of city diplomacy. *Economic and Political Studies*, *10*(2), 228–249.

Mansfeld, Y. (2006). The role of security information in tourism crisis management: The missing link. In Y. Mansfeld & A. Pizam (Eds.), *Tourism, security and safety* (pp. 271–290). Routledge.

Mark, S. L. (2010). Rethinking cultural diplomacy: The cultural diplomacy of New Zealand, the Canadian Federation and Quebec. *Political Science*, *62*(1), 62–83.

Minardi, A., Afriantari, R., & Hasanah, N. U. (2021). Indonesian tourism diplomacy to India. *Indonesian Tourism Diplomacy to India*, *1*(1), 1–13.

Miño, P. (2023). Power imbalances and contested notions of the nation: Latin American nation branding through the lens of the cultural-economic model of public relations. *Journal of Public Relations Research*, *35*(5–6), 307–320.

Moilanen, T., & Rainisto, S. K. (2009). *How to brand nations, cities and destinations*. Palgrave Macmillan UK.

Okafor, L. E., Tan, C. M., & Khalid, U. (2021). Does panda diplomacy promote Chinese outbound tourism flows? *Journal of Hospitality and Tourism Management*, *49*, 54–64.

Okano-Heijmans, M. (2012). Japan's new economic diplomacy: Changing tactics or strategy? *Asia-Pacific Review*, *19*(1), 62–87.

Oliver, A. (2016). Travelling responsibly, but further to go: Australia's new consular diplomacy. *Australian Journal of International Affairs*, *70*(6), 681–694.

Ormerod, N., & Wood, E. H. (2021). Regional event tourism funding policies: A strategic-relational critique of current practice. *Journal of Travel Research*, *60*(4), 860–877.

Özlem, K. (2019). The place of public diplomacy in Bulgaria's Balkans policy during the GERB governments. *The Journal of Diplomatic Research*, *1*(1), 85–97.

Pack, S. D. (2006). Tourism and international engagement, 1945–1957. In S. D. Pack (Ed.), *Tourism and dictatorship: Europe's peaceful invasion of Franco's Spain* (pp. 39–56). Palgrave Macmillan US.

Pack, S. D. (2010). Revival of the pilgrimage to Santiago de Compostela: The politics of religious, national, and European patrimony, 1879–1988. *The Journal of Modern History*, *82*(2), 335–367.

Qiu, S., Li, M., Huang, Z., & Dang, N. (2015). Impact of tourism openness across the Taiwan strait: Perspective of mainland Chinese tourists. *Asia Pacific Journal of Tourism Research*, *20*(1), 76–93.

Quer, D. (2021). Location decisions of Chinese firms in the global tourism industry: The role of prior international experience and diplomatic relations. *Journal of Hospitality and Tourism Management*, *46*, 62–72.

Quer, D. (2024). Diplomatic relations and investment location of Chinese Multinationals: An international political economy perspective. *China and World Economy*, *32*(5), 87–112.

Rana, K. S. (2013). Economic diplomacy: What might best serve a developing country? *International Journal of Diplomacy and Economy*, *1*(3–4), 232–247.

Rosendorf, N. M., & Rosendorf, N. M. (2014). The Franco Regime's postwar US public relations strategies: Media, messages and relationships in America. In *Franco sells Spain to America: Hollywood, tourism and public relations as postwar Spanish soft power* (pp. 80–118).

Salman, Y. (2023). Tourism and classic diplomacy: The case of strengthening Israeli–Tanzanian bilateral relations. *Tourism Review International*, *27*(2), 125–139.

Şen, O. (2019). Targeted soft power in Turkish new foreign policy and its impact on origins of inbound tourists. *Journal of Tourism Theory and Research*, *5*(1), 65–74.

Senbeto, D. L., Mamo, Y., & Seyfi, S. (2024). Light in the middle of the tunnel? A sentimental analysis of tourist responses to ongoing crisis. *Current Issues in Tourism*, *27*(6), 838–846.

Shanks, C. (2009). The global compact: The conservative politics of international tourism. *Futures*, *41*(6), 360–366.

Singh, R. P., & Rana, P. S. (2021). Cultural diplomacy in India: Dispersal, heritage representation, contestation, and development. In O. Niglio & E. Y. J. Lee (Eds.), *Transcultural diplomacy and international law in heritage conservation: A dialogue between ethics, law, and culture* (pp. 231–256). Springer.

Sorzano, O. L., & Miller, T. (2018). Odd bedfellows? US Pub (l) ic diplomacy, Colombian industry policy, and sex tourism in Cartagena. In J. Pamment & K. G. Wilkins (Eds.) *Communicating national image through development and diplomacy: The politics of foreign aid* (pp. 99–121). Palgrave.

Spies, Y. K. (2019). *Global south perspectives on diplomacy*. Palgrave Macmillan.

Stachowiak, K., Janta, H., Kozina, J., & Sunngren-Granlund, T. (2024). Introduction: Film and place from an intercultural perspective. In K. Stachowiak, H. Hania Janta, J. Kozina, & T. Sunngren-Granlund (Eds.), *Film and place in an intercultural perspective* (pp. 3–15). Routledge.

Strömbom, L. (2019). Exploring prospects for agonistic encounters in conflict zones: Investigating dual narrative tourism in Israel/Palestine. *Alternatives*, *44*(2–4), 75–93.

Su, J. J., Pham, T. D., & Dwyer, L. (2022). Political relations and bilateral tourism demand: The case of China and Japan. *International Journal of Tourism Research*, *24*(3), 337–346.

Sulaiman, M. Z., & Wilson, R. (2018). Translating tourism promotional materials: A cultural-conceptual model. *Perspectives*, *26*(5), 629–645.

Tessema, G. A., & Haile, E. A. (2022). Urban tourism development in Africa: Evidence from Addis Ababa, Ethiopia. In J. van der Borg (Ed.), *A research agenda for urban tourism* (pp. 177–200). Edward Elgar Publishing.

Thirumaran, K., Sabacan, R. F., Pourabedin, Z., Nguyen, H. H., Jang, H., Atkinson, B., & Wood, J. (2021). The Eurasian economic union and silk road tourism: Qualifying resources, amplifying messages. In *International conference on silk road sustainable tourism development and cultural heritage* (pp. 265–271). Springer Nature Switzerland.

UNESCO. (2024). *World heritage*. https://whc.unesco.org. Accessed 10 22, 2024.

UNWTO. (2024). *UN tourism*. https://www.unwto.org. Accessed 10 22, 2024.

Van Noort, C. (2021). *China's communication of the belt and road initiative: Silk road and infrastructure narratives*. Routledge.

Wang, J., Feng, J., & Zhao, J. (2023). Chinese tourism enterprises' host country choice for overseas investment: Influencing factors, interactive effects, and national heterogeneity. *Current Issues in Tourism*, *26*(10), 1688–1705.

Wang, H., Ye, X., & Shi, J. (2019). Study on development of Chinese cruise industry in 2017–2018: Steady operation, high quality and favorable situation. In H. Wang (Ed.), *Report on the development of cruise industry in China (2018)* (pp. 37–72). Springer.

Wigley, A. (2015). Against the wind: The role of Belgian colonial tourism marketing in resisting pressure to decolonize from Africa. *Journal of Tourism History*, *7*(3), 193–209.

Winter, T. (2016). Heritage diplomacy and tourism in Asia. In C. M. Hall & S. J. Page (Eds.), *The Routledge Handbook of Tourism in Asia* (pp. 45–53). Routledge.

Xu, H., Wang, K., & Song, Y. M. (2020). Chinese outbound tourism and soft power. *Journal of Policy Research in Tourism, Leisure and Events*, *12*(1), 34–49.

Ye, F., Park, J., Li, C., & He, Y. (2020). The relationship between China-South Pacific Island countries tourism and trade in the belt and road initiative context. *Island Studies Journal*, *15*(2), 73–92.

Zhang, X., Song, W., & Peng, L. (2020). Investment by Chinese enterprise in infrastructure construction in Malaysia. *Pacific Focus*, *35*(1), 109–140.

Chapter 4

Tourism Partnership Models for Tourism Diplomacy

Abstract

Tourism diplomacy thrives on robust partnerships that transcend traditional boundaries, fostering collaboration among diverse stakeholders. This chapter comprehensively analyzes partnership models that support tourism diplomacy, encompassing governmental, private, community-based, regional, technological, educational, and corporate actors. Government-to-government (G2G) partnerships are examined to highlight their structured frameworks and strategic benefits in shaping international tourism policies alongside the challenges of bureaucratic complexities. Public–private partnerships (PPPs) are explored as dynamic models that leverage private sector innovation and public sector oversight to enhance tourism initiatives despite potential risks like misaligned objectives. Community-based tourism (CBT) partnerships are presented as mechanisms for grassroots empowerment, showcasing successful examples while addressing sustainability challenges. Cross-border regional partnerships emerge as pivotal in harmonizing tourism strategies across national boundaries, illustrated by notable cases of transnational cooperation. Technology integration is emphasized, detailing technology-driven partnerships that revolutionize tourism diplomacy through digital platforms and innovative tools yet necessitate equity and data security considerations. The involvement of educational and cultural institutions underscores the role of intellectual and cultural exchange in fostering mutual understanding, though these partnerships may face financial and logistical constraints. Finally, corporate social responsibility (CSR) partnerships are discussed as ethical and sustainable avenues for private sector involvement in tourism diplomacy, focusing on their societal impact and implementation challenges. By synthesizing these diverse partnership models, the chapter underscores their collective importance in advancing tourism diplomacy while addressing each framework's inherent complexities and opportunities.

Tourism Diplomacy, 69–95

Copyright © 2025 Mahmut Demir and Şirvan Şen Demir

Published under exclusive licence by Emerald Publishing Limited
doi:10.1108/978-1-83708-676-420251004

Keywords: Tourism diplomacy; public–private partnerships; community-based tourism; cross-border cooperation; technology-driven tourism

1. Introduction

Tourism diplomacy relies heavily on strategic partnerships as a multifaceted tool for fostering international cooperation and cultural exchange. These partnerships bring together a range of stakeholders – governments, private enterprises, local communities, and other institutions – to create synergies that amplify tourism's reach and impact as a diplomatic instrument. Tourism diplomacy addresses global challenges through various partnership models, promotes sustainable development, and enhances mutual understanding between nations (Fig. 8). Government-to-government (G2G) partnerships form the cornerstone of tourism diplomacy, offering a structured approach to policy alignment and cooperation. These partnerships typically involve bilateral or multilateral agreements focusing on areas such as visa facilitation, customs cooperation, and joint promotional campaigns. G2G partnerships strengthen diplomatic ties and promote cross-border tourism flows by harmonizing tourism policies and leveraging shared resources. However, challenges such as geopolitical tensions, varying priorities, and administrative complexities often hinder their effectiveness. Effective G2G partnerships require diplomatic finesse and a shared vision to address these obstacles and maximize their potential for mutual benefit.

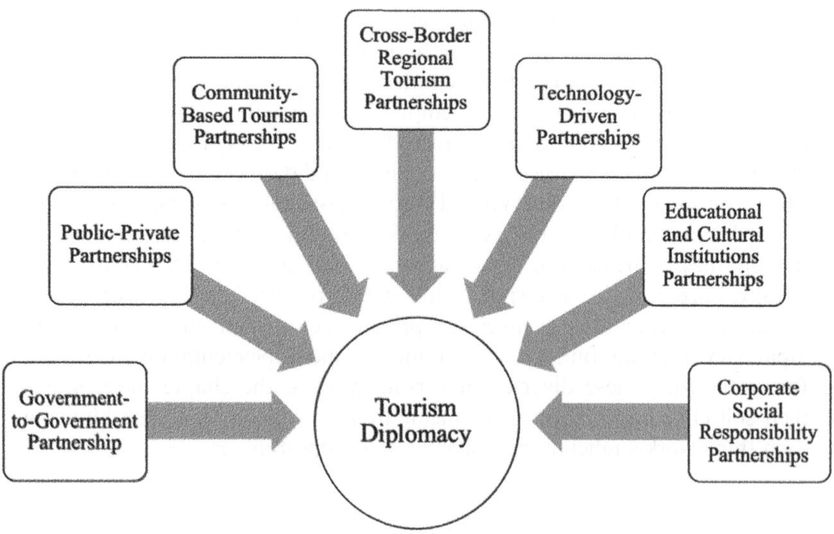

Fig. 8. Tourism Partnership Models for Tourism Diplomacy.

Public–private partnerships (PPPs) have emerged as a dynamic model in tourism diplomacy, combining the strategic oversight of governments with the innovation and efficiency of private enterprises. PPPs are characterized by their collaborative approach to developing tourism infrastructure, organizing large-scale events, and implementing marketing campaigns. These partnerships benefit from shared investments and risk distribution, fostering sustainable tourism development. Nevertheless, the challenges associated with PPPs, such as aligning divergent objectives and ensuring accountability, require robust governance frameworks. Successful PPPs demonstrate the potential of blending public and private interests to create impactful tourism initiatives. Community-based tourism (CBT) partnerships emphasize the active involvement of local communities in tourism development, positioning them as key stakeholders in tourism diplomacy. These partnerships prioritize the preservation of cultural heritage, environmental sustainability, and equitable economic benefits. CBT initiatives often highlight a community's unique cultural and natural assets, creating authentic tourism experiences that promote cross-cultural understanding. Examples of successful CBT partnerships underscore their potential to enhance local livelihoods while contributing to the broader objectives of tourism diplomacy. However, challenges such as inadequate funding, limited capacity, and community resistance can undermine these efforts, necessitating targeted interventions to support their success.

Cross-border regional tourism partnerships foster cooperation between neighboring countries, particularly in regions with shared cultural and natural resources. These partnerships facilitate the development of transnational tourism routes, joint marketing campaigns, and coordinated infrastructure investments. By transcending political boundaries, cross-border partnerships promote regional integration and mutual prosperity. Notable examples include collaborative initiatives in regions such as the European Union and ASEAN. However, these partnerships often face challenges such as political instability, uneven resource distribution, and differing regulatory environments, requiring a comprehensive approach to negotiation and implementation. Technology-driven partnerships are reshaping tourism diplomacy in the digital age by enhancing connectivity, communication, and marketing capabilities. These partnerships leverage digital tools, such as online platforms, artificial intelligence, and big data analytics, to improve destination management, customer engagement, and promotional efforts. Examples include collaborations between governments and tech companies to create smart tourism solutions or virtual reality campaigns. While technology-driven partnerships offer immense benefits, such as cost-efficiency and global reach, they also raise concerns regarding data privacy, digital divides, and cybersecurity. Addressing these challenges is critical to harnessing the full potential of technology in tourism diplomacy.

Educational and cultural institutions play a vital role in tourism diplomacy by fostering academic exchanges, cultural awareness, and intellectual collaborations. Partnerships with universities, museums, and cultural organizations promote knowledge sharing and intercultural dialogue, enhancing tourism's diplomatic value. These collaborations often involve student exchange programs, cultural festivals, and heritage preservation projects. Despite their benefits, such partnerships may face challenges such as limited funding, bureaucratic barriers, and competing priorities. Strengthening these alliances requires long-term commitment and effective resource management. Corporate social responsibility (CSR) partnerships align businesses' social and environmental objectives with tourism diplomacy goals. CSR initiatives in tourism often focus on sustainability, community development, and ethical practices. These partnerships demonstrate the potential of private sector engagement in addressing global challenges while enhancing a country's soft power. However, implementing CSR partnerships effectively requires overcoming obstacles such as greenwashing, lack of transparency, and limited scalability. Encouraging authentic and impactful CSR practices is essential for leveraging their potential in tourism diplomacy.

2. G2G Partnerships in Tourism Diplomacy

G2G partnerships play a foundational role in tourism diplomacy, creating frameworks for international cooperation that enhance tourism and foster deeper diplomatic ties (Demir & Alper, 2021; Suntikul, 2019). These partnerships, often established through bilateral or multilateral agreements, allow nations to collectively promote tourism, improve travel accessibility, and support each other's cultural promotion efforts. These partnerships, formed through agreements, policy alignment, and coordinated strategies, help nations work collaboratively to address mutual goals in tourism development, cultural promotion, and regional stability (Demir & Alper, 2021; Labonté et al., 2018). By establishing direct connections between governments, G2G partnerships support tourism diplomacy in ways that benefit both the nations involved and their citizens. They offer a means to increase cross-border travel, boost economic benefits, promote sustainable practices, and facilitate cultural exchange, all essential for building positive global relations.

2.1 Key Characteristics of G2G Partnerships

G2G partnerships in tourism diplomacy are built on formal agreements that define shared goals, responsibilities, and strategic initiatives (Kalbaska et al., 2017). They are commonly established through bilateral or multilateral tourism agreements, visa relaxation programs, travel corridors, and marketing alliances. Typically, these agreements aim to streamline travel regulations, improve tourism infrastructure, and promote destinations collectively on the global stage. The collaborative nature of G2G partnerships ensures that each country's cultural and economic objectives are respected and that any differences are addressed through diplomacy. One of the most defining aspects of G2G partnerships is their ability to transcend political boundaries, focusing instead on shared interests like regional stability, economic cooperation, and environmental preservation (Özlem, 2019; Suntikul, 2019). For instance, many European Union countries collaborate on tourism policies that promote free movement within the Schengen Area. This structure allows tourists to explore multiple nations easily, strengthening regional tourism appeal and fostering a sense of unity among member states.

2.2 Types of G2G Partnerships in Tourism Diplomacy

G2G partnerships in tourism diplomacy can take many forms, depending on the objectives and geographic context of the countries involved. Here are some of the most common types.

- *Bilateral Agreements:* Bilateral tourism agreements between two nations directly form a G2G partnership. These agreements typically address travel ease, visa relaxation, tourism promotion, and sometimes the development of joint events or cultural programs (Minardi et al., 2021; Ormond & Mainil, 2015). For example, a bilateral agreement between Japan and Australia simplifies travel procedures for citizens of both countries, promoting tourism and enhancing cultural ties.
- *Multilateral Alliances:* When multiple countries share common tourism goals, they may form multilateral alliances (Singh & Marwah, 2022). The Caribbean Community (CARICOM) is one example, where several nations in the Caribbean region collaborate to attract international tourists through joint marketing and tourism infrastructure development. These alliances allow smaller nations to leverage shared branding and resources, strengthening their presence in the global tourism market.
- *Travel Corridors and Free Movement Zones:* G2G partnerships often include the establishment of travel corridors or free movement zones that facilitate cross-border tourism (Demir & Alper, 2021; Salman, 2023). The Schengen Area in Europe is a prime example, where travelers can move freely between member countries without border checks. This type of partnership not only makes travel more convenient but also strengthens regional tourism by allowing tourists to experience multiple destinations within a single trip. Similarly, ASEAN countries have formed tourism partnerships to create a unified brand for Southeast Asia, marketing the region collectively to international tourists. These collaborations help bolster mutual interests, create stable travel corridors, and establish frameworks for addressing shared challenges, such as environmental protection and visitor management.
- *Joint Tourism Marketing Initiatives:* Governments frequently engage in joint marketing campaigns that promote a region or cultural theme shared by multiple countries (Kozak & Buhalis, 2019). For instance, countries along the Silk Road have come together to promote the ancient trade route as a unified tourism destination. These marketing initiatives highlight shared heritage and cultural landmarks, presenting a cohesive story that appeals to international travelers.

2.3 Benefits of G2G Partnerships in Tourism Diplomacy

G2G partnerships in tourism diplomacy provide a range of benefits that contribute to stronger diplomatic ties and sustainable tourism development.

- *Enhanced Cultural Exchange:* G2G partnerships are pivotal in promoting cultural exchange and often prioritize cultural promotion. They allow each country to showcase its unique heritage (Kalbaska et al., 2017; Labonté et al., 2018), fostering mutual understanding and respect among nations and contributing to more harmonious international relations. Cultural festivals, joint exhibitions, and heritage site collaborations are often outcomes of such partnerships, giving travelers a broader view of each participating country's culture.
- *Economic Growth and Stability:* Tourism is a significant economic driver, and G2G partnerships help to optimize this sector for mutual benefit (Demir & Alper, 2021; Minardi et al., 2021). By simplifying travel restrictions and coordinating marketing efforts, these partnerships can significantly increase tourist arrivals and economic revenue for all involved countries. Furthermore, the economic stability fostered by tourism partnerships can contribute to regional stability, promoting sustained tourism growth and economic prosperity.
- *Support for Sustainable Tourism:* Many G2G partnerships are committed to sustainable tourism practices that address environmental and social impacts (Ormond & Mainil, 2015; Suntikul, 2019). By working together, governments can promote eco-friendly tourism initiatives, preserve shared natural resources, and create policies that minimize tourism's negative effects. For example, the "Amazon Pact" among countries in the Amazon Basin encourages eco-tourism and conservation efforts to protect this biodiverse region.
- *Improved Crisis Management:* G2G partnerships facilitate coordinated responses to tourism crises, such as natural disasters, health emergencies, or security threats (Demir et al., 2020). During the COVID-19 pandemic, travel corridors established between countries with low infection rates allowed safe tourism to resume, providing a model for future crisis management in tourism. By establishing joint protocols and sharing resources, G2G partnerships improve resilience and preparedness in the face of global challenges, ensuring the safety and security of tourists.

2.4 Challenges in G2G Partnerships

While G2G partnerships offer substantial benefits, they also face challenges that can complicate their effectiveness (Demir & Alper, 2021; Özlem, 2019; Salman, 2023). Political changes, economic shifts, and policy differences can disrupt established agreements or hinder new partnerships. Balancing national interests with regional or global tourism objectives requires diplomacy and negotiation, as each country has unique priorities. Environmental concerns are another consideration, as increased tourism can lead to resource depletion and habitat disruption.

For G2G partnerships to remain sustainable, they must incorporate environmental protections and prioritize responsible tourism practices. Otherwise, the long-term viability of tourism destinations may be compromised, undermining the diplomatic benefits these partnerships aim to achieve.

3. PPPs in Tourism Diplomacy

In tourism diplomacy, PPPs play a pivotal role by blending the strengths of government and private sector stakeholders to foster economic and cultural exchange. PPPs are a strategic means to leverage resources, expertise, and networks that neither public nor private entities could harness alone (Bäckstrand & Kylsäter, 2014; Li et al., 2019). By aligning government policies and private sector innovation, PPPs enhance the appeal, accessibility, and sustainability of destinations while also promoting international goodwill. Tourism diplomacy gains momentum through such partnerships, with both sectors working together to shape how nations present themselves to the world. These partnerships enable leveraging governmental resources, such as cultural assets and regulatory support, alongside private companies' expertise, funding, and marketing strength.

3.1 Characteristics of PPPs in Tourism Diplomacy

PPPs are characterized by a shared commitment to promoting tourism in ways that align with national interests while meeting the business goals of private partners (Tomazzoni et al., 2022). Unlike purely commercial ventures, PPPs in tourism diplomacy often focus on long-term objectives, such as increasing destination attractiveness, supporting local communities, and fostering a country's global image. These partnerships typically involve collaborative marketing campaigns, infrastructure development, and digital initiatives showcasing a nation's unique heritage, environments, and cultural identity. The synergy created by PPPs allows for comprehensive tourism strategies that are both economically viable and diplomatically beneficial (Litheko, 2022).

Another defining characteristic of PPPs in tourism diplomacy is their adaptability to changing global trends. In an era when travelers prioritize sustainability, cultural authenticity, and responsible tourism, PPPs can quickly respond by integrating eco-friendly and culturally respectful initiatives into tourism offerings. This adaptability is essential in tourism diplomacy (Li et al., 2019), as it enables destinations to maintain a positive international image while catering to the evolving expectations of global travelers.

3.2 Forms of PPPs in Tourism Diplomacy

There are various models of PPPs within tourism diplomacy, each designed to achieve different strategic objectives.

- *Joint Marketing Initiatives:* Tourism boards often partner with private companies, such as airlines, hotel chains, and online travel agencies, to launch marketing campaigns that target specific demographics or regions (Hall, 1999). For example, a country might collaborate with an international airline to promote cultural festivals or natural attractions, increasing awareness and travel interest. Joint marketing enhances diplomatic outreach by shaping the destination's image in global markets.
- *Infrastructure Development Projects:* Many PPPs involve developing essential tourism infrastructure, from airports and ports to roads and accommodations (Gerlitz et al., 2021; Tomazzoni et al., 2022). Governments may partner with private developers to build resorts, transportation facilities, or tourist information centers in underserved areas. This type of partnership not only boosts tourism by improving accessibility but also enhances a country's soft power by showcasing its ability to provide safe and modern facilities to international travelers.
- *Sustainable Tourism Initiatives:* Given the growing global emphasis on sustainability, many PPPs in tourism focus on environmental conservation and responsible tourism (Gerlitz et al., 2021). Private enterprises can support government-led conservation efforts by funding eco-parks, promoting zero-waste policies, or offering incentives for sustainable accommodations. This approach aligns with tourists' preference for eco-friendly travel and strengthens the diplomatic message that a nation is committed to global environmental goals.
- *Heritage Conservation Projects:* PPPs uniquely preserve a country's cultural and historical assets, pivotal in tourism diplomacy (Hall, 1999; Litheko, 2022). Private sponsorships for museum renovations, heritage site restorations, or cultural festivals not only demonstrate a commitment to maintaining a nation's identity but also invite tourists to engage with its traditions. This partnership model is diplomatically valuable, as it positions a nation as both proud of and responsible for its cultural legacy.

3.3 Benefits of PPPs in Tourism Diplomacy

PPPs offer several advantages that amplify the impact of tourism diplomacy efforts.

- *Resource Pooling and Risk Sharing:* One of the key advantages of PPPs is their ability to pool resources and share risks (Bäckstrand & Kylsäter, 2014; Gerlitz et al., 2021). By combining the resources of government and private entities, PPPs can execute large-scale projects without overburdening either sector. For instance, constructing a new international airport or developing a high-profile tourist attraction is made feasible through shared investment and responsibilities. This risk-sharing aspect of PPPs enables ambitious projects that can attract a high volume of tourists and elevate a destination's international standing. Take the UK's GREAT Campaign, for instance. This pioneering initiative seamlessly blends the efforts of the government and the private sector to position Britain as a top-tier travel destination. Its partnership model allows for co-branded international campaigns that showcase iconic British companies like Rolls-Royce and British Airways, enhancing the destination's allure through globally recognized brands. The synergy created in PPPs benefits both sectors: governments can achieve diplomatic goals of showcasing the nation's appeal, while private entities gain from increased business opportunities and market reach.

- *Enhanced Innovation and Efficiency:* The private sector brings expertise, technological advancement, and efficiency that may be lacking in public institutions (Hall, 1999; Li et al., 2019). Tourism boards can incorporate innovations like digital marketing strategies, mobile applications, and data analytics through PPPs to enhance visitor experience. This modernized approach to tourism resonates well in diplomatic contexts, as it shows the country's commitment to embracing technology and enhancing tourist satisfaction.
- *Strengthened Cultural Diplomacy:* PPPs support preserving and celebrating local culture and heritage by directing funds and attention toward these assets (Litheko, 2022; Tomazzoni et al., 2022). This aligns with tourism diplomacy objectives by creating meaningful cultural exchanges and fostering mutual understanding. For example, a private company may sponsor a government-led cultural initiative, such as a national festival, allowing tourists to engage more deeply with the host country's culture.
- *Local Economic Development:* PPPs support economic development by providing jobs, training, and business opportunities for local communities (Gerlitz et al., 2021; Hall, 1999). When communities benefit directly from tourism, they are more likely to participate in and support tourism initiatives. This community support creates a stable foundation for tourism diplomacy, ensuring that local people become ambassadors of their culture and heritage to international visitors.

3.4 Challenges of PPPs in Tourism Diplomacy

While PPPs are beneficial, they also present challenges that require careful navigation (Gerlitz et al., 2021; Hall, 1999; Tomazzoni et al., 2022). One such challenge is maintaining a balance between economic interests and public good. This balance is essential for the long-term success of PPPs, particularly when commercial objectives conflict with cultural or environmental values. Additionally, PPPs must be transparent and equitable, ensuring local communities benefit from tourism initiatives and minimize adverse effects. Without proper oversight, there is a risk of over-commercialization or exploitation of cultural assets, which can undermine diplomatic goals.

4. CBT Partnerships in Tourism Diplomacy

CBT partnerships are an innovative approach within tourism diplomacy, emphasizing local community involvement in tourism planning, management, and benefits

(Chassagne & Everingham, 2024; Sofield, 2007). CBT partnerships typically involve collaborations between residents, small businesses, nongovernmental organizations (NGOs), and sometimes local governments. CBT partnerships prioritize sustainable practices and cultural authenticity by integrating local voices, traditions, and economies into tourism initiatives (Scott, 2012). By empowering communities as primary stakeholders, CBT partnerships promote cultural exchange, environmental stewardship, and economic development while fostering mutual respect and understanding between local populations and international visitors. As a diplomatic tool, CBT partnerships enable host countries to project a positive image internationally while supporting local livelihoods, protecting cultural heritage, and preserving natural resources.

4.1 Characteristics of CBT Partnerships

Focusing on local ownership, collaboration, and sustainable management of resources distinguishes CBT partnerships (Demir & Alper, 2021). Rather than treating the community as a passive backdrop to tourism, these partnerships actively involve residents in decision-making processes, ensuring that tourism activities align with community values and needs. This model often incorporates homestays, local guided tours, and cultural exchanges, allowing visitors to experience a more authentic and personal connection to the area. By doing so, CBT partnerships support the goals of tourism diplomacy by showcasing the country's cultural depth and commitment to sustainable practices.

The emphasis on sustainable tourism is extreme in CBT partnerships (Movono & Hughes, 2022; Muntifering et al., 2020). Such alliances often include eco-friendly accommodations, low-impact activities, and locally sourced products that reflect the community's heritage and environmental priorities. These characteristics appeal to modern travelers who prioritize responsible tourism and help shape the destination's international reputation as a responsible and ethically conscious host.

4.2 Benefits of CBT Partnerships in Tourism Diplomacy

CBT partnerships offer several benefits that align with the broader goals of tourism diplomacy.

- *Cultural Exchange and Mutual Understanding:* CBT partnerships create direct interactions between locals and international visitors, facilitating meaningful cultural exchanges (Scott, 2012; Sofield, 2007). These interactions promote understanding and appreciation for diverse traditions and play a crucial role in reducing stereotypes. By fostering a welcoming environment, CBT partnerships contribute to the nation's soft power and present a positive image to the international community.
- *Economic Empowerment and Local Development:* CBT aims to ensure that tourism benefits flow directly to the local community (Demir & Alper, 2021;

Movono & Hughes, 2022). Profits from tourism activities, such as accommodation, dining, and tours, are reinvested into local infrastructure, education, and health services. This economic empowerment aligns with diplomatic goals by improving local quality of life, reducing poverty, and creating stable communities supporting tourism diplomacy's broader goals. When communities experience tangible benefits from tourism, they become ambassadors for their culture, sharing stories and perspectives that enrich the visitor experience.

- *Environmental Conservation:* Many CBT initiatives are in rural or ecologically sensitive areas (Chassagne & Everingham, 2024; Scott, 2012). CBT partnerships often incorporate environmental conservation efforts, such as waste management, wildlife protection, and eco-friendly accommodations. By educating visitors and locals on sustainable practices, these partnerships protect natural assets and promote a global awareness of environmental challenges. This environmental emphasis enhances the host country's reputation as a steward of nature, resonating with international travelers who prioritize sustainable tourism.
- *Protection and Promotion of Intangible Cultural Heritage:* By centering local traditions and knowledge, CBT partnerships help preserve and promote intangible cultural heritage, such as oral histories, craft making, and traditional cuisine (Muntifering et al., 2020; Scott, 2012). These cultural expressions are key to creating a unique tourism experience that attracts international visitors and fosters cultural understanding. Through CBT, a nation can share its cultural richness with the world respectfully, authentically, and sustainably.

4.3 Examples of Successful CBT Partnerships

Several countries have leveraged CBT partnerships as a core tourism diplomacy strategy. For example:

- *Thailand's Village Homestay Program* has successfully introduced visitors to rural communities, allowing them to experience Thai culture firsthand (Aboe et al., 2023). Visitors participate in activities like rice farming, cooking classes, and traditional festivals through homestays. This program supports local economies and strengthens Thailand's reputation as a welcoming and culturally rich destination.
- *Costa Rica's Ecotourism in Rural Communities* involves partnerships with Indigenous groups to offer guided tours and accommodations in biodiversity-rich areas (Miller, 2016). These partnerships have reinforced Costa Rica's image as an ecotourism leader and raised global awareness of the country's commitment to environmental conservation.
- *Nepal's Community Trekking Initiatives* engage local communities in the Himalayan region. Residents manage guesthouses and offer trekking services (Sapkota, 2020). This initiative supports local economies and strengthens Nepal's tourism diplomacy by highlighting the nation's cultural and environmental diversity.

4.4 Challenges of CBT Partnerships

Despite their benefits, CBT partnerships face several challenges that must be managed to achieve sustainable success (Chassagne & Everingham, 2024; Movono & Hughes, 2022; Scott, 2012). A primary challenge is ensuring that local communities are not overshadowed by external stakeholders, who may prioritize commercial gains over community welfare. Ensuring fair profit distribution and maintaining cultural integrity are the essence of these partnerships and are crucial to maintaining the partnership's sustainability and reputation. Another challenge is the potential impact of globalization on local cultures. As CBT destinations grow in popularity, there is a risk of cultural commodification, where traditions are altered or oversimplified to suit tourist expectations. Proper training and community input are essential to preserving authenticity and avoiding the dilution of cultural heritage.

5. Cross-Border Regional Tourism Partnerships in Tourism Diplomacy

Cross-border regional tourism partnerships are a collaborative model in which neighboring countries promote tourism across shared geographical or cultural areas (Beck, 2008; Tosun et al., 2005). These partnerships emphasize cooperation in marketing, infrastructure development, visa facilitation, and resource-sharing to attract international tourists interested in experiencing multiple regional countries. By pooling resources and aligning promotional strategies, cross-border tourism initiatives allow regions to leverage their shared assets, such as historical ties, environmental landmarks, or cultural heritage, making them an effective instrument for tourism diplomacy.

In an increasingly interconnected world, cross-border tourism partnerships strengthen diplomatic ties, foster mutual understanding, and encourage sustainable economic growth across borders. These partnerships enable nations to showcase their commitment to regional stability, cooperation, and cultural appreciation, projecting a united image that appeals to global audiences (Birrell & Hayes, 2004; Timothy & Saarinen, 2013). Furthermore, they help create more comprehensive and appealing tourism experiences, providing tourists with an enriched perspective of the region.

5.1 Characteristics of Cross-Border Regional Tourism Partnerships

Cross-border tourism partnerships are known for their convenience and ease of travel. Shared branding, collective marketing, and joint itineraries simplify cross-border journeys (Brunet-Jailly, 2022). For instance, multi-country passes, streamlined visa processes, and cross-border transportation links are often introduced, making travel seamless. These initiatives allow tourists to enjoy diverse experiences within a single trip, exploring each nation's unique offerings without the logistical challenges of independent travel.

Cross-border partnerships often develop thematic tourism circuits that connect destinations through a shared cultural or natural theme (Birrell & Hayes, 2004; Slusarciuc, 2013). This approach creates a compelling travel narrative that enriches the visitor experience and distinguishes the region as a collaborative and culturally rich destination. Additionally, cross-border tourism partnerships frequently focus on conserving shared natural resources, recognizing that environmental assets, such as rivers, mountains, and forests, span borders and require cooperative management.

5.2 Benefits of Cross-Border Regional Tourism Partnerships

Cross-border tourism partnerships offer various benefits that support the objectives of tourism diplomacy.

- *Strengthening Diplomatic Relations:* Cross-border partnerships demonstrate a commitment to peace and cooperation between neighboring nations. These collaborations are often seen as a symbol of diplomatic goodwill and regional stability, attracting tourists who value secure and cooperative destinations (Beck, 2008; Tosun et al., 2005). Such partnerships promote a positive international image and reinforce the message that tourism can create unity.
- *Expanding Market Reach and Competitiveness:* By pooling resources and aligning marketing efforts, cross-border partnerships enhance the region's visibility on the global tourism stage (Birrell & Hayes, 2004; Timothy & Saarinen, 2013). Rather than competing individually, partner countries present a united front that appeals to international travelers interested in multi-country experiences. This collaborative approach increases the region's competitiveness, especially against more prominent tourism destinations, and attracts more diverse tourists seeking in-depth and cross-cultural experiences.
- *Cultural Exchange and Preservation:* Cross-border tourism partnerships enable countries to celebrate and share their cultural heritage, strengthening cross-cultural bonds and preserving unique traditions (Brunet-Jailly, 2022; Slusarciuc, 2013). By promoting heritage sites, festivals, and cultural landmarks that span borders, these partnerships encourage a deepened understanding of the region's interconnected histories and cultures. Such initiatives also serve as a diplomatic tool, showing respect for cultural diversity and fostering international appreciation.
- *Shared Economic Growth and Development:* Joint tourism initiatives benefit all participating countries by creating new business opportunities, jobs, and revenue (Sofield, 2006; Timothy & Saarinen, 2013). The cross-border flow of tourists supports local businesses, from accommodation and dining to arts and crafts, driving economic development in urban and rural areas. This shared growth reduces economic disparities between border regions, contributing to the overall stability and prosperity of the area.

5.3 Examples of Successful Cross-Border Tourism Partnerships

Several regions worldwide have implemented successful cross-border tourism initiatives that illustrate the benefits of collaborative tourism diplomacy.

- *The European Alps (Austria, France, Germany, Italy, Switzerland, and Slovenia):* The Alpine region partnership between Switzerland, France, Austria, and Italy is a leading example (Ruzicic-Kessler, 2015). Cross-border partnerships also play a diplomatic role by fostering collaboration on environmental conservation and visitor management. They underscore the commitment to sustainable tourism while enhancing international relations. This partnership promotes the Alps as a single destination, transcending national boundaries to highlight the region's shared natural beauty and outdoor recreation opportunities.
- *Greater Mekong Subregion (Cambodia, China, Laos, Myanmar, Thailand, and Vietnam):* Through the Greater Mekong Tourism Strategy, these countries collaborate on tourism infrastructure, visa facilitation, and marketing initiatives (Sofield, 2007). The partnership emphasizes ecotourism and cultural tourism, drawing attention to the region's biodiversity, historic temples, and unique cultural experiences. This initiative has successfully increased visitor numbers and promoted regional harmony.
- *East African Community (EAC) Visa (Kenya, Rwanda, and Uganda):* The EAC Visa allows tourists to travel within these three countries on a single visa, simplifying cross-border travel (Kigali, 2018). This initiative supports regional tourism by promoting wildlife safaris that span multiple countries, benefiting each nation's tourism sector while providing tourists with a rich and varied experience.

5.4 Challenges of Cross-Border Regional Tourism Partnerships

Despite their benefits, cross-border tourism partnerships face various challenges (Sofield, 2006; Timothy & Saarinen, 2013; Tosun et al., 2005). Political instability, visa and border control issues, and infrastructural disparities hinder effective collaboration. For example, regional conflicts or political disagreements may lead to restrictive policies or border closures, disrupting tourist flow and harming the partnership's image. Effective communication and trust-building between governments are essential to overcoming these obstacles and ensuring the partnership's long-term success. Another challenge is balancing promoting tourism and protecting local communities and natural environments. Increased tourism traffic can strain shared resources, particularly in ecologically sensitive areas. Environmental management and regulatory alignment across borders are crucial to prevent over-tourism and protect the destinations' sustainability.

6. Technology-Driven Partnerships in Tourism Diplomacy

Technology-driven partnerships have become a cornerstone in advancing tourism diplomacy, enabling destinations to enhance global visibility, streamline services, and offer innovative experiences that align with travelers' growing expectations. In an increasingly digital world, partnerships centered on technological integration allow for unprecedented collaboration between public and private entities, including governments, tech companies, tourism boards, and hospitality businesses (Kalbaska et al., 2017; Rana, 2013). This approach not only improves operational efficiency but also strengthens diplomatic ties by promoting seamless travel experiences and showcasing a country's commitment to innovation. In the context of tourism diplomacy, technology-driven partnerships foster mutual understanding, cultural exchange, and the global sharing of resources, setting a standard for modern tourism collaborations.

6.1 The Role of Technology in Tourism Diplomacy

The tourism industry has witnessed significant technological transformations, from online booking systems and virtual reality (VR) tours to data-driven marketing and AI-based personalization (Ergen, 2020). Countries can strengthen their tourism appeal by fostering partnerships focused on these innovations while positioning themselves as forward-thinking destinations. Such alliances often support tourism diplomacy goals by enhancing the accessibility and appeal of cross-border tourism, improving the quality of traveler experiences, and promoting sustainable tourism practices.

Through technology, tourism organizations are better equipped to communicate and cooperate across borders (Nag & Mishra, 2024; Salam, 2024). For instance, digital platforms and data analytics provide insights into visitor preferences, enabling more targeted marketing campaigns. Digital tools also make it easier to create content that reflects the unique cultural values of each destination, which is essential for tourism diplomacy as it allows countries to present an authentic image to a global audience. In this way, technology-driven partnerships not only enhance the appeal of a region but also build connections that encourage cultural appreciation and understanding.

6.2 Examples of Technology-Driven Partnerships in Tourism

Several key examples illustrate the value of technology-driven partnerships in tourism diplomacy, demonstrating how they can be applied to improve visitor experiences and promote international cooperation.

- *Digital Visa Platforms and E-Visas:* Many countries now offer e-visas and digital travel authorizations through partnerships with tech companies specializing in digital security and automation (Mathur, 2019; Shrestha et al., 2022). These initiatives simplify the visa application process, making it more accessible to international travelers while maintaining security standards. For example, the ASEAN Single Visa initiative, though still in development, aims to simplify travel within Southeast Asia through a single electronic visa, reducing visitor barriers and promoting regional tourism.

- *Smart Cities and IoT Integration:* Smart city projects incorporate IoT devices and data analytics to enhance urban areas for locals and tourists (Kolotouchkina & Seisdedos, 2018). In destinations like Singapore and Dubai, government and private sectors collaborate to install sensors and data-collecting devices that improve transportation, monitor environmental impact, and ensure traveler safety. These projects make cities more attractive to visitors while demonstrating a country's commitment to high-tech solutions and sustainable tourism.
- *Augmented and Virtual Reality (AR/VR):* Tourism boards can offer virtual experiences that showcase key cultural and historical sites by partnering with technology firms (Ergen, 2020). AR and VR experiences give potential visitors an immersive preview of a destination, sparking interest and promoting cultural knowledge before arriving. Countries such as Japan and Italy have partnered with tech companies to create VR tours of heritage sites, allowing people worldwide to experience these landmarks virtually. This cultural outreach is invaluable for tourism diplomacy, enabling destinations to share their cultural treasures globally.
- *Blockchain for Secure Transactions and Transparency:* Tourism has adopted blockchain technology to increase transaction transparency and security (Yang, 2022). Partnerships between tourism boards and fintech firms have led to blockchain implementation for secure payments, verification of traveler identities, and tracking visitor activity data. This technology promotes trust between tourists and destinations, which is particularly valuable in diplomacy as it demonstrates a commitment to security and integrity.

6.3 Benefits of Technology-Driven Partnerships for Tourism Diplomacy

Technology-driven partnerships offer unique benefits that contribute to the goals of tourism diplomacy.

- *Enhanced Accessibility and Inclusivity:* Digital platforms and mobile apps help make tourism accessible to a broader audience (Carayannis, 2013; Kalbaska et al., 2017). For example, websites and applications that provide information in multiple languages or offer AI-driven translation services make it easier for non-native speakers to navigate and appreciate a destination. This accessibility reinforces tourism diplomacy by making destinations more inclusive and welcoming.
- *Data-Driven Decision Making:* Through partnerships in data analytics, governments and tourism boards analyze trends, monitor visitor satisfaction, and predict future travel patterns (Nag & Mishra, 2024; Rana, 2013). This data-driven approach helps optimize tourism management and develop targeted strategies that appeal to specific demographics. By understanding what attracts international tourists, destinations can tailor experiences that promote cultural exchange and align with diplomatic goals.
- *Sustainable Tourism Management:* Partnerships centered on technology also support sustainability in tourism (Salam, 2024; Shrestha et al., 2022). For example, data-driven systems for managing visitor flow help reduce

overcrowding at popular sites, and eco-friendly apps can guide tourists toward sustainable practices during their stay. Demonstrating a commitment to sustainability aligns with global diplomatic efforts, as many countries seek to promote environmentally responsible tourism.

6.4 Challenges and Considerations

Despite their benefits, technology-driven partnerships in tourism diplomacy come with challenges (Kalbaska et al., 2017; Nag & Mishra, 2024; Rana, 2013). Data privacy and cybersecurity are primary concerns, as destinations collect and store vast amounts of traveler information. Protecting this data is crucial to maintaining trust and fulfilling diplomatic obligations, primarily as international tourists rely on safe, seamless experiences. Another challenge is the digital divide, as not all regions have equal access to technological infrastructure. To create a globally inclusive tourism experience, countries must work to bridge this gap by investing in their digital infrastructure or forming partnerships that can provide these resources.

7. Educational and Cultural Institution Partnerships in Tourism Diplomacy

Educational and cultural institution partnerships are pivotal in advancing tourism diplomacy by fostering understanding, promoting cross-cultural interactions, and preserving heritage. These partnerships often involve collaboration between universities, museums, cultural organizations, and tourism boards, providing research, education, and cultural exchange platforms. Such alliances aim to create mutual appreciation, build intercultural competency, and promote tourism as a channel for diplomacy. In a world where cultural identity and preservation are increasingly relevant to diplomatic relations, partnerships with educational and cultural institutions have become crucial to shaping positive international perceptions and strengthening bonds.

7.1 The Role of Educational and Cultural Institutions in Tourism Diplomacy

Educational and cultural institutions serve as custodians of heritage, knowledge, and culture, vital for effective tourism diplomacy. By partnering with these institutions, governments and tourism organizations gain access to academic research, cultural resources, and innovative ways to engage global audiences (Abahre, 2021; Setyagung et al., 2013). For example, museums and cultural centers offer exhibitions and educational programs that showcase a country's historical and cultural assets, helping to create a deeper understanding and appreciation of its heritage among international visitors. Universities also contribute by researching visitor demographics, behaviors, and preferences, enabling tourism boards to tailor their strategies for better engagement. Collaborations with cultural institutions provide opportunities to showcase unique traditions, art, and customs that enhance a destination's appeal and strengthen its cultural brand.

7.2 Types of Partnerships With Educational and Cultural Institutions

Several types of partnerships with educational and cultural institutions illustrate their value in tourism diplomacy.

- *University and Research Collaborations:* Partnerships between universities and tourism boards support tourism diplomacy by driving research that shapes marketing, destination management, and policy-making (Abahre, 2021; Eilat, 2024). These collaborations often involve studies on tourism trends, visitor satisfaction, and sustainable practices, which are crucial for destinations that appeal to a diverse audience. For example, research conducted by academic institutions may reveal insights into what international visitors value in a destination, enabling tourism agencies to highlight specific cultural aspects or offer targeted experiences. Furthermore, educational exchanges and tourism-focused university programs encourage students from different backgrounds to become cultural ambassadors, contributing to long-term diplomatic relationships.
- *Museum and Exhibition Partnerships:* Museums and cultural centers are integral to tourism diplomacy as they preserve and present a country's cultural heritage (Demir & Dalgıç, 2022; Kornbluth, 2002). Partnerships with these institutions allow for the creation of joint exhibitions, cultural festivals, and international art exchanges that attract tourists and promote cultural understanding. For example, traveling exhibitions featuring artifacts or art from a specific region allow global audiences to connect with that culture before visiting the destination. By fostering cross-cultural appreciation, these partnerships help lay the groundwork for diplomatic goodwill and a positive national image.
- *Study Abroad and Cultural Exchange Programs:* Study abroad and cultural exchange programs connect students with host countries, allowing for immersive cultural experiences that foster mutual respect and understanding (Demir et al., 2023). Educational institutions work with tourism boards to promote these programs, often designing tours or activities emphasizing local culture and history. Such initiatives are crucial for tourism diplomacy because they provide young people with first-hand experiences of different cultures, often inspiring them to return as tourists or advocates for the destination. Programs like the Fulbright and Erasmus exchanges exemplify the success of educational partnerships in promoting international cooperation through immersive cultural experiences.
- *Language and Cultural Learning Initiatives:* Language is a critical component of cultural identity, and language learning programs represent an effective partnership strategy in tourism diplomacy. By promoting language courses and

cultural workshops, institutions help international visitors connect with the local culture on a deeper level. For instance, programs like Japan's JET (Japan Exchange and Teaching) program allow foreigners to live in Japan, learn the language, and immerse themselves in Japanese culture, encouraging tourism and building a long-term appreciation of the country (Abbasi & Maher, 2022). Such programs bridge tourists and local communities, enhancing diplomatic relations and creating lasting connections.

7.3 Benefits of Educational and Cultural Institution Partnerships

Educational and cultural partnerships in tourism diplomacy yield numerous benefits that extend beyond immediate tourism growth.

- *Enhanced Cultural Understanding:* By partnering with cultural institutions, tourism boards can provide visitors with a more authentic and in-depth understanding of a country's traditions, values, and history, which is required for effective diplomacy (Eilat, 2024; Setyagung et al., 2013). These experiences foster a lasting appreciation and respect for the culture among visitors.
- *Promotion of Cultural Preservation:* Partnerships with educational institutions and museums support the preservation of cultural heritage by encouraging responsible tourism practices and educating visitors on the significance of local traditions (Kornbluth, 2002; Sandersen, 2017). This commitment to heritage preservation enhances a country's reputation for valuing cultural assets, which is crucial in tourism diplomacy.
- *Development of Cultural Ambassadors:* Study abroad and cultural exchange programs often produce "cultural ambassadors" who share positive experiences about a destination in their home countries (Richard, 2024; Setyagung et al., 2013). These ambassadors help promote tourism and foster diplomatic goodwill, advocating for cultural exchange and mutual understanding.
- *Economic and Social Impact:* Partnerships with educational and cultural institutions can have significant economic and social benefits (Abahre, 2021; Sandersen, 2017). For example, museums, cultural festivals, and language programs attract international visitors, boosting local economies and creating job opportunities. Additionally, these partnerships can lead to a greater appreciation of cultural heritage among local communities, strengthening social cohesion and identity.

7.4 Challenges and Considerations

While educational and cultural institution partnerships offer many advantages, they also come with challenges (Eilat, 2024; Richard, 2024). Securing funding for programs and exhibitions is often tricky, as cultural projects may not receive the same level of investment as other tourism initiatives. Challenges can also relate to balancing the representation of cultural narratives in a way that is authentic yet accessible to international visitors. Institutions must be sensitive to cultural nuances, ensuring their heritage portrayal respects local traditions while engaging a global audience.

8. CSR Partnerships in Tourism Diplomacy

In recent years, CSR partnerships have become a key model in tourism diplomacy, focusing on promoting sustainable tourism practices, environmental protection, and social equity. CSR has emerged as a fundamental component in modern business practices, particularly in the tourism industry. As travelers increasingly seek authentic experiences and socially responsible options, tourism stakeholders – such as governments, NGOs, and private companies – recognize CSR partnerships' importance. Private companies with CSR initiatives in tourism often collaborate with NGOs and government bodies to support projects that benefit local communities and protect cultural and natural resources. These partnerships serve as a vehicle for promoting sustainable tourism practices, enhancing cultural preservation, and contributing positively to the communities that host tourists. By aligning business objectives with social and environmental goals, CSR partnerships play a critical role in tourism diplomacy, fostering goodwill, trust, and mutual understanding among nations.

8.1 The Role of CSR in Tourism Diplomacy

CSR in tourism encompasses a wide range of initiatives to promote sustainable practices, protect the environment, and support local communities. As tourism can significantly impact cultural and natural resources, companies are increasingly held accountable for their operations. CSR partnerships enable tourism stakeholders to collaborate on initiatives that enhance their reputations while addressing social issues (Bier & White, 2021; Hayes, 2019; Karaman, 2015). These collaborations often result in improved community relations, increased tourist satisfaction, and enhanced diplomatic ties between countries as they commit to ethical practices.

8.2 Types of CSR Partnerships in Tourism

Various models of CSR partnerships illustrate the diverse ways stakeholders can collaborate in tourism diplomacy.

- *Business and Community Partnerships:* One of the most direct forms of CSR in tourism is the partnership between businesses and local communities (Levy & Hawkins, 2009; Ordeix-Rigo & Duarte, 2009). Hotels, tour operators, and travel companies often engage in initiatives that support local economies, such as sourcing goods and services from local suppliers, hiring local staff, and investing in community projects. For example, a hotel chain may partner with a local artisans' cooperative to showcase traditional crafts, providing income for artisans while enhancing the guest experience. These partnerships boost local economies and contribute to cultural preservation, fostering a sense of pride and ownership among community members. By demonstrating genuine commitment to local well-being, businesses can enhance their reputation and establish stronger ties with the communities in which they operate.

- *NGO Collaborations:* Tourism companies frequently partner with nongovernmental organizations (NGOs) to implement sustainable practices and address pressing social and environmental challenges (Westermann-Behaylo et al., 2015; White et al., 2011). Such partnerships can involve various initiatives, including wildlife conservation, habitat restoration, and community development. For instance, a wildlife tour operator may collaborate with an NGO focused on endangered species to promote ethical wildlife tourism. This partnership can result in educational programs for tourists, raising awareness of conservation issues while generating funds for preservation efforts. By working alongside NGOs, tourism businesses can enhance their credibility and demonstrate a commitment to responsible practices, ultimately contributing to diplomatic relationships by showcasing a unified approach to global challenges.
- *Government and Private Sector Partnerships:* Governments play a crucial role in facilitating CSR partnerships by creating favorable policies and incentives for businesses to engage in socially responsible practices (Karaman, 2015; Ordeix-Rigo & Duarte, 2009). These partnerships often focus on promoting sustainable tourism development, regulatory compliance, and enhancing the overall visitor experience. For example, a national tourism board may collaborate with hotels and restaurants to implement sustainability certifications, ensuring that tourism operations adhere to environmentally friendly practices. These partnerships can create a sustainable development framework that benefits the industry and the community by aligning government objectives with private sector initiatives. Moreover, showcasing successful CSR initiatives can bolster a country's image, enhancing its attractiveness as a travel destination.
- *Cross-Industry Collaborations:* Cross-industry partnerships can also amplify the impact of CSR initiatives in tourism diplomacy (Levy & Hawkins, 2009; White et al., 2011). For instance, collaborations between tourism companies and sectors such as agriculture, technology, or education can foster innovative solutions to common challenges. A travel company might partner with a tech firm to develop apps that promote sustainable tourism practices, such as eco-friendly travel options or guides to local conservation efforts. These partnerships can help disseminate valuable information to travelers while promoting responsible tourism behaviors. Furthermore, by showcasing collaborative efforts across industries, countries can highlight their commitment to sustainability and social responsibility on a global scale.

8.3 Benefits of CSR Partnerships

The benefits of CSR partnerships in tourism diplomacy extend beyond immediate business gains (Bier & White, 2021; Karaman, 2015; Ordeix-Rigo & Duarte, 2009).

- *Enhanced Reputation and Brand Loyalty:* Companies engaged in CSR initiatives often experience improved reputations, leading to greater brand loyalty among consumers who prioritize social and environmental responsibility.
- *Increased Tourist Satisfaction:* Tourists are increasingly drawn to destinations committed to sustainable practices. By engaging in CSR partnerships, tourism stakeholders can enhance the visitor experience and foster positive memories of their travels.
- *Community Empowerment:* CSR partnerships can empower local communities by providing economic opportunities, preserving cultural heritage, and improving overall quality of life. As local communities thrive, they are more likely to support tourism initiatives, creating a mutually beneficial relationship.
- *Strengthened Diplomatic Relations:* Countries engaging in CSR partnerships foster goodwill and mutual respect, enhancing diplomatic relations. By demonstrating a commitment to shared values, nations can work together to address global challenges such as climate change, poverty, and social inequality.

8.4 Challenges in Implementing CSR Partnerships

Despite the benefits, several challenges (Hayes, 2019; Westermann-Behaylo et al., 2015; White et al., 2011) can hinder the effectiveness of CSR partnerships in tourism diplomacy. First, a lack of awareness or understanding of CSR principles among stakeholders can impede collaborative efforts. Ensuring that CSR initiatives benefit local communities rather than merely serving as marketing tools can be challenging. Companies must engage in meaningful dialogue with community members to identify their needs and preferences. Moreover, measuring the impact of CSR initiatives can be complex, requiring robust evaluation frameworks to assess effectiveness and make necessary adjustments.

9. Conclusion

G2G partnerships are not just essential in tourism diplomacy but also are pivotal in promoting peace through tourism. These partnerships foster mutual benefits through collaboration and shared tourism initiatives. From creating seamless travel experiences to promoting regional identities, G2G partnerships strengthen diplomatic ties and enhance all involved nations' cultural and economic environments. While challenges exist, the benefits of these partnerships – cultural exchange, economic growth, sustainability, and crisis resilience – demonstrate their value as an effective model for cooperation in tourism diplomacy. As global travel grows, G2G partnerships will play an increasingly crucial role in connecting nations and promoting peace through tourism.

PPPs are integral to the success of tourism diplomacy, as they blend the strengths of government oversight with the efficiency and innovation of the private sector. Through joint marketing, sustainable tourism initiatives, and infrastructure development, PPPs enable countries to effectively promote their cultural and natural attractions globally. Despite challenges, the benefits of PPPs – including resource sharing, enhanced innovation, and local economic impact – make them invaluable tools in pursuing tourism diplomacy goals. As tourism continues as a bridge between nations, PPPs will remain a crucial model for cooperation, helping countries build mutual understanding and goodwill in an interconnected world.

CBT partnerships influence tourism diplomacy, fostering cultural exchange, environmental stewardship, and economic empowerment. By placing local communities at the center of tourism development, CBT partnerships present a model that aligns the interests of communities, governments, and visitors. Through these partnerships, nations can promote their culture, heritage, and values globally, enhancing their soft power and contributing to mutual understanding. When implemented thoughtfully, CBT partnerships create lasting benefits for all involved, helping host countries achieve the dual goals of tourism development and diplomatic outreach and ensuring a sustainable future for the communities involved.

Cross-border regional tourism partnerships embody the essence of tourism diplomacy by fostering cooperation, cultural exchange, and shared economic growth between neighboring nations. These partnerships enhance the region's appeal as a cohesive, multi-country destination through collaborative marketing, streamlined travel procedures, and joint conservation efforts. Cross-country tourism partnerships can provide long-lasting diplomatic and economic benefits by overcoming political coordination and environmental protection challenges. Ultimately, they demonstrate the power of tourism as a tool for peace, cooperation, and regional prosperity, helping to bridge divides and promote mutual understanding on a global scale.

Technology-driven partnerships are essential in modern tourism diplomacy, offering tools that enhance the accessibility, security, and appeal of destinations on an international scale. Through collaborations focused on digital solutions, countries can streamline travel experiences, highlight cultural assets, and promote sustainable practices. These partnerships underscore the diplomatic value of tourism as a means to foster mutual understanding, economic growth, and environmental responsibility. As technology evolves, technology-driven partnerships will remain at the forefront of tourism diplomacy, providing a framework for countries to engage meaningfully with the world.

Educational and cultural institution partnerships represent a dynamic approach to tourism diplomacy, blending academic research, cultural heritage, and international collaboration to promote understanding and cooperation. By leveraging the resources and expertise of these institutions, countries can enhance their tourism appeal, foster cross-cultural dialogue, and strengthen diplomatic relations. As destinations continue to invest in these partnerships, they not only boost tourism but also contribute to a more interconnected, culturally aware global community. Through thoughtful collaboration with educational and cultural institutions, tourism diplomacy can achieve its goal of building bridges between nations and celebrating humanity's shared heritage.

CSR partnerships represent a significant opportunity for tourism stakeholders to engage in meaningful collaboration that promotes sustainable practices and fosters diplomatic relations. These partnerships can positively impact communities, enhance the tourism experience, and improve global perceptions by aligning business goals with social and environmental objectives. As the tourism industry continues to evolve, the importance of CSR partnerships will only grow, underscoring the need for stakeholders to embrace responsible practices that prioritize the well-being of communities and the planet. Through these efforts, tourism diplomacy can contribute to a more sustainable, equitable, and interconnected world.

References

Abahre, J. S. H. (2021). Reforming tourism and archaeology education in Palestine to meet industry expectations. *Journal of Teaching in Travel & Tourism*, *21*(3), 248–267.

Abbasi, I. A., & Maher, N. (2022). Cultural diplomacy: The case study of Pakistan-Japan cultural relations. *Asia-Pacific-Annual Research Journal of Far East & South East Asia*, *40*, 65–81.

Aboe, R. M., Beazley, H., Livingstone, P., Prasad, M., Ramsay, W., Syamsudin, K., & Carter, R. W. (2023). Women's empowerment in a community-based tourism project: A case study from the 'Spice Islands' of North Maluku, Indonesia. In C. Baldwin & S. van Bommel (Eds.), *Rural development for sustainable social-ecological systems: Putting communities first* (pp. 229–262). Springer International Publishing.

Bäckstrand, K., & Kylsäter, M. (2014). Old wine in new bottles? The legitimation and delegitimation of UN public–private partnerships for sustainable development from the Johannesburg summit to the Rio+ 20 summit. *Globalizations*, *11*(3), 331–347.

Beck, J. (2008). Patterns of administrative culture in cross-border cooperation. In J. Beck & F. Thedieck (Eds.), *The European dimension of administrative culture* (pp. 179–214). Nomos Verlagsgesellschaft mbH & Co. KG.

Bier, L. M., & White, C. L. (2021). Cultural diplomacy as corporate strategy: An analysis of Pasona group's "New Tohoku" program in Japan. *Place Branding and Public Diplomacy*, *17*(2), 180–192.

Birrell, D., & Hayes, A. (2004). Managing cross-border cooperation between voluntary organizations in Ireland. *Nonprofit Management and Leadership*, *15*(1), 41–53.

Brunet-Jailly, E. (2022). Cross-border cooperation: A global overview. *Alternatives*, *47*(1), 3–17.

Carayannis, E. G. (2013). Innovation diplomacy as driver of democracy, innovation and development: The case of Greece. In E. G. Carayannis (Ed.), *The innovation union in Europe* (pp. 123–143). Edward Elgar Publishing.

Chassagne, N., & Everingham, P. (2024). Rethinking tourism transformation for the sustainable development goals through buen vivir. In K. A. Boluk, F. Higgins-Desbiolles, & M. Akhoundoghli (Eds.), *The elgar companion to tourism and the sustainable development goals* (pp. 162–177). Edward Elgar Publishing.

Demir, M., & Alper, P. (2021). G20 summit menus as a means of gastrodiplomacy: Messages to the world via menus. *International Journal of Gastronomy and Food Science, 25*, 1–8. https://doi.org/10.1016/j.ijgfs.2021.100368

Demir, M., & Dalgıç, A. (2022). Examining gastronomy festivals as the attractiveness factor for tourism destinations: The case of Turkey. *Journal of Convention & Event Tourism, 23*, 412–434. https://doi.org/10.1080/15470148.2022.2089797

Demir, M., Demir, Ş. Ş., & Aktürk, O. (2023). The effects of distance education capabilities and competencies on learning outcomes during COVID-19 in higher education institutions. *Journal of Hospitality and Tourism Education*, 1–12.

Demir, M., Günaydın, Y., & Demir, Ş. Ş. (2020). Koronavirüs (Covid-19) salgınının Türkiye'de turizm üzerindeki öncülleri, etkileri ve sonuçlarının değerlendirilmesi. *International Journal of Social Sciences and Education Research, 6*(1), 80–107.

Eilat, O. (2024). David Yellin, Muhammad Kurd'Ali and the great library of damascus during the first world war. *British Journal of Middle Eastern Studies*, 1–17.

Ergen, F. D. (2020). Artırılmış ve sanal gerçeklik teknolojilerinin Isparta ilinin kültürel miras alanlarında uygulanabilirliği üzerine bir literatür taraması. *Journal of Tourism Theory and Research, 6*(1), 62–74.

Gerlitz, L., Meyer, C., & Prause, G. (2021). Marketing and branding strategy for the South Baltic sea region: Reinforcing regional innovation in SMEs through cross-border collaboration models in the age of transformation. *Entrepreneurship and Sustainability Issues*, (4), 467–478.

Hall, C. M. (1999). Rethinking collaboration and partnership: A public policy perspective. *Journal of Sustainable Tourism, 7*(3–4), 274–289.

Hayes, R. (2019). Linking public relations and public diplomacy: Creating a new cadre of public and corporate diplomats. In K. Sriramesh & D. Verčič (Eds.), *The global public relations handbook* (pp. 235–245). Routledge.

Kalbaska, N., Janowski, T., Estevez, E., & Cantoni, L. (2017). When digital government matters for tourism: A stakeholder analysis. *Information Technology & Tourism, 17*, 315–333.

Karaman, Z. T. (2015). Corporate social responsibilities of stakeholders in terms of secure tourism at disasters and sustainable tourism governance. *Journal of Tourism Theory and Research, 3*(2), 66–78.

Kigali, R. (2018). Abuya Joshua Olang'o & Aime Muyombano Irivuzimana. *African Journal of Business and Industry, 2*(4), 236–248.

Kolotouchkina, O., & Seisdedos, G. (2018). Place branding strategies in the context of new smart cities: Songdo IBD, Masdar and Skolkovo. *Place Branding and Public Diplomacy, 14*, 115–124.

Kornbluth, D. (2002). Jordan and the anti-normalization campaign, 1994–2001. *Terrorism and Political Violence, 14*(3), 80–108.

Kozak, M., & Buhalis, D. (2019). Cross–border tourism destination marketing: Prerequisites and critical success factors. *Journal of Destination Marketing & Management, 14*, 1–9.

Labonté, R., Crooks, V. A., Valdés, A. C., Runnels, V., & Snyder, J. (2018). Government roles in regulating medical tourism: Evidence from Guatemala. *International Journal for Equity in Health, 17*, 1–10.

Levy, S. E., & Hawkins, D. E. (2009). Peace through tourism: Commerce based principles and practices. *Journal of Business Ethics, 89*, 569–585.

Li, L., Chen, X., & Hanson, E. C. (2019). Private think tanks and public–private partnerships in Chinese public diplomacy. *The Hague Journal of Diplomacy*, *14*(3), 293–318.

Litheko, A. (2022). Management of eco-tourism through public-private partnerships in South Africa. *African Journal of Hospitality, Tourism and Leisure*, *11*(6), 2103–2127.

Mathur, A. N. (2019). *Finland–India business opportunities: Connecting the Swan and the Elephant*. Springer.

Miller, A. P. (2016). *Sustainable ecotourism in central America: Comparative advantage in a globalized world*. Lexington Books.

Minardi, A., Afriantari, R., & Hasanah, N. U. (2021). Indonesian tourism diplomacy to India. *Indonesian Tourism Diplomacy to India*, *1*(1), 1–13.

Movono, A., & Hughes, E. (2022). Tourism partnerships: Localizing the SDG agenda in Fiji. *Journal of Sustainable Tourism*, *30*(10), 2318–2332.

Muntifering, J. R., Clark, S., Linklater, W. L., Uri-Khob, S., Hebach, E., Cloete, J., Jacobs, S., & Knight, A. T. (2020). Lessons from a conservation and tourism cooperative: The Namibian black rhinoceros case. *Annals of Tourism Research*, *82*, 1–12.

Nag, A., & Mishra, S. (2024). Sustainable competitive advantage in heritage tourism: Leveraging cultural legacy in a data-driven world. In R. P. Singh Kaurav & V. Mishra (Eds.), *Review of technologies and disruptive business strategies* (Vol. 3, pp. 137–162). Emerald Publishing Limited.

Ordeix-Rigo, E., & Duarte, J. (2009). From public diplomacy to corporate diplomacy: Increasing corporation's legitimacy and influence. *American Behavioral Scientist*, *53*(4), 549–564.

Ormond, M., & Mainil, T. (2015). Government and governance strategies in medical tourism. In N. Lunt, D. Horsfall, & J. Hanefeld (Eds.), *Handbook on medical tourism and patient mobility* (pp. 154–163). Edward Elgar Publishing.

Özlem, K. (2019). The place of public diplomacy in Bulgaria's Balkans policy during the GERB governments. *The Journal of Diplomatic Research*, *1*(1), 85–97.

Rana, K. S. (2013). Economic diplomacy: What might best serve a developing country? *International Journal of Diplomacy and Economy*, *1*(3–4), 232–247.

Richard, B. (2024). Confucius institute and the spread of Chinese culture in Cameroon. *International Journal of Research and Innovation in Social Science*, *8*(6), 1672–1680.

Ruzicic-Kessler, K. (2015). Regional cooperation in Europe: Austria, Italy, Yugoslavia and the "Alpsadriatic" region. *Europske studije*, *1*(2), 91–110.

Salam, U. (2024). The dynamic of ASEAN tourism development within the travel & tourism competitiveness index/travel & tourism development index (TTCI–TTD) throughout 2017–2023. *Sosio Dialektika*, *9*(1), 31–59.

Salman, Y. (2023). Tourism and classic diplomacy: The case of strengthening Israeli–Tanzanian bilateral relations. *Tourism Review International*, *27*(2), 125–139.

Sandersen, H. T. (2017). Success by necessity? Educational partnerships between individual initiatives and institutional frameworks. In M. Sundet, P. A. Forstorp, & A. Örtenblad (Eds.), *Higher education in the high North: Academic exchanges between Norway and Russia* (pp. 105–126). Springer International Publishing.

Sapkota, R. (2020). *Community-based homestay tourism as a tool for community empowerment: A case study of two community-managed homestay destinations in Nepal*. Liverpool John Moores University.

Scott, J. (2012). Tourism, civil society and peace in Cyprus. *Annals of Tourism Research*, *39*(4), 2114–2132.

Setyagung, E., Hani, U., Azzadina, I., Sianipar, C., & Ishii, T. (2013). Preserving cultural heritage: The harmony between art idealism, commercialization, and triple-helix collaboration. *American Journal of Tourism Management*, *2*(1), 22–28.

Shrestha, S. B., Parajuli, L. K., & Shrestha, M. V. (2022). Science diplomacy: An overview in the global and national context. *Journal of Foreign Affairs*, *2*(01), 41–51.

Singh, S., & Marwah, R. (2022). *Multilateralism in the Indo-Pacific: Conceptual and operational challenges*. Taylor & Francis.

Slusarciuc, M. (2013). Partnership and cooperation models in cross-border areas. *Acta Universitatis Danubius - Œconomica*, *9*(4), 267–280.

Sofield, T. H. (2006). Border tourism and border communities: An overview. *Tourism Geographies*, *8*(2), 102–121.

Sofield, T. H. (2007). The role of tourism in transition economies of the Greater Mekong Subregion. In T. H. B. Sofield (Ed.), *Asian tourism: Growth and change* (pp. 39–53). Routledge.

Suntikul, W. (2019). Gastrodiplomacy in tourism. *Current Issues in Tourism*, *22*(9), 1076–1094.

Timothy, D. J., & Saarinen, J. (2013). Cross-border co-operation and tourism in Europe. *Trends in European Tourism Planning and Organisation*, *60*, 64–75.

Tomazzoni, E. L., Abrahão, C. M. D. S., & Lumertz, J. S. (2022). The performance of the private initiative of the Brazilian tourism, in the framework of mercosur, on the perspectives of diplomacy and international technical cooperation. *Podium Sport, Leisure and Tourism Review*, *11*(2), 353–380.

Tosun, C., Timothy, D. J., Parpairis, A., & MacDonald, D. (2005). Cross-border cooperation in tourism marketing growth strategies. *Journal of Travel & Tourism Marketing*, *18*(1), 5–23.

Westermann-Behaylo, M. K., Rehbein, K., & Fort, T. (2015). Enhancing the concept of corporate diplomacy: Encompassing political corporate social responsibility, international relations, and peace through commerce. *Academy of Management Perspectives*, *29*(4), 387–404.

White, C., Vanc, A., & Coman, I. (2011). Corporate social responsibility in transitional countries: Public relations as a component of public diplomacy in Romania. *International Journal of Strategic Communication*, *5*(4), 281–292.

Yang, Y. (2022). *Digital economy and the sustainable development of ASEAN and China* (Vol. 9). World Scientific.

Chapter 5

Tourism Diplomacy Through Cultural Values, Understanding, and Exchange

Abstract

Cultural values, understanding, and exchange play a pivotal role in tourism diplomacy by fostering international cooperation, enhancing mutual respect, and promoting sustainable cultural heritage. The interplay between culture and diplomacy strengthens national identity, as heritage preservation becomes a tool for soft power and economic empowerment through cultural tourism. Furthermore, tourism diplomacy facilitates intercultural dialogue, enhancing communication and tolerance among diverse communities while addressing social cohesion and conflict resolution. By fostering global citizenship and ethical practices, cultural exchange initiatives contribute to deeper intellectual and emotional connections across borders. This chapter explores the multifaceted roles of culture in tourism diplomacy, examining its influence on national identity, the promotion of tolerance, and the development of shared heritage-based initiatives. Key themes include integrating art, language, and cuisine as mediums for cultural understanding, as well as the ethical considerations underpinning the effective use of tourism diplomacy to navigate global challenges. The analysis underscores the potential of tourism to build bridges between nations while respecting the nuances of cultural diversity.

Keywords: Tourism diplomacy; cultural exchange; heritage preservation; intercultural dialogue; soft power

1. Introduction

Tourism diplomacy has emerged as a vital avenue for promoting cultural values, fostering intercultural understanding, and encouraging global exchange. In an increasingly interconnected world, tourism has the power to bridge cultural divides and create a platform for communication, empathy, and appreciation of

Tourism Diplomacy, 97–112

Copyright © 2025 Mahmut Demir and Şirvan Şen Demir

Published under exclusive licence by Emerald Publishing Limited
doi:10.1108/978-1-83708-676-420251005

diversity (Abbasi & Maher, 2022; Zugasti, 2019). Beyond its economic benefits, tourism can act as a vehicle for peace and collaboration, helping societies to transcend their differences and celebrate their shared humanity.

One of the primary roles of tourism diplomacy is the promotion of cultural values and heritage (Cai, 2020; Lähdesmäki, 2021). Nations, regions, and communities each hold unique cultural attributes that can enrich and enlighten others. By sharing these aspects through tourism, countries promote a narrative that fosters national pride while educating visitors about their history, art, traditions, and lifestyle. The showcasing of cultural heritage often extends beyond historical monuments or traditional events; it includes intangible elements like language, folklore, and culinary practices that shape the collective identity of a society (Cameron, 2015; Nag & Mishra, 2024). When respectfully and authentically shared with visitors, these cultural dimensions enable countries to project a nuanced image to the world. Thus, tourism has become a tool for preserving cultural heritage and communicating values such as respect, hospitality, and unity. Through dedicated efforts to protect and share their heritage, countries use tourism as a form of "soft power," cultivating positive perceptions and goodwill on the global stage.

Tourism plays a crucial role in fostering intercultural dialogue and understanding, helping to bridge communication gaps, reducing prejudice, and enhancing tolerance among people from different backgrounds (Abbasi & Maher, 2022; Zugasti, 2019). This is a significant contribution, as tourism enables individuals to interact directly with diverse cultures, breaking down stereotypes and promoting empathy. When tourists and hosts engage in open dialogue, they gain insights into each other's beliefs, practices, and values. This interaction encourages tolerance and broadens worldviews, creating a foundation for mutual respect. Intercultural dialogue through tourism is particularly impactful because it involves face-to-face exchanges that are often spontaneous and genuine (Carbone, 2017; Wüst & Nicolai, 2023). Such experiences allow people to see past preconceived notions and find common ground with others. Furthermore, destinations promoting intercultural exchange create an environment where visitors are encouraged to learn about and appreciate the local way of life. This process enriches the tourist experience and fosters a sense of solidarity, contributing to a more harmonious global community.

At the heart of tourism diplomacy is cultural exchange – sharing ideas, information, arts, language, and other cultural elements across borders (Del Campo, 2015; Shannon, 2024). This is a significant role, as this exchange is crucial in fostering mutual understanding and respect among nations. When people travel, they bring their perspectives, ideas, and customs while also absorbing those of the places they visit. These interactions cultivate a cross-pollination of knowledge and creativity, enriching both visitors and hosts. Cultural exchange in tourism is not limited to the physical movement of people; it can also include digital platforms, educational programs, and partnerships that connect people from different parts of the world (Hjorthén, 2021; Zreik, 2023). Through such exchanges, individuals and communities gain a deeper appreciation of cultural diversity, leading to a world that values inclusivity and dialogue. Tourism diplomacy encourages a global culture of peace and understanding by creating opportunities for people to connect and exchange cultural insights.

2. Promotion of Cultural Values and Heritage in Tourism Diplomacy

Tourism diplomacy offers a powerful platform for promoting cultural values and preserving heritage, serving as an instrument to connect nations and foster mutual understanding. By showcasing the unique characteristics of a nation's culture, history, and way of life, tourism diplomacy attracts visitors and builds positive international relationships (Fig. 9). The promotion of cultural values and heritage extends beyond mere displays of traditional artifacts or performances; it involves a more profound commitment to preserving and sharing the essence of a nation's identity in ways that resonate globally. This focus on culture and heritage is fundamental to tourism diplomacy, where the primary goal is not merely economic gain but fostering a spirit of global cooperation and respect.

2.1 The Role of Culture and Heritage in Shaping National Identity

Cultural heritage, comprising tangible and intangible elements, is a key player in shaping national identity. For countries involved in tourism diplomacy, promoting cultural heritage helps construct a narrative highlighting values such as respect, unity, and historical continuity (Cai, 2020; Winter, 2016). Monuments, historical sites, traditional practices, art, and local customs tell the story of a nation and convey the values that have shaped its people over generations. By sharing these aspects with international visitors, countries share their past and vision for the future. The intentional promotion of cultural values through tourism diplomacy counters homogenization in a globalized world, preserving each culture's uniqueness while encouraging diversity (Cameron, 2015; Wiktor-Mach, 2019). For example, the Japanese government's effort to promote the tea ceremony as a symbol of peace, discipline, and tranquility demonstrates how a specific cultural practice can communicate core national values to an international audience. By framing such traditions within the context of tourism diplomacy, nations can shape their global identity and foster deeper connections with other countries.

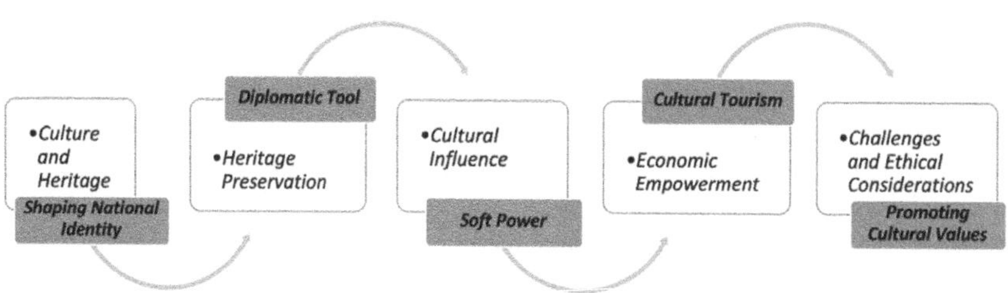

Fig. 9. Tourism Diplomacy Through Cultural Values.

2.2 Heritage Preservation as a Diplomatic Tool

Heritage preservation is crucial to tourism diplomacy, as it maintains the authenticity and integrity of the promoted cultural elements (Folmer et al., 2016; Singh & Rana, 2021). Countries that actively preserve their heritage not only protect their cultural resources but also position themselves as custodians of global history and knowledge. International organizations like UNESCO are essential in supporting countries in identifying, preserving, and promoting World Heritage Sites. These sites become symbols of global unity, showcasing humanity's shared history and accomplishments. In tourism diplomacy, promoting well-preserved heritage sites enhances a country's reputation on the global stage (García, 2024; Setyagung et al., 2013). Tourists are increasingly interested in authentic experiences that allow them to engage with the history and traditions of a place. For instance, Egypt's efforts to preserve and promote the Pyramids of Giza or Italy's dedication to safeguarding Venice as a cultural treasure highlight how heritage preservation reinforces tourism diplomacy. These countries do not simply attract tourists; they communicate a message of cultural pride and historical responsibility that resonates worldwide.

Heritage preservation involves collaboration with other nations, fostering international cooperation in protecting cultural landmarks and practices (Grenet, 2019; Platts et al., 2023). Cross-border efforts, such as the collaboration between Germany and Poland to preserve Auschwitz as a reminder of World War II atrocities, show how shared cultural heritage can become a foundation for reconciliation and mutual respect. This form of tourism diplomacy transforms cultural sites into symbols of unity and peace, emphasizing the shared responsibilities of nations toward preserving humanity's collective history.

2.3 Soft Power and Cultural Influence Through Tourism

One of the most influential aspects of promoting cultural values and heritage through tourism diplomacy is the soft power it generates. Soft power refers to the ability to influence other nations through attraction rather than coercion, and cultural diplomacy is a primary instrument of this influence (Lähdesmäki, 2021; Nag & Mishra, 2024). By sharing culture and heritage, countries create a favorable image in the minds of international audiences, building trust and goodwill that can lead to more robust political and economic relationships.

Countries like South Korea have successfully harnessed soft power by promoting aspects of their culture – such as K-pop, traditional cuisine, and fashion – within their tourism campaigns. This strategy has made South Korean culture popular worldwide, increasing its appeal and positively associating with the nation. Similarly, France's promotion of its wine regions and culinary heritage attracts millions of tourists annually, cementing its image as a center of refined culture and sophistication. Tourism diplomacy that leverages cultural heritage for soft power does not only benefit national image; it also creates pathways for deeper understanding and cooperation (Cai, 2020; Grenet, 2019). Tourists who experience another culture firsthand are more likely to appreciate and respect its values. This appreciation can break down stereotypes and encourage a more balanced perspective, contributing to a more peaceful and inclusive global society.

2.4 Economic Empowerment Through Cultural Tourism

While the primary aim of promoting cultural values and heritage may not be financial, the economic benefits are undeniable. Cultural tourism generates significant revenue for many countries, supporting local communities and creating employment opportunities (Bier & White, 2021; Grincheva, 2024). By focusing on sustainable tourism practices that highlight cultural assets, countries can attract high-value tourists interested in immersive experiences rather than superficial visits. This economic potential of cultural tourism offers a promising avenue for growth and development.

Local artisans, performers, and guides benefit directly from tourism that centers around cultural values, as their skills and knowledge are in demand. In places like Bali, where the culture and religion of the Balinese people are central to tourism, visitors gain insights into the local way of life while contributing to the economy. This economic empowerment extends to rural areas and smaller communities, which rely on cultural tourism for development. Cultural tourism bridges economic growth and cultural preservation for countries engaged in tourism diplomacy. Governments increasingly recognize the importance of developing tourism policies that protect cultural assets while generating income (Abuan, 2021; Linardaki & Aslanides, 2020). Initiatives like heritage festivals, craft markets, and culinary tours allow tourists to participate in cultural experiences in ways that are respectful and economically beneficial to the host communities. This balance ensures that economic growth does not come at the cost of cultural preservation, reassuring the audience.

2.5 Challenges and Ethical Considerations in Promoting Cultural Values

While promoting cultural values and heritage in tourism diplomacy has many advantages, it also raises challenges and ethical considerations (García, 2024; Platts et al., 2023). Commercializing cultural assets can lead to the commodification of traditions, where their market value overshadows the intrinsic value of cultural practices. Cultural performances, rituals, or artifacts risk being altered or simplified to meet tourist expectations, potentially losing authenticity. The popularity of specific cultural sites can lead to overcrowding and environmental degradation, threatening the promotion of heritage (Cameron, 2015; Singh & Rana, 2021). For example, the over-tourism at Machu Picchu has led to strict regulations to protect the site from damage. Countries must balance the desire to share their heritage with the need to protect it, ensuring that tourism remains sustainable and respectful.

Another ethical challenge in tourism diplomacy is representing cultural practices. Some nations might face pressure to present a "sanitized" version of their culture, omitting complex or controversial aspects. For tourism diplomacy to be genuinely effective, countries must embrace the full spectrum of their cultural identity, including its challenges and diversity. This emphasis on authenticity and diversity in cultural representation ensures that tourism diplomacy contributes to mutual understanding rather than reinforcing stereotypes, enlightening the audience about the need for a comprehensive portrayal of cultural identity.

3. Intercultural Dialogue and Understanding in Tourism Diplomacy: Developing Communication and Tolerance

The need for intercultural dialogue and understanding has never been more critical in today's interconnected world. Tourism diplomacy, with its inherent emphasis on people-to-people interactions, is pivotal in fostering intercultural communication and tolerance. By facilitating encounters between individuals from diverse backgrounds, tourism enables a richer appreciation of cultural diversity and offers an invaluable platform for reducing prejudice and promoting tolerance. This form of diplomacy goes beyond governmental interactions, reaching citizens directly and nurturing relationships based on respect, empathy, and a shared sense of humanity. Tourism diplomacy is uniquely positioned to foster intercultural dialogue and understanding in this context.

3.1 The Importance of Intercultural Dialogue in Global Society

Intercultural dialogue is not just a means for peaceful coexistence and mutual respect but also a path to personal growth and more profound understanding in a multicultural world (Abbasi & Maher, 2022; Grincheva, 2013). As individuals immerse themselves in different customs, languages, and traditions through travel, they encounter the richness and complexity of human culture. These encounters highlight the similarities and differences between people and invite them to consider perspectives beyond their own. This is where tourism diplomacy becomes crucial, as it fosters the notion that engaging with other cultures can lead to personal growth and a more profound understanding, ultimately contributing to global harmony (Fig. 10).

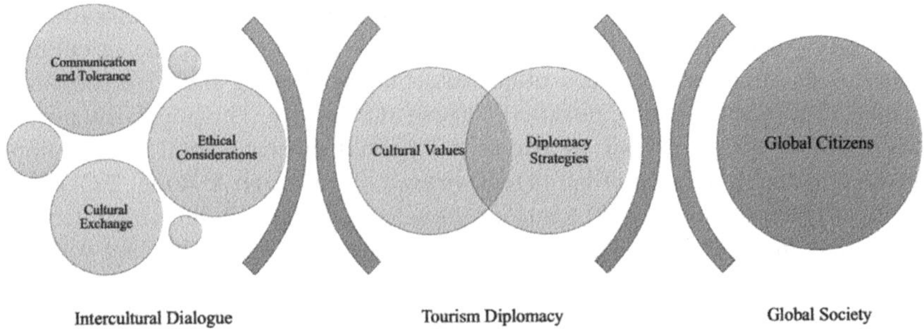

Fig. 10. Intercultural Dialogue and Understanding in Tourism Diplomacy.

Intercultural dialogue is a powerful tool in dispelling stereotypes and fostering a more balanced perception of other cultures (Bier & White, 2021; Wüst & Nicolai, 2023). Without direct interaction, misunderstandings and biases are more likely to thrive. However, when tourists actively engage with local communities, they begin to appreciate the nuances of another culture, often challenging preconceived notions. For instance, tourists visiting a predominantly Muslim country may gain a more informed understanding of Islamic culture by participating in local festivals, tasting traditional foods, or simply conversing with residents. These seemingly simple interactions, facilitated by tourism, build bridges of understanding that have long-term benefits for international relations and foster a more accepting and appreciative attitude toward cultural diversity.

3.2 Tourism as a Catalyst for Intercultural Communication

Tourism diplomacy utilizes traveling to foster dialogue across cultures (Abuan, 2021; Zugasti, 2019). Tourism provides an organic setting for intercultural communication, where individuals can learn about cultural differences rather than theoretical ones in real-life contexts. These experiences encourage tourists and locals to engage in meaningful conversations and overcome language or cultural barriers. This communication contributes to a global dialogue in which both visitors and hosts exchange knowledge, challenge assumptions, and enrich each other's perspectives.

Developing intercultural communication skills through tourism is a significant benefit for global citizens. Communication goes beyond mere words; it involves understanding nonverbal cues, cultural practices, and social norms that vary widely from one culture to another. Tourists exposed to these differences become more adept at adapting their communication style and learning to navigate intercultural interactions with greater sensitivity and respect. For example, personal space or appropriate greetings may differ across cultures; tourists learning these subtleties develop a more nuanced understanding of communication, enhancing their ability to relate to people from diverse backgrounds.

3.3 Promoting Tolerance Through Tourism Diplomacy

Tolerance is not just a byproduct but a key goal of successful intercultural dialogue and communication (Carbone, 2017; Isar, 2020). Tourism diplomacy is crucial in reducing ethnocentrism and fostering acceptance by exposing individuals to new cultures and perspectives. When tourists experience a culture firsthand, they are less likely to hold onto negative stereotypes and more likely to develop an appreciation for diversity. This direct experience often shifts perspectives, making travelers more open-minded and respectful toward cultural differences.

Tourism diplomacy initiatives can specifically target the promotion of tolerance by creating programs that encourage cultural immersion. For example, homestay programs where tourists live with local families provide deeper insight into daily life, customs, and traditions. These programs offer a more intimate and genuine experience than traditional hotel stays and contribute to a greater understanding of cultural differences. Additionally, educational tourism programs that focus on the host country's history, art, and social customs encourage tourists to recognize the value of cultural diversity.

Tolerance can also be fostered by encouraging locals to view tourists as partners in cultural exchange rather than outsiders. Communities that welcome tourists with open-mindedness and a willingness to share their traditions are likely to gain respect from visitors, who, in turn, feel more connected to the culture they are exploring. This mutual tolerance, fostered by tourism, lays a promising foundation for global solidarity and peace as individuals learn to see value in other ways of life without feeling threatened or diminished (Del Campo, 2015; Grincheva, 2024).

3.4 Tourism as a Tool for Social Cohesion and Conflict Resolution

Tourism diplomacy offers a path toward reconciliation by fostering social cohesion in areas where political or religious conflicts have created barriers (Faucher, 2016; Zreik, 2023). Tourism can act as a neutral ground where individuals from conflicting backgrounds meet and engage in constructive dialogue. For instance, peace tourism initiatives in historically contentious regions have helped build connections between people by highlighting shared heritage and history. This approach shifts the focus from divisive narratives to commonalities, fostering a sense of shared humanity. Tourism diplomacy programs that promote intercultural dialogue in conflict regions have shown promise in reducing hostility and promoting mutual understanding (Gripentrog, 2015; Winter, 2016). An example of this is the joint tourism initiatives between Israel and Jordan, where cross-border tourism projects allow tourists to experience the cultures of both nations. By highlighting common historical sites and fostering shared tourism spaces, such initiatives inspire people from both sides to view each other through a lens of shared history rather than division. This exposure to diverse perspectives has the potential to break down prejudices and cultivate empathy, laying a foundation for more peaceful interactions.

3.5 Developing Global Citizens Through Cultural Exchange

Tourism diplomacy plays a pivotal role in creating global citizens – individuals who are not only aware of their own culture but also empathetic toward other cultures (Hjorthén, 2021; Shannon, 2024). Exposure to different ways of life encourages tourists to reflect on their values and behaviors, leading to a greater sense of self-awareness and adaptability. This process is essential in developing intercultural sensitivity, where individuals can navigate cultural differences with respect and understanding, empowering them to be ambassadors of tolerance and understanding.

Programs encouraging cultural exchange, such as student exchange programs, volunteer tourism, and language immersion experiences, are particularly effective in cultivating global citizens. These programs allow participants to live in foreign countries for extended periods, creating opportunities for sustained intercultural dialogue (Linardaki & Aslanides, 2020; Mark, 2010). They build friendships across borders and instill a sense of global responsibility and respect for cultural diversity. Individuals who participate in these exchanges often return to their home countries with a broader perspective, making them advocates for tolerance and understanding. For example, the Erasmus program in Europe has allowed millions of students to study and live in different countries, exposing them to many cultures. This experience fosters a European identity that transcends national borders, promoting values of unity and mutual respect. Similarly, the Peace Corps program has enabled Americans to serve in communities worldwide, facilitating cultural exchange and understanding on a grassroots level. These experiences profoundly impact individuals, making them ambassadors of peace and tolerance in their communities.

3.6 Challenges and Ethical Considerations in Intercultural Dialogue Through Tourism

While tourism diplomacy has significant potential for fostering intercultural dialogue, there are challenges and ethical considerations to address (Abbasi & Maher, 2022; Carbone, 2017; Grincheva, 2024). One major challenge is the risk of cultural appropriation, where elements of a culture are adopted superficially without respect or understanding. This can lead to the commodification of culture, where traditional practices and artifacts are marketed to tourists without regard for their deeper meaning. To avoid this, tourism diplomacy must emphasize authenticity and respect, encouraging tourists to appreciate and understand cultures rather than consume them.

Another challenge lies in managing the expectations of both tourists and hosts (Del Campo, 2015; Winter, 2016). While tourists may desire genuine cultural experiences, locals may feel pressure to perform or alter their traditions to meet these expectations. This dynamic can lead to a loss of cultural authenticity as traditions are modified to cater to the tourist market. Ethical tourism practices must prioritize the integrity of local customs and encourage tourists to engage respectfully.

Language barriers pose a significant challenge to intercultural dialogue, as effective communication is the cornerstone of meaningful interactions. While translation services and language guides are increasingly accessible, the subtleties of cultural expression can often be lost in translation. Tourism diplomacy initiatives must support language learning and cultural education to bridge these gaps and foster more authentic connections, thereby underscoring the crucial role of language in this context.

4. Cultural Exchange in Tourism Diplomacy: Fostering Mutual Understanding Through Shared Heritage

Cultural exchange is one of the most potent tools in tourism diplomacy, enabling individuals and communities from different nations to share and learn from each other's customs, values, and ways of life. Cultural exchange goes beyond mere travel; it embodies a meaningful interaction where participants gain deeper insight into another culture's traditions, languages, art, and perspectives. Tourism diplomacy facilitates mutual understanding and fosters stronger global relationships by promoting these exchanges.

Fostering intercultural respect and cooperation is more crucial than ever in an era of rapid globalization and increasing interdependence. Through various forms of cultural exchange, including the sharing of ideas, information, art, language, and lifestyle, tourism diplomacy offers a pathway to creating a more harmonious and connected world. Cultural exchange underpins the purpose of tourism diplomacy, turning what could be passive encounters into transformative experiences that build bridges between individuals and societies.

4.1 The Role of Cultural Exchange in Tourism Diplomacy

Cultural exchange forms the foundation of tourism diplomacy, enabling people to engage in immersive experiences that deepen their understanding of other cultures (Bier & White, 2021; Cai, 2020). Unlike economic or political diplomacy, which often takes place between governments or institutions, tourism diplomacy operates at a more personal level. It harnesses the power of cultural exchange to transcend borders, encouraging tourists and locals alike to explore each other's values, practices, and identities.

Through tourism diplomacy, cultural exchange encourages people to see beyond their perspectives and appreciate the richness of other cultures (Carbone, 2017; Wiktor-Mach, 2019). This interaction reduces prejudice and promotes a more inclusive mindset, exposing travelers to new languages, arts, religious practices, and social norms. For example, a tourist visiting Japan may witness traditional tea ceremonies, Japanese calligraphy, and Zen gardens, providing them with insight into Japanese esthetics, mindfulness, and spirituality. Such exposure allows tourists to appreciate the complexity and depth of another culture, fostering respect and admiration.

4.2 Exchanging Ideas and Information: Building Intellectual Connections

One of the key elements of cultural exchange is the sharing of ideas and information, which can profoundly impact international understanding (Del Campo, 2015; García, 2024). As stated by some researchers (e.g., Linardaki & Aslanides, 2020; Mark, 2010; Singh & Rana, 2021), when people travel, they bring their perspectives, knowledge, and experiences, which can broaden the worldview of those they encounter. Conversely, tourists also absorb new ideas, philosophies, and ways of thinking from the places they visit. This reciprocal exchange creates intellectual bonds contributing to a more informed and empathetic global society. For instance, tourism diplomacy initiatives often involve educational exchanges, where students, scholars, or professionals visit other countries to learn about their fields from different cultural standpoints. These exchanges expose participants to diverse methods and theories, enhancing their academic or professional expertise. For example, a biologist studying wildlife conservation may visit Kenya to understand African approaches to conservation, learning from local knowledge and practices that prioritize community involvement and ecological preservation. The ideas and insights from such experiences are invaluable, broadening the participants' outlooks and inspiring innovative solutions incorporating global perspectives.

4.3 Art and Cultural Expression: Bridging Differences Through Creativity

Art is a universal language that transcends borders and provides a profound means of cultural expression. Cultural exchange enables individuals to communicate ideas and emotions that may be difficult to express verbally by sharing music, visual art, dance, theater, and literature (Grincheva, 2024; Lähdesmäki, 2021). Tourism diplomacy encourages the exchange of artistic traditions, which allows for a deeper appreciation of cultural differences and similarities. Artistic exchange often brings people together, inspiring a shared sense of humanity through creativity and self-expression.

Festivals, exhibitions, and performances are platforms for this exchange, drawing tourists eager to experience another culture's art (Demir & Dalgıç, 2022). For example, the annual Venice Biennale attracts artists and audiences worldwide, providing a venue for global artistic dialogue. Such events expose participants to various cultural expressions, challenging stereotypes and encouraging a more nuanced understanding of each nation's unique cultural environment. Similarly, jazz festivals in New Orleans or carnival celebrations in Rio de Janeiro invite international visitors to experience the artistic soul of these cities, fostering a global appreciation for cultural diversity.

Beyond traditional art forms, the exchange of contemporary art allows nations to communicate their social issues, aspirations, and collective identities (Wüst & Nicolai, 2023; Zreik, 2023). Street art, for instance, often reflects local communities' struggles and aspirations. Visitors viewing street art in cities like Berlin, Mexico City, or Cape Town gain insight into local perspectives on historical trauma, political struggle, or social change. This exposure fosters empathy and understanding, as art speaks to universal themes in ways that words sometimes cannot.

4.4 Language Exchange: Unlocking Cultural Nuances and Fostering Communication

Language is a gateway to understanding a culture's intricacies. Through language, individuals gain insight into a society's values, beliefs, and social norms.

Tourism diplomacy often promotes language exchange to facilitate communication and build mutual respect. When tourists attempt to learn the language of their host country, even at a basic level, they demonstrate respect for the culture and create a foundation for meaningful interactions (Platts et al., 2023; Shannon, 2024).

Programs encouraging language learning as part of tourism experiences can deepen cultural appreciation and foster stronger connections. For example, language immersion programs in Spain allow tourists to live with Spanish-speaking families, participate in daily routines, and practice conversational Spanish. This exposure enables participants to understand better the culture's social structure, humor, and idiomatic expressions, often lost in translation. Similarly, Japanese language immersion programs for tourists provide insights into Japanese politeness and honorifics, reinforcing the importance of respect and humility in Japanese society.

Moreover, language exchange fosters tolerance by reducing the potential for misunderstandings. When individuals communicate effectively, they are more likely to navigate cultural differences with patience and empathy. This skill becomes particularly valuable in multicultural societies or international settings where diverse cultural perspectives are represented. By learning each other's languages, people not only communicate better but also develop a sense of respect for each other's cultural identities (Isar, 2020; Nag & Mishra, 2024).

4.5 Culinary Tourism: Experiencing Culture Through Food

Food is one of the most direct and enjoyable ways to experience another culture (Demir & Alper, 2021). Culinary tourism, which involves exploring a destination through food and beverages, allows tourists to connect with local traditions and customs. The cuisine reflects a culture's history, resources, and values, and sharing a meal can be a profound form of cultural exchange. In many countries, food preparation and consumption are deeply embedded in cultural identity, and tourists can learn much about a society by engaging with its culinary traditions.

Tourism diplomacy often promotes culinary exchanges, allowing tourists to attend cooking classes, food tours, or wine tastings. For instance, Italy offers pasta-making classes where tourists learn not only about the ingredients and techniques but also about the significance of family and tradition in Italian culture. In Thailand, visitors can participate in cooking classes highlighting the balance of flavors in Thai cuisine, reflecting the harmony central to Thai philosophy. Such experiences go beyond eating; they involve learning about the ingredients, cultural practices, and social rituals associated with food.

Culinary tourism also fosters mutual respect by encouraging tourists to embrace local customs (Demir & Alper, 2021; Zreik, 2023). For instance, dining etiquette varies widely across cultures, and understanding these customs demonstrates respect. In Japan, tourists may learn the significance of not leaving food on the plate as a sign of gratitude, while in India, they might be introduced to the tradition of eating with hands to connect more closely with the food. Through these encounters, culinary tourism promotes understanding and acceptance of cultural differences.

4.6 Tourism Diplomacy Initiatives Promoting Cultural Exchange

Governments and international organizations have recognized the value of cultural exchange in fostering mutual understanding and have implemented various initiatives under the umbrella of tourism diplomacy (Grenet, 2019; Hjorthén, 2021). Programs such as UNESCO's World Heritage Sites aim to protect cultural treasures and make them accessible to global audiences, promoting a shared appreciation for humanity's collective heritage. By designating and preserving landmarks of cultural significance, UNESCO encourages tourists to explore and learn about different histories, art forms, and social traditions.

Exchange programs like those sponsored by Fulbright and Erasmus encourage students and professionals to live and study in other countries, fostering cultural exchange and understanding. These programs are instrumental in promoting diplomacy at the grassroots level, allowing participants to become cultural ambassadors who share their experiences and insights upon returning home. These exchange participants often become advocates for international collaboration and continue to promote cross-cultural understanding in their future careers.

5. Conclusions

Tourism diplomacy can significantly contribute to global harmony when guided by a commitment to cultural values, understanding, and exchange. Tourism fosters an environment where nations and people unite in cooperation and mutual respect by promoting cultural heritage, facilitating intercultural dialogue, and enabling cultural exchange. In a time of global challenges and increasing cultural diversity, tourism diplomacy is crucial for building connections, fostering tolerance, and enhancing the shared understanding essential for a peaceful and interconnected world. Through thoughtful and intentional efforts, tourism can continue to strengthen international relationships, laying the groundwork for a future where cultural appreciation and empathy prevail.

Promoting cultural values and heritage in tourism diplomacy is a powerful means of building international relationships based on respect, empathy, and shared history. By embracing their cultural heritage, countries can foster a positive image, support local communities, and contribute to a more connected world. However, this promotion must be carefully managed to ensure authenticity, sustainability, and respect for shared cultural practices.

As the world becomes increasingly interconnected, the role of cultural values in tourism diplomacy will continue to grow in importance. With thoughtful approaches, nations can use tourism to celebrate their unique heritage, enrich global culture, and contribute to a more harmonious international community. Focusing on cultural values and heritage strengthens national identity and emphasizes the universal elements of humanity, fostering peace and understanding in a complex world.

Intercultural dialogue and understanding are essential to tourism diplomacy, fostering communication, tolerance, and global unity. Tourism diplomacy promotes mutual respect and appreciation by facilitating encounters between diverse cultures, making it an invaluable tool for building a more harmonious world. Tourists and hosts engage in dialogue and exchange, breaking down barriers and building bridges that transcend political or cultural divides. Tourism diplomacy cultivates global citizens' awareness of and active involvement in fostering cultural understanding and tolerance.

Tourism diplomacy's role in promoting intercultural dialogue is indispensable in a world where misunderstandings can lead to conflict. Through tourism, nations can showcase the richness of their culture while learning from others. As intercultural communication and tolerance continue to develop through these interactions, tourism diplomacy will remain a cornerstone in the journey toward global peace and solidarity.

Cultural exchange, facilitated through tourism diplomacy, fosters mutual understanding by creating platforms for sharing and learning about diverse ways of life. Tourism diplomacy nurtures empathy, breaks down stereotypes, and builds bridges across cultural divides by promoting exchanges of ideas, information, art, language, and cuisine. Tourists and locals better understand humanity's shared values and diverse expressions through these interactions.

Cultural exchange offers peace and unity in a world where divisions often lead to conflict. Tourism diplomacy, by promoting these exchanges, cultivates a global citizenry that values diversity, seeks understanding, and upholds respect for cultural heritage. Tourism diplomacy will remain invaluable in building a more connected and compassionate world as nations and individuals continue to participate in and support cultural exchange.

References

Abbasi, I. A., & Maher, N. (2022). Cultural diplomacy: The case study of Pakistan–Japan cultural relations. *Asia-Pacific-Annual Research Journal of Far East & South East Asia*, *40*, 65–81.

Abuan, R. E. M. (2021). Cultural diplomacy of Thailand and Indonesia in the Philippines. *MJIR| Malaysian Journal of International Relations*, *9*(1), 88–104.

Bier, L. M., & White, C. L. (2021). Cultural diplomacy as corporate strategy: An analysis of Pasona Group's "New Tohoku" program in Japan. *Place Branding and Public Diplomacy*, *17*(2), 180–192.

Cai, Y. (2020). *Staging Indigenous heritage: Instrumentalisation, brokerage, and representation in Malaysia*. Routledge.

Cameron, C. (2015). UNESCO and cultural heritage: Unexpected consequences. In W. Logan, M. N. Craith, & U. Kockel (Eds.), *A companion to heritage studies* (pp. 322–336). John Wiley & Sons.

Carbone, F. (2017). International tourism and cultural diplomacy: A new conceptual approach towards global mutual understanding and peace through tourism. *Tourism: An International Interdisciplinary Journal*, *65*(1), 61–74.

Del Campo, L. G. M. (2015). *Cultural diplomacy: A hundred years of the British-Spanish society*. Oxford University Press.

Demir, M., & Alper, P. (2021). G20 summit menus as a means of gastrodiplomacy: Messages to the world via menus. *International Journal of Gastronomy and Food Science*, *25*, 1–8. https://doi.org/10.1016/j.ijgfs.2021.100368

Demir, M., & Dalgıç, A. (2022). Examining gastronomy festivals as the attractiveness factor for tourism destinations: The case of Turkey. *Journal of Convention & Event Tourism*, *23*, 412–434. https://doi.org/10.1080/15470148.2022.2089797

Faucher, C. (2016). Cultural diplomacy and international cultural relations in twentieth-century Europe. *Contemporary European History*, *25*(2), 373–385.

Folmer, A., Revier, H., & Cupido, T. (2016). Sustainable tourism development and the world heritage status of the Wadden Sea: The case of Terschelling. *Research in Hospitality Management*, *6*(1), 45–50.

García, P. (2024). Diplomatic heritage: The involvement of the world monuments fund in the Sacred Valley of the Incas, Cuzco, Peru 1. In G. Bozoğlu, G. Campbell, L. Smith, & C. Whitehead (Eds.), *The Routledge international handbook of heritage and politics* (pp. 552–567). Routledge.

Grenet, S. (2019). Heritage of display: Interculturality and cultural diplomacy in the 2010 UNESCO falconry file. *International Journal of Heritage Studies*, *25*(6), 553–564.

Grincheva, N. (2013). Cultural diplomacy 2.0: Challenges and opportunities in museum international practices. *Museum & Society*, *11*(1), 39–49.

Grincheva, N. (2024). The past and future of cultural diplomacy. *International Journal of Cultural Policy*, *30*(2), 172–191.

Gripentrog, J. (2015). Power and culture: Japan's cultural diplomacy in the United States, 1934–1940. *Pacific Historical Review*, *84*(4), 478–516.

Hjorthén, A. (2021). Old world homecomings: Campaigns of ancestral tourism and cultural diplomacy, 1945–66. *Journal of Contemporary History*, *56*(4), 1147–1170.

Isar, Y. R. (2020). Cultural diplomacy: India does it differently. *Cultural Diplomacy and International Cultural Relations*, *I*, 47–58.

Lähdesmäki, T. (2021). Heritage diplomacy discourses in the EU: Notions on cultural diplomacy, cultural heritage, and intercultural dialogue among EU officials and heritage practitioners. *Ethnologia Europaea*, *51*(2), 48–71.

Linardaki, C., & Aslanides, A. (2020). From poem and song to cultural diplomacy: Challenges and opportunities for place branding and tourism promotion. *Place Branding and Public Diplomacy*, *16*(4), 304–315.

Mark, S. L. (2010). Rethinking cultural diplomacy: The cultural diplomacy of New Zealand, the Canadian Federation and Quebec. *Political Science*, *62*(1), 62–83.

Nag, A., & Mishra, S. (2024). Sustainable competitive advantage in heritage tourism: Leveraging cultural legacy in a data-driven world. In R. P. Singh Kaurav & V. Mishra (Eds.), *Review of technologies and disruptive business strategies* (Vol. 3, pp. 137–162). Emerald Publishing Limited.

Platts, E. J., Keifer, H. L., & Samuels, K. L. (2023). Carbon footprints of travel to world heritage sites: Communicating climate to potential tourists through a consumption-based life-cycle assessment. *Journal of Heritage Tourism*, *18*(4), 407–426.

Setyagung, E., Hani, U., Azzadina, I., Sianipar, C., & Ishii, T. (2013). Preserving cultural heritage: The harmony between art idealism, commercialization, and triple-helix collaboration. *American Journal of Tourism Management*, *2*(1), 22–28.

Shannon, J. H. (2024). Melodies heard and unheard: The promise and limits of cultural diplomacy through music. In M. R. Lopes da Cunha, J. Shannon, S. M. Sørensen, & V. Danielson (Eds.), *Music and cultural diplomacy in the Middle East: Geopolitical re-configurations for the 21st century* (pp. 71–92). Springer International Publishing.

Singh, R. P., & Rana, P. S. (2021). Cultural diplomacy in India: dispersal, heritage representation, contestation, and development. In O. Niglio and E. Y. J. Lee (Eds.). *Transcultural diplomacy and international law in heritage conservation: A dialogue between ethics, law, and culture* (pp. 231–256). Springer Nature Pte Ltd.

Wiktor-Mach, D. (2019). Cultural heritage and development: UNESCO's new paradigm in a changing geopolitical context. *Third World Quarterly*, *40*(9), 1593–1612.

Winter, T. (2016). Heritage diplomacy and tourism in Asia. In C. M. Hall & S. J. Page (Eds.), *The Routledge Handbook of Tourism in Asia* (pp. 45–53). Routledge.

Wüst, A., & Nicolai, K. (2023). Cultural diplomacy and the reconfiguration of soft power: Evidence from Morocco. *Mediterranean Politics*, *28*(4), 554–579.

Zreik, M. (2023). Stirring up soft power: The role of Chinese Cuisine in China's cultural diplomacy. In K. Kankaew (Ed.), *Global perspectives on soft power management in business* (pp. 292–306). IGI Global.

Zugasti, J. E. S. (2019). Casa México: Promotion, innovation and cultural diplomacy in south by Southwest (SXSW). *Revista Mexicana de Política Exterior*, (117), 85–98.

Chapter 6

Tourism Diplomacy Through International Brandings

Abstract

Tourism diplomacy plays a transformative role in shaping international branding by enhancing destination image, promoting cultural heritage, and fostering competitive advantages in the global tourism market. Integrating destination, city, and institutional branding strategies, this approach amplifies national and regional identities, leveraging tourism as a powerful tool for diplomatic engagement. City branding and urban diplomacy highlight the strategic promotion of urban centers on international platforms, showcasing their cultural, economic, and social assets to attract global attention. Tour operators, international hotel chains, and airlines are critical contributors to tourism diplomacy, utilizing innovative branding strategies to enhance global brand perception and strengthen their roles in destination promotion. Tourism diplomacy significantly influences brand image, adding value to destinations and institutions while fostering resilience in competitive environments. Through the analysis of successful international branding initiatives, this chapter offers insights into best practices and lessons learned, emphasizing the pivotal role of tourism diplomacy in global branding efforts. Exploring these dynamics underscores the synergies between diplomacy and branding, contributing to a deeper understanding of their combined impact on international tourism development.

Keywords: Tourism diplomacy; destination branding; city branding; international competition; brand image

1. Introduction

In the interconnected world of the 21st century, tourism has emerged as a potent diplomatic tool, significantly influencing how nations, cities, and institutions project their identities on a global stage. Tourism diplomacy is at the core of this

Tourism Diplomacy, 113–134

Copyright © 2025 Mahmut Demir and Şirvan Şen Demir

Published under exclusive licence by Emerald Publishing Limited
doi:10.1108/978-1-83708-676-420251006

influence, a concept where travel and tourism act as conduits for nurturing international relations, promoting cultural understanding, and fostering economic growth. A crucial aspect of tourism diplomacy is international branding. This strategy empowers destinations, cities, tour operators, hotel chains, and airline companies to craft unique identities that resonate with global travelers and contribute to national and regional narratives.

Tourism diplomacy and destination branding is foundational in establishing a nation's or region's global identity. Effective destination branding goes beyond mere advertising; it encapsulates the essence of a place's cultural heritage, natural attractions, and values, crafting an image that resonates with tourists and international audiences. Tourism diplomacy enhances national and regional branding through strategic initiatives by promoting a cohesive identity and highlighting a destination's unique attributes. These branding efforts boost tourism, attract foreign investment, and foster goodwill, demonstrating how tourism diplomacy supports economic and diplomatic goals.

The concept of city branding and urban diplomacy underscores the strategic role of individual cities in global tourism diplomacy. Urban centers are increasingly promoted internationally as iconic national identity and cultural expression symbols. City branding enhances tourist appeal and diplomatic clout by associating it with particular experiences or values, such as innovation, tradition, or natural beauty. Through city branding, urban environments can serve as ambassadors of cultural diversity and regional pride, and strategic branding initiatives have empowered cities to become significant players in diplomacy. Case studies reveal how cities like Barcelona, Tokyo, and Istanbul have successfully crafted global identities that draw tourists while influencing diplomatic relations.

Tour operators and international branding play a pivotal role in tourism diplomacy by orchestrating travel experiences that showcase cultural and natural landmarks. Local and international tour operators are not just intermediaries but are instrumental in shaping tourists' perceptions of a destination. With tailored branding strategies, tour operators enhance the appeal of specific regions and create narratives that align with broader tourism diplomacy objectives. Their branding efforts significantly contribute to a destination's global image, directly influencing the effectiveness of tourism diplomacy in promoting international understanding. In hotel chains and global brand perception, international hotels are extensions of a destination's identity. Hotel chains like Marriott, Hilton, and Accor have invested substantially in building brands that mirror the values and appeal of the regions they represent. These brands play a significant role in tourism diplomacy by fostering a sense of place and consistency across locations, offering travelers a familiar yet locally inspired experience. Hotel chains actively participate in destination branding, playing a pivotal role in shaping the image and reputation of the cities and countries where they operate.

Airline companies and international tourism diplomacy underscore the significance of air travel in enhancing national and regional brands. Airlines like Emirates, Turkish Airlines, and Singapore Airlines are more than transportation providers; they are ambassadors of their home countries, promoting culture and values on a global scale. Through strategic alliances and international branding, airlines not only make destinations accessible and attractive but also facilitate cultural exchange, thereby enhancing national identity. The impact of tourism diplomacy on brand image and global competition is evident in a competitive international arena. A strong brand image adds significant value to destinations, cities, and tourism-related institutions, distinguishing them in a crowded market (Fig. 11). Backed by tourism diplomacy, branding strategies are essential in building competitive advantages that attract international visitors. Tourism diplomacy thus plays a critical role in reinforcing these branding efforts, helping destinations and institutions remain relevant and attractive in a globalized world. This chapter delves into the intricate relationship between tourism diplomacy and international branding, showcasing how diverse actors in the tourism sector contribute to shaping global perceptions, fostering cultural connections, and advancing economic and diplomatic objectives.

2. Tourism Diplomacy and Destination Branding

Countries and regions seek to distinguish themselves in an increasingly interconnected world by crafting distinctive destination brands that appeal to

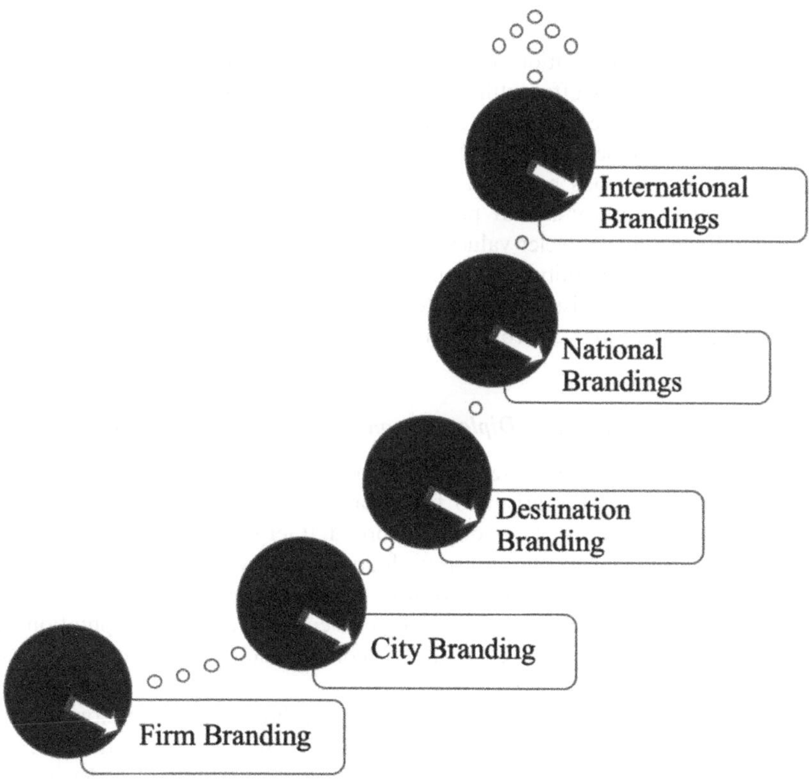

Fig. 11. Tourism Diplomacy Through Brandings.

international audiences. Tourism diplomacy plays a pivotal role in this endeavor, acting as a bridge to communicate a location's unique culture, heritage, and attractions to global travelers. By leveraging destination branding, governments and tourism boards aim to shape perceptions, attract visitors, and establish long-term economic benefits. In this context, strategic approaches to destination branding, the influence of tourism diplomacy on national and regional branding, and the effective use of cultural heritage and natural attractions all contribute significantly to successful tourism brands.

2.1 The Role and Strategies of Destination Branding

Destination branding involves creating and promoting a unique identity for a place, aiming to influence how it is perceived and attract a desired demographic (Clancy, 2011; Ermann & Hermanik, 2018). Successful branding requires a deep understanding of what sets the location apart and what appeals to potential visitors. Common strategies include highlighting natural landmarks, cultural icons, cuisine, or historical significance (Demir & Tür, 2019). For instance, Greece emphasizes its ancient heritage and idyllic environments, while Japan often promotes its cultural uniqueness and natural beauty. Effective destination branding addresses target audiences through carefully curated imagery, slogans, and narratives.

In branding a destination, consistent and compelling storytelling is crucial. Marketing campaigns often utilize social media, targeted advertising, and partnerships with influencers or travel agencies to reach wider audiences (Kolotouchkina & Seisdedos, 2018; Linardaki & Aslanides, 2020). Increasingly, sustainable tourism has become a central theme as destinations highlight their commitment to environmental preservation and responsible travel. This shift aligns with changing traveler values, as eco-conscious visitors prefer destinations that prioritize sustainability and cultural preservation. For example, Costa Rica's brand as an "eco-paradise" has attracted visitors who value conservation, directly supporting tourism and environmental initiatives.

2.2 The Impact of Tourism Diplomacy on National and Regional Branding

Tourism diplomacy is an essential tool for enhancing national and regional branding, as it utilizes tourism to foster favorable international relations and improve the perception of a country abroad (Gerlitz et al., 2021; White & Kolesnicov, 2015). Through tourism diplomacy, governments can showcase their nation's appeal to tourists, investors, foreign businesses, and international policymakers. A strong destination brand helps cultivate a positive reputation and establishes the country or region as welcoming, stable, and culturally rich (Bouzanis, 2009).

Countries like Spain and Thailand illustrate how tourism diplomacy can significantly enhance national branding. Spain's focus on art, architecture, and culinary tourism reinforces its image as a vibrant, culturally rich destination, attracting millions yearly. Likewise, Thailand's "Land of Smiles" campaign has positioned it as a warm and friendly destination. Regional branding within countries also benefits from tourism diplomacy, as local governments promote their distinct cultural and natural attributes. For instance, Catalonia in Spain or Bali in Indonesia leverage unique cultural aspects that set them apart, creating sub-brands under the national tourism umbrella that appeal to specific interests and add depth to the national brand.

2.3 Utilizing Cultural Heritage and Natural Attractions as Destination Brands

Cultural heritage and natural attractions are the most potent assets in creating destination brands (Cameron, 2015; García, 2024). They offer tangible and intangible elements that can attract diverse visitor profiles, including those interested in history, nature, adventure, or leisure. Many countries recognize that preserving and promoting their heritage can differentiate them in the competitive tourism market. Italy, for example, capitalizes on its rich Roman history, Renaissance art, and cuisine, while New Zealand has successfully built its brand around its dramatic environments and outdoor adventure experiences.

Natural attractions like mountains, beaches, forests, and wildlife sanctuaries are solid foundations for destination brands. The Grand Canyon in the United States, the Great Barrier Reef in Australia, and the Northern Lights in Scandinavia are all-natural wonders that have been instrumental in attracting global tourism. Simultaneously, destinations with well-preserved cultural heritage sites, such as Angkor Wat in Cambodia or Machu Picchu in Peru, become cultural symbols that embody national pride and identity.

Moreover, these heritage and natural elements can be woven into a destination's broader brand story. Tourism diplomacy efforts emphasize preserving these treasures, appealing to travelers seeking meaningful and sustainable experiences (Pop et al., 2020; Therkelsen & Gram, 2010). When countries invest in maintaining and showcasing their cultural and natural heritage, they not only attract tourists but also position themselves as custodians of world heritage, gaining respect and positive recognition on the global stage.

3. City Branding and Urban Diplomacy

City branding and urban diplomacy have become critical for cities aiming to enhance their global presence, attract tourism, and foster international partnerships. Cities today compete for tourists, investors, and residents, leading local governments to create distinctive brands that highlight their unique qualities. In this context, promoting cities on international platforms, developing strategic tourism appeal, and examining the impact of successful city brands in tourism diplomacy are essential to understanding how cities can achieve global influence and economic growth.

3.1 The Promotion of Cities on International Platforms and Their Role in Diplomacy

Cities increasingly use urban diplomacy to position themselves as global players, showcasing their unique identities on international platforms (Gerlitz et al., 2021; Iwabuchi, 2018). Events such as trade fairs, cultural festivals, and international sports tournaments allow cities to present their brand to a diverse audience. These platforms allow cities to promote cultural heritage, economic opportunities, and urban lifestyle, building relationships with other cities and international organizations. For example, hosting events like the Olympics or the World Expo places a town on the global stage, attracting visitors and media attention, which boosts its reputation and economic prospects. Urban diplomacy goes beyond attracting tourists; it fosters inter-city collaborations on shared challenges such as climate change, urban development, and innovation (Miño, 2023; Tijani et al., 2024). Organizations like the United Cities and Local Governments (UCLG) and initiatives like the C40 Cities Climate Leadership Group encourage cities to collaborate on issues that transcend national borders. In this way, urban diplomacy enables cities to participate in global policy discussions and advocate for sustainable and inclusive urbanization, adding depth to their brands as responsible, forward-thinking places.

3.2 Strategies to Enhance Cities' Tourist Appeal

To attract tourists, cities need targeted strategies that appeal to both domestic and international visitors (Kobierecka & Kobierecki, 2024; Therkelsen & Halkier, 2008). These strategies often emphasize cultural diversity, historical landmarks, gastronomy, nightlife, and unique experiences. For example, cities like Paris, Rome, and Istanbul highlight their historical and cultural assets, while cities like Tokyo and New York capitalize on their modernity, cultural melting pots, and vibrant entertainment scenes. Each city's brand focuses on specific qualities that resonate with tourists' desires for unique and memorable experiences. Investing in cultural and infrastructure development is also critical. Cities that build or renovate cultural sites, such as museums, theaters, and public spaces, add to their appeal as vibrant destinations (Grincheva, 2013). Hosting arts festivals, food fairs, or film festivals can draw niche tourist groups, generating year-round tourism outside traditional peak seasons. Innovative city technology, including efficient public transportation and digital tourism resources, can significantly enhance the tourist experience. Cities like Singapore and Amsterdam, known for integrating technology and sustainability in urban life, have strengthened their brands by prioritizing visitor-friendly innovations.

3.3 The Impact of City Brands in Tourism Diplomacy: Case Studies

Successful city brands can substantially impact tourism diplomacy, transforming cities into symbols of culture, innovation, and diplomacy (Kolotouchkina & Seisdedos, 2018; Tudor, 2022; White & Kolesnicov, 2015). Case studies of cities like Barcelona, Dubai, and Melbourne reveal the power of a substantial city brand in attracting international attention and fostering diplomatic ties. Barcelona, for example, has established a reputation for culture, architecture, and creativity. The city's tourism diplomacy emphasizes its vibrant lifestyle, bolstered by events like the Barcelona Design Week and music festivals, creating a brand that appeals to culturally inclined visitors. This brand identity also attracts international businesses, contributing to Barcelona's status as an economic hub.

Dubai provides another striking example of effective city branding and tourism diplomacy. Dubai has become a top global tourist destination by positioning itself as a luxurious, forward-thinking city with cutting-edge architecture and world-class shopping. Initiatives like the Dubai Expo 2020 showcased its capacity for hosting large-scale international events and reinforced its brand as an innovative and welcoming city. The city's brand communicates ambition, luxury, and openness, which appeals to tourists and investors alike and has cemented Dubai's role as a diplomatic leader in the Gulf region.

Melbourne, on the other hand, focuses on quality of life, cultural diversity, and education, making it one of the most livable cities in the world. This city brand attracts tourists interested in urban life, arts, and education and has positioned Melbourne as a leader in urban diplomacy within the Asia-Pacific region. Its brand values of inclusivity and cultural vibrancy appeal to visitors and international partners, furthering its soft power influence.

4. Tour Operators and International Branding

Tour operators are instrumental in shaping and promoting tourism on a global scale, acting as the bridge between travelers and destinations. Through well-developed branding strategies and cross-border partnerships, tour operators not only boost tourism but also contribute significantly to tourism diplomacy by creating cultural connections. Exploring the role of tour operators in global tourism, their branding strategies, and their contributions to tourism diplomacy highlights how these organizations drive international tourism while fostering positive intercultural relationships.

4.1 The Role of Tour Operators in Global Tourism

Tour operators play a central role in global tourism by designing, promoting, and delivering travel experiences tailored to diverse interests and demographics (Demir, 2017). Their primary function is to create seamless, curated travel packages that often combine accommodation, transportation, excursions, and other services, making travel more accessible and convenient (Becker, 2016; Demir, 2017). Large tour operators such as TUI and Intrepid Travel are global facilitators, encouraging international tourism by catering to mainstream and niche markets, from adventure tourism to cultural immersion. Through partnerships with local businesses, tour operators provide visitors with curated experiences that showcase the destination's unique attractions, culture, and lifestyle. Promoting regions that may otherwise be overlooked contributes to a more balanced distribution of tourism and fosters economic development in local communities. Additionally, tour operators act as mediators between travelers and foreign cultures, educating clients on responsible travel practices and helping them appreciate local customs. In doing so, they help manage and mitigate the cultural impact of tourism, which is essential for fostering sustainable tourism.

4.2 Branding Strategies for Local and International Tour Operators

Branding is essential for tour operators to distinguish themselves in a highly competitive industry and appeal to a global audience (Fayard, 2024; Webster et al., 2014). For local tour operators, branding often emphasizes authenticity and specialized knowledge of the destination. These operators leverage their deep local connections to offer unique experiences, such as homestays, guided cultural tours, or eco-friendly excursions, which appeal to tourists seeking meaningful and immersive experiences. Local operators focus on communicating their intimate knowledge of the area, the cultural values they promote, and their commitment to supporting the local community.

On the other hand, international tour operators often adopt branding strategies that emphasize trust, convenience, and variety, appealing to travelers who prioritize reliable services and a seamless travel experience (Demir, 2017). These operators highlight their global reach, experience in handling logistics, and broad service range that meets various travel interests and budgets. TUI, for example, has successfully branded itself as a global leader in travel by emphasizing high-quality service, sustainable tourism initiatives, and diverse destination offerings across continents. Similarly, brands like G Adventures appeal to socially conscious travelers by emphasizing sustainability and responsible tourism, setting them apart in a crowded marketplace. Digital branding has also become increasingly important, with many operators investing in online platforms, social media, and user-generated content. Tour operators often engage with customers on digital platforms, sharing travel stories, testimonials, and immersive visuals that strengthen brand identity and create an emotional connection with prospective clients. In this way, digital branding helps tour operators broaden their reach and engage with international travelers on a personal level.

4.3 Contributions of Tour Operators to Tourism Diplomacy

Tour operators contribute significantly to tourism diplomacy by promoting intercultural understanding and positive interactions between tourists and local communities (Gordon, 2024; Kim et al., 2016). By organizing group tours, cultural exchange programs, and community-based experiences, tour operators create opportunities for visitors to gain authentic insights into foreign cultures. This fosters goodwill and mutual respect between visitors and hosts, which is essential for establishing a positive image of the destination abroad. In destinations that may be less well-known or have limited international exposure, tour operators often collaborate with local tourism boards to promote the location's unique features and attractions. This contributes to nation-branding efforts. Tour operators help build international recognition and improve a country's soft power by increasing global visibility and facilitating sustainable tourism (Minardi et al., 2021; Oliver, 2016). Tour operators that emphasize responsible tourism contribute to positive perceptions of a destination by educating travelers on respecting local traditions, supporting eco-friendly practices, and minimizing their environmental footprint (Becker, 2016; Webster et al., 2014). In doing so, they support a form of tourism diplomacy that aligns with global values of sustainability and ethical travel. This approach enhances the travel experience and creates lasting impressions that can impact how travelers perceive and discuss the destination in their home countries.

5. Hotel Chains and Global Brand Perception

Hotel chains significantly shape the global tourism environment and influence destinations' perceptions. Through structured brand-building processes, strategic involvement in tourism diplomacy, and active contributions to destination branding, international hotel chains strengthen their reputation and the attractiveness of the regions in which they operate. Examining the process of building brands within international hotel chains, their role in tourism diplomacy, and examples of their contributions to destination branding provide insight into how these companies impact global tourism and hospitality.

5.1 The Process of Building Brands in International Hotel Chains

Building a global brand is the main goal for international hotel chains, aiming to ensure consistent quality, recognition, and customer loyalty across diverse markets (Demir & Tür, 2019). Branding typically involves establishing a unique brand identity that reflects the chain's values, service standards, and target customer demographics. A key component of this identity is consistency; whether in İstanbul, Tokyo, or New York, guests expect the same level of service, ambiance, and amenities from a hotel chain. This consistency builds trust and reinforces brand loyalty, as guests rely on familiar standards, regardless of location. Hotel chains often develop signature experiences emphasizing unique cultural elements to differentiate themselves. For example, Marriott's "Marriott Bonvoy" program offers experiences tailored to the destination, including culinary experiences, city tours, and cultural engagements, which give travelers a sense of place while maintaining brand reliability. Other chains, like Hilton, use digital platforms to enhance convenience, offering seamless check-ins, room selection, and customized services through their apps. This combination of brand consistency, cultural sensitivity, and digital convenience strengthens a chain's brand perception on a global scale, making it a preferred choice for travelers seeking familiarity without sacrificing local immersion (Bose et al., 2022; Watts & Parks, 2018).

5.2 The Role of Hotel Chains in Tourism Diplomacy

Hotel chains contribute to tourism diplomacy by promoting cross-cultural understanding and creating positive first impressions for travelers (Hung, 2013; Sun et al., 2017). Often, hotels serve as the initial point of cultural interaction between foreign visitors and local communities, with staff acting as cultural ambassadors who introduce guests to the local language, customs, and cuisine. For example, Accor's commitment to employing and training local staff boosts the local economy. It enhances cultural exchanges, as visitors interact with local employees who can share insights about the destination.

Moreover, hotel chains often partner with local governments and tourism boards to help position the destination favorably on the global stage. By hosting international events, conferences, and exhibitions, hotel chains create opportunities for diplomacy and business exchange (Demir & Dalgıç, 2022). These events attract tourists, government officials, investors, and business professionals, strengthening diplomatic ties and positioning the hotel as a venue that supports global cooperation. Many hotel chains actively promote sustainable tourism practices, enhancing their image as responsible entities and reflecting positively on the destinations they represent (Hung, 2013; Lee et al., 2017). Chains like InterContinental Hotels Group (IHG) implement eco-friendly initiatives and support local environmental programs, conveying a commitment to sustainability that aligns with global tourism values and diplomacy efforts focused on environmental responsibility.

5.3 Examples of Hotel Chains' Contributions to Destination Branding

Hotel chains play a pivotal role in destination branding by helping to shape how travelers perceive and remember a location (Demir & Tür, 2019). By partnering with local entities and creating culturally immersive experiences, hotel chains contribute to building a unique identity for the region. For instance, the Ritz-Carlton's "Community Footprints" program allows guests to participate in community projects, such as coral reef restoration in Bali or cooking classes with local chefs in Mexico. These initiatives enable travelers to engage meaningfully with the destination, leaving them with positive, authentic memories that enhance the region's brand.

Similarly, Four Seasons hotels are renowned for their location-specific luxury experiences that highlight local culture through art installations, culinary experiences, or local architecture integrated into their hotel design. Their Hawaiian properties, for instance, feature traditional Polynesian design elements, Hawaiian cultural programs, and locally sourced menus, which make the Four Seasons brand synonymous with authentic and luxurious experiences that reflect the destination's culture. Another example is Hilton Hotels' role in contributing to the image of destinations in the Middle East. By promoting Arabian hospitality traditions, Hilton hotels in the UAE and Saudi Arabia offer experiences that blend luxury with local customs, creating a distinct brand for the region that appeals to global travelers. This branding approach also extends to international marketing campaigns, where Hilton highlights each destination's attractions and cultural uniqueness, enhancing regional appeal globally.

6. Airline Companies and International Tourism Diplomacy

Airline companies play a pivotal role in facilitating international tourism and shaping perceptions of destinations on the global stage. Airlines act as ambassadors of their home countries by promoting national identity, forming strategic alliances, contributing directly to tourism diplomacy, and helping create positive impressions among international travelers. Examining the role of airlines in national promotion and brand building, their strategic alliances, and their contributions to tourism diplomacy illustrates how airlines influence international tourism dynamics.

6.1 The Role of Airlines in National Promotion and Brand Building

Airlines are uniquely positioned to promote their home country's culture, values, and attractions, acting as "flying embassies" that introduce travelers to a destination before arriving. National carriers, in particular, play a significant role in building and promoting the country's brand image globally (Demir, 2017; Doz & Hamel, 1998). For instance, Emirates, Etihad, and Qatar Airways emphasize the luxury and warmth of Middle Eastern hospitality, using premium services, cabin design, and amenities to represent the culture and appeal of their home countries. Through these elements, they not only elevate their brand but also enhance the image of their nations as luxurious and welcoming destinations.

Branding initiatives often include in-flight experiences that reflect the airline's country of origin. Japan Airlines offers Japanese cuisine and cultural content on its flights, giving passengers a taste of Japan, while Turkish Airlines includes local cuisine and Turkish-inspired interiors to promote Turkey's heritage and traditions (Demir, 2017). Moreover, airlines participate in international advertising campaigns showcasing the beauty and uniqueness of their home countries. Airlines like Singapore Airlines and Air New Zealand incorporate local culture and environments into their marketing, connecting the idea of the airline with the appeal of the destination. This approach strengthens the national brand in the global market, encouraging potential travelers to choose the country as their next travel destination (Stephens Balakrishnan, 2008; Tijani et al., 2024; White & Kolesnicov, 2015).

6.2 Strategic Alliances of National and International Airline Brands

Strategic alliances and partnerships between airline companies enhance their reach and impact on international tourism (Egan, 2005; Lee & Yang, 2003). Global alliances like Star Alliance, SkyTeam, and Oneworld allow airlines to expand their networks through code-sharing agreements, mutual loyalty programs, and streamlined services. These partnerships make international travel more accessible and convenient by offering passengers a more comprehensive range of destinations, simplified ticketing, and enhanced connectivity. These alliances benefit tourism diplomacy by fostering cooperation between countries and promoting travel benefits (Ermann & Hermanik, 2018; Liu et al., 2000). Airlines can introduce travelers to new destinations through partnerships with foreign carriers and increase tourist flows to lesser-known regions. For instance, United Airlines' partnership with Japan's All Nippon Airways (ANA) promotes tourism between the United States and Japan, supporting diplomatic and economic ties between the two nations.

Airline alliances also strengthen branding efforts by allowing smaller or newer airlines to benefit from the reputation of more prominent, well-established brands (Gerlitz et al., 2021; Olivares, 2023). For example, Ethiopian Airlines, a member of Star Alliance, benefits from the network, resources, and global recognition associated with Star Alliance, helping it increase tourist access to Africa and elevate its brand status. By uniting under a shared brand or alliance, airlines create a consistent travel experience, reinforcing their brands and the destinations they represent.

6.3 Contributions of Airline Companies to Tourism Diplomacy

Airlines significantly contribute to tourism diplomacy by connecting people across borders and fostering cross-cultural understanding. By facilitating global mobility, airlines support international exchanges, cultural tourism, and economic development, essential to tourism diplomacy (Stephens Balakrishnan, 2008; White & Kolesnicov, 2015). Airlines also frequently work with national tourism boards and governments to promote their home countries through joint campaigns, sponsorships, and event hosting. Airlines like Qatar Airways and Emirates, closely tied to their governments, actively participate in tourism diplomacy initiatives by supporting large-scale events such as sports tournaments, global expositions, and cultural festivals. Emirates' sponsorship of major sports teams, including Real Madrid and Arsenal, has promoted Dubai as a global tourism hub, attracting visitors from Europe, Asia, and beyond. Similarly, Qatar Airways' sponsorship of international sporting events, including the FIFA World Cup 2022, raised global awareness of Qatar, highlighting the country as a capable host for large-scale international events and a worthy tourist destination.

In-flight offerings and programs also support tourism diplomacy by fostering an appreciation for the airline's home culture (Demir, 2017; Steinhilber, 2008). Air Canada, for example, showcases Canadian environments and local tourism attractions through in-flight entertainment and promotional content, inviting travelers to explore Canada's rich culture and natural beauty. Airlines also contribute to social and environmental diplomacy by adopting sustainable practices and engaging in charitable initiatives. KLM, for instance, has been a leader in eco-friendly practices, including reducing in-flight waste, promoting carbon offset programs, and operating some flights with biofuels, thus promoting the Netherlands as an environmentally conscious destination.

7. The Impact of Tourism Diplomacy on Brand Image and Global Competition

Tourism diplomacy has become a significant factor in shaping the brand image of destinations and institutions and plays a vital role in a globally competitive tourism environment. By leveraging brand identity and strategically positioning destinations on the international stage, tourism diplomacy enhances brand value and helps countries and regions distinguish themselves amid fierce competition. Exploring the added value of brand image, branding strategies within an international context, and the role of tourism diplomacy in global competition reveals how diplomacy has evolved as an essential tool for tourism.

7.1 The Added Value of Brand Image for Destinations and Institutions

Brand image is a critical asset for destinations and tourism-related institutions, as it influences tourists' perceptions and likelihood of visiting a location (Bouzanis, 2009; Pop et al., 2020). A strong, positive brand image attracts travelers by evoking trust, excitement, and cultural allure. A well-established brand image for destinations can increase visitor numbers, bring economic benefits, support local businesses, and foster job creation. Take, for example, Italy's successful branding as the home of art, history, and cuisine or Japan's positioning as a center for high-tech innovation paired with cultural traditions. These brand images have made these countries popular choices for tourists worldwide. Institutions like national tourism boards or travel organizations benefit from an established brand image, enhancing their credibility and effectiveness in promoting the destination. For instance, the "Incredible India" campaign not only brought visibility to India's cultural diversity but also positioned the country as a must-see destination, increasing tourist interest and awareness on a global level. Practical tourism diplomacy efforts contribute to this brand-building process, allowing destinations to present their unique identities in ways that resonate with international audiences (Clancy, 2011; Tijani et al., 2024).

7.2 Branding Strategies in an International Competitive Environment

In a globally competitive tourism environment, branding strategies are a potent tool for destinations to stand out (Demir & Tür, 2019; Miño, 2023). Destinations employ various approaches, including highlighting unique cultural or natural assets, emphasizing hospitality, or promoting specific experiences like adventure tourism or eco-tourism. Many countries also brand themselves based on niche tourism, such as medical tourism in Thailand or wellness retreats in Bali, appealing to specific travel interests.

Strategically, tourism boards and diplomatic bodies work together to create a cohesive brand narrative that reflects the values and characteristics of the destination (Ermann & Hermanik, 2018; Kobierecka & Kobierecki, 2024). Public–private partnerships are often formed to support these efforts, leveraging resources and insights from both sectors to design and execute impactful campaigns. One approach to differentiating destinations is incorporating sustainability and responsible tourism in branding. Costa Rica, for example, brands itself as a leader in eco-tourism and conservation, which appeals to environmentally conscious travelers and strengthens its reputation as a sustainable destination. This type of branding strategy is not only attractive to specific tourist segments but also creates a positive impression of the country's values on the world stage.

Promotional activities, including international expos, partnerships with global influencers, and large-scale media campaigns, are often employed to ensure that a destination's brand is seen and recognized worldwide (Demir & Dalgıç, 2022; Gerlitz et al., 2021). Through these efforts, destinations are better positioned to compete internationally, offering unique experiences that distinguish them from other tourism markets (Demir & Tür, 2019; Iwabuchi, 2018).

7.3 The Role of Tourism Diplomacy in International Competition

Tourism diplomacy enhances a country's competitive position by fostering international goodwill and promoting cultural exchange (Linardaki & Aslanides, 2020; Therkelsen & Halkier, 2008). Through diplomatic engagement, countries can build connections with potential tourists, strengthen economic ties, and enhance cooperation with other nations. Events like trade fairs, cultural festivals, and international tourism summits are vital platforms where countries can showcase their tourism offerings, build global partnerships, and attract tourists worldwide.

Moreover, tourism diplomacy enables countries to counteract negative perceptions that may impact their brand image. By engaging in public diplomacy initiatives, destinations address issues related to safety, political stability, or environmental concerns, helping to rebuild or enhance their brand reputation (Kobierecka & Kobierecki, 2024; Tijani et al., 2024). For example, after a natural disaster, countries often use tourism diplomacy to reassure potential visitors that the destination is safe and ready to welcome tourists again. Japan's tourism diplomacy efforts post-2011 earthquake and tsunami effectively communicated the country's recovery, preserving its tourism brand and maintaining international tourist interest.

Countries also utilize tourism diplomacy to highlight their cultural heritage and shared values, which fosters a sense of understanding and connection with potential visitors (Bouzanis, 2009; Therkelsen & Halkier, 2008; Tijani et al., 2024). The United Arab Emirates, through tourism and cultural diplomacy, has established itself as a top destination for luxury tourism and a bridge between Eastern and Western cultures. Hosting global events like the Dubai Expo has showcased the UAE's cultural heritage, infrastructure, and openness to international tourists, reinforcing its brand image and competitiveness in global tourism.

8. Successful International Branding Examples and Case Studies

International branding has become a powerful tool for countries, cities, hotels, tour operators, and airlines to attract tourists, investors, and residents. Successful examples demonstrate the importance of creating a robust and unique brand image that resonates with target audiences globally. Examining key case studies across different tourism sectors reveals valuable lessons about establishing and maintaining a memorable brand identity, ultimately contributing to a destination's or organization's appeal on the global stage.

8.1 Case Studies: Countries, Cities, Hotels, Tour Operators, and Airline Companies

8.1.1 Countries: New Zealand's "100% Pure New Zealand"

New Zealand's tourism brand, "100% Pure New Zealand," launched in 1999, is one of the world's most recognized and effective destination campaigns (Lewis, 2011; Maydell, 2020). Showcasing New Zealand's stunning natural environments, outdoor adventures, and unique cultural heritage, the campaign has evolved with digital storytelling techniques to capture the essence of the destination. By positioning itself as a haven for eco-tourism and adventure, New Zealand attracts millions of nature-loving tourists yearly, reinforcing its identity as a top destination for clean, green, and serene travel experiences.

8.1.2 Cities: Amsterdam's "I Amsterdam"

Amsterdam's iconic "I Amsterdam" campaign, initiated in 2004, has effectively shaped the city's brand by promoting it as a cultural, diverse, and open destination (Belabas et al., 2020; Pareja-Eastaway et al., 2013). The "I Amsterdam" sign became an attraction, with tourists from around the world posing in front of it, turning the slogan into a globally recognized symbol of Amsterdam. This branding initiative not only highlights Amsterdam's heritage and lively spirit but also boosts the city's international profile, attracting visitors, businesses, and creative talent alike.

8.1.3 Hotels: Marriott's Bonvoy Program

Marriott International successfully rebranded its rewards program as "Bonvoy," merging multiple loyalty programs into one unified brand with over 30 hotel brands under the Marriott umbrella (Duziak, 2023). Bonvoy emphasizes exclusive experiences, worldwide accessibility, and premium customer service. By offering personalized loyalty incentives and memorable travel experiences, Marriott has strengthened its global brand and increased customer loyalty, setting a high standard for brand integration in the hotel industry.

8.1.4 Tour Operators: TUI Group's Focus on Sustainability

TUI Group, one of the world's largest tour operators, has successfully built its brand around responsible and sustainable tourism. With programs like "TUI Care Foundation," TUI actively contributes to local communities and environmental initiatives in their locations. Their commitment to sustainable travel has resonated with eco-conscious travelers, establishing TUI as a leader in responsible tourism (Demir, 2017). This positioning has enhanced TUI's brand image and given it a competitive edge in an increasingly eco-aware travel market.

8.1.5 Airline Companies: Emirates' "Hello Tomorrow"

Emirates Airlines has consistently leveraged luxury and global connectivity in its brand image. The "Hello Tomorrow" campaign showcases the airline's role as a bridge across cultures and a gateway to new experiences (Funk, 2018; Nickerson, 2022). With innovative onboard services and partnerships with events like the FIFA World Cup, Emirates has positioned itself as more than an airline – it's a lifestyle choice. This campaign solidified Emirates' brand as a top-tier, cosmopolitan airline with luxury, innovation, and world-class service.

8.2 Lessons Learned from Successful Branding Initiatives

Consistency and Authenticity: Successful brands maintain consistent messaging and delivery while remaining authentic to their core values. For instance, New Zealand's "100% Pure" campaign remains true to the country's natural beauty and adventure appeal, which align perfectly with the destination's offerings. A consistent, authentic message builds audience trust, making it easier for potential tourists to identify with the brand.

Harnessing the Power of Storytelling: Memorable brands tell a story that resonates with people's desires, values, and aspirations. Amsterdam's "I Amsterdam" campaign used a simple, relatable message that tourists could physically engage with, turning the brand into an interactive experience. As exemplified by Emirates' "Hello Tomorrow" campaign, storytelling connects travelers to the brand's vision, creating a sense of excitement around global exploration.

Adaptation to Emerging Trends: Brands that adapt to trends like sustainability or digital engagement stay relevant in a rapidly changing industry. TUI Group's emphasis on sustainable tourism addresses the growing demand for eco-friendly travel, enhancing its reputation and meeting consumer expectations. By responding to evolving interests, TUI has become a responsible tour operator.

Leveraging Technology and Social Media: The digital age has transformed how brands connect with audiences. Campaigns like "I Amsterdam" became viral on social media, amplifying brand visibility. Similarly, Marriott's Bonvoy program uses a seamless digital platform that makes rewards more accessible and enhances the customer experience, keeping the brand competitive in a tech-driven market.

Engaging Local Communities: Successful tourism brands actively involve local communities to create authentic experiences. TUI's work with the TUI Care Foundation to support local communities and Emirates' collaborations with major global events fosters goodwill and inclusivity. By engaging locals, these brands strengthen their appeal and contribute positively to the destination's or company's broader brand image.

9. Conclusions

Tourism diplomacy has become a powerful means of shaping a nation's global image, fostering mutual understanding, and enhancing international relationships in an increasingly interconnected world. Through carefully crafted destination branding and strategic alliances, tourism is both a soft power tool and a competitive asset, empowering countries, cities, and private sector stakeholders such as hotels, airlines, and tour operators to position themselves distinctively on the global stage. Examining the multifaceted impact of tourism diplomacy through various branding efforts provides valuable insight into how destinations and organizations can harness their cultural, historical, and natural assets to enhance their global appeal.

Destination branding forms the foundation of tourism diplomacy, enabling nations to craft an image that reflects their unique cultural and environmental assets. This approach attracts tourists and fosters positive perceptions among international audiences, facilitating diplomatic relations through cultural and economic exchange. For instance, leveraging cultural heritage and natural attractions allows destinations to present an authentic narrative that resonates with tourists' desire for meaningful and immersive experiences. Countries that successfully implement destination branding showcase the essence of their national identity, creating a lasting impression that drives both tourism and goodwill globally.

Tourism diplomacy, in this context, elevates national and regional branding by connecting cultural storytelling with strategic marketing, allowing destinations to align their promotional efforts with their foreign policy objectives. Through careful and consistent destination branding, tourism diplomacy builds national pride, fosters local economic growth, and enhances a destination's global competitiveness. This alignment has led to iconic branding campaigns, such as New Zealand's "100% Pure" initiative, which promotes the country's natural beauty and strengthens New Zealand's diplomatic ties by appealing to sustainability and environmental stewardship values.

Cities have emerged as vital players in tourism diplomacy, with city branding initiatives designed to project urban identities and values to international audiences. These efforts are significant for cities that strive to be recognized as cultural, economic, or political hubs. Through global expos, arts festivals, and trade fairs, cities can communicate their unique offerings, elevating their international profiles and attracting tourism, investment, and talent. For example, Amsterdam's "I Amsterdam" campaign effectively transformed the city into a symbol of openness, culture, and creativity, resonating with tourists and enhancing the city's global influence.

To sustain tourist appeal, city branding strategies often incorporate urban diplomacy, positioning cities as attractive, vibrant destinations that meet diverse visitor expectations. Local governments frequently emphasize cultural events, infrastructural improvements, and environmental initiatives to appeal to the modern traveler's values, with case studies from cities like Barcelona and Tokyo illustrating how local cultures and city policies can significantly shape international perceptions. This city-centered approach to tourism diplomacy underscores the significance of urban branding in projecting a positive image that transcends borders, establishing cities as diplomatic actors on the world stage.

Tour operators serve as essential conduits for international tourism, acting as cultural mediators who design and promote travel experiences that reflect a destination's brand. Tour operators contribute to a richer and more authentic brand image by crafting itineraries that highlight well-known attractions and lesser-explored areas. They also amplify the impact of tourism diplomacy by allowing travelers to experience the culture, history, and people behind a destination, fostering greater intercultural understanding and respect.

Tour operators utilize branding strategies catering to global and local audiences, positioning themselves as trusted ambassadors of their destinations. For example, large international tour operators such as TUI have successfully integrated responsible tourism into their branding, advocating sustainable travel practices that reflect their commitment to environmental and cultural preservation. Through such initiatives, tour operators strengthen tourism diplomacy, as their dedication to responsible tourism reinforces the positive image of the destinations they represent, ultimately contributing to sustainable tourism development and improved international relations.

Global hotel chains play a significant role in tourism diplomacy by shaping the perceptions of destinations through hospitality excellence, brand consistency, and cultural adaptation. Building an international hotel brand involves creating a recognizable identity that resonates across diverse markets while adapting to local preferences and cultural norms. Marriott's Bonvoy loyalty program exemplifies this approach, merging multiple brands under a single, globally recognized identity while offering localized experiences that appeal to a range of guests.

Hotel chains contribute to tourism diplomacy by emphasizing high service standards and cultural respect, which enhances the overall visitor experience and promotes a positive perception of the host country. Through collaborations with local businesses and cultural events, hotel brands like Hilton and Accor actively participate in destination branding efforts, presenting an image of inclusivity and international appeal. These contributions attract visitors and create an environment conducive to diplomatic engagement, positioning hotels as key players in promoting cross-cultural exchange and understanding.

Airlines are ambassadors for their home countries, often embodying the national image through service quality, branding, and strategic alliances. National airlines, like Emirates and Turkish Airlines, play a crucial role in national promotion and brand building, offering travelers a first impression of the culture, hospitality, and values of their countries of origin. These airlines leverage tourism diplomacy by highlighting their national identities through inflight experiences, destination partnerships, and advertising campaigns, such as Emirates' "Hello Tomorrow" campaign, which presents the airline as a gateway to global exploration.

Strategic alliances between international airline brands, such as the Star Alliance and Oneworld, further contribute to tourism diplomacy by enhancing connectivity and accessibility across regions, fostering increased travel and cultural exchange. By collaborating within these alliances, airlines expand their reach and bolster their national branding efforts, creating networks reinforcing tourism diplomacy initiatives and strengthening relationships between member countries.

Tourism diplomacy significantly enhances the brand image in a competitive global tourism environment and provides destinations and institutions with a unique added value. Destinations that engage in tourism diplomacy initiatives tend to cultivate strong brand identities that distinguish them from competitors. For example, Scotland's "Spirit of Scotland" campaign connects visitors to the nation's cultural heritage, thereby enhancing Scotland's reputation as a destination for immersive cultural experiences.

Branding strategies in tourism diplomacy extend beyond promotion; they foster international relationships and promote cooperation. By positioning themselves as open, inclusive, and culturally rich destinations, countries and cities can build trust and respect among foreign audiences. Tourism diplomacy thus plays a pivotal role in navigating international competition, creating a cooperative environment where destinations and institutions can showcase their strengths while benefiting from global tourism's economic and cultural impact.

Case studies from countries, cities, hotels, tour operators, and airlines reveal valuable lessons in successful international branding. New Zealand's "100% Pure," Amsterdam's "I Amsterdam," and Emirates' "Hello Tomorrow" campaigns exemplify how tourism diplomacy can effectively promote destinations, create emotional connections, and enhance brand loyalty. These initiatives underscore the importance of authenticity, storytelling, and sustainability in building a brand that resonates globally and appeals to diverse audiences.

Each successful branding example highlights a strategic approach to tourism diplomacy, demonstrating the significance of cultural integration, community involvement, and consistent messaging. For instance, TUI's dedication to sustainable tourism strengthens its brand and reinforces the destination's reputation for environmental responsibility, benefiting both the operator and the host community.

The intersection of tourism diplomacy and international branding illustrates tourism's profound impact on cultural understanding, economic growth, and diplomatic relations. By effectively employing destination branding, city promotion, and strategic alliances across the tourism sector, stakeholders contribute to a shared global narrative of openness, diversity, and sustainability. As international tourism continues to grow, tourism diplomacy will play an increasingly important role.

References

Becker, E. (2016). *Overbooked: The exploding business of travel and tourism*. Simon & Schuster.

Belabas, W., Eshuis, J., & Scholten, P. (2020). Re-imagining the city: Branding migration-related diversity. *European Planning Studies*, *28*(7), 1315–1332.

Bose, S., Pradhan, S., Bashir, M., & Roy, S. K. (2022). Customer-based place brand equity and tourism: A regional identity perspective. *Journal of Travel Research*, *61*(3), 511–527.

Bouzanis, J. (2009). The economic face of public diplomacy: International business promotion and tourism. In E. H. Potter (Ed.), *Branding Canada: Projecting Canada's soft power through public diplomacy* (pp. 173–193). McGill-Queen's University Press.

Cameron, C. (2015). UNESCO and cultural heritage: Unexpected consequences. In W. Logan, M. N. Craith, & U. Kockel (Eds.), *A companion to heritage studies* (pp. 322–336). John Wiley & Sons, Inc.

Clancy, M. (2011). Re-presenting Ireland: Tourism, branding and national identity in Ireland. *Journal of International Relations and Development*, *14*, 281–308.

Demir, M. (2017). *Seyahat Acentacılığı ve Tur Operatörlüğü: İlkeler ve Yönetim*. Detay Yayıncılık.

Demir, M., & Dalgıç, A. (2022). Examining gastronomy festivals as the attractiveness factor for tourism destinations: The case of Turkey. *Journal of Convention & Event Tourism*, *23*, 412–434. https://doi.org/10.1080/15470148.2022.2089797

Demir, Ş. Ş., & Tür, E. (2019). Otel logosu ne söyler? Tüketiciler ne algılar? *Journal of Tourism Theory and Research*, *5*(1), 51–64.

Doz, Y. L., & Hamel, G. (1998). *Alliance advantage: The art of creating value through partnering*. Harvard Business Press.

Duziak, D. (2023). The metaverse. In D. Duziak (Ed.), *Blockchain for hospitality and tourism: A guide to the future* (pp. 87–113). Apress.

Egan, M. P. (2005). *Creating a transatlantic marketplace: Government policies and business strategies*. Manchester University Press.

Ermann, U., & Hermanik, K. J. (2018). *Branding the nation, the place, the product*. Routledge.

Fayard, G. (2024). The geopolitics of outbound travel: Theorizing outgoing tourism as state strategy. *Environment and Planning C: Politics and Space*, *42*(5), 881–900.

Funk, K. (2018). Between freedom and futility: On the political uses of corporate globalizing discourses. *Journal of Cultural Economy*, *11*(6), 565–590.

García, P. (2024). Diplomatic heritage: The involvement of the world monuments fund in the Sacred Valley of the Incas, Cuzco, Peru 1. In G. Bozoğlu, G. Campbell, L. Smith, & C. Whitehead (Eds.), *The routledge international handbook of heritage and politics* (pp. 552–567). Routledge.

Gerlitz, L., Meyer, C., & Prause, G. (2021). Marketing and branding strategy for the South Baltic Sea Region: Reinforcing regional innovation in SMEs through cross-border collaboration models in the age of transformation. *Entrepreneurship and Sustainability Issues*, (4), 467–478.

Gordon, R. (2024). Concepts and strategies required to develop the professional integration of travel and tourism. In B. Prideaux & D. Beirman (Eds.), *Handbook on crisis and disaster management in tourism* (pp. 280–294). Edward Elgar Publishing.

Grincheva, N. (2013). Cultural diplomacy 2.0: Challenges and opportunities in museum international practices. *Museum & Society*, *11*(1), 39–49.

Hung, K. (2013). Chinese hotels in the eyes of Chinese hoteliers: The most critical issues. *Asia Pacific Journal of Tourism Research*, *18*(4), 354–368.

Iwabuchi, K. (2018). Pop-culture diplomacy in Japan: Soft power, nation branding and the question of 'international cultural exchange. In L. Ang, Y. Isar, & P. Mar (Eds.), *Cultural diplomacy: Beyond the national interest?* (pp. 65–78). Routledge.

Kim, S. S., Prideaux, B., & Timothy, D. (2016). Factors affecting bilateral Chinese and Japanese travel. *Annals of Tourism Research*, *61*, 80–95.

Kobierecka, A., & Kobierecki, M. M. (2024). Public diplomacy and nation branding in action: Swiss Embassy's participation in the night of museums event in Warsaw. *Place Branding and Public Diplomacy*, *20*(2), 204–217.

Kolotouchkina, O., & Seisdedos, G. (2018). Place branding strategies in the context of new smart cities: Songdo IBD, Masdar and Skolkovo. *Place Branding and Public Diplomacy*, *14*, 115–124.

Lee, S., Oh, H., & Hsu, C. H. (2017). Country-of-operation and brand images: Evidence from the Chinese hotel industry. *International Journal of Contemporary Hospitality Management*, *29*(7), 1814–1833.

Lee, H., & Yang, H. M. (2003). Strategies for a global logistics and economic hub: Incheon international airport. *Journal of Air Transport Management*, *9*(2), 113–121.

Lewis, N. (2011). Packaging political projects in geographical imaginaries: The rise of nation branding. In E. Pike (Ed.), *Brands and branding geographies*. Edward Elgar Publishing.

Linardaki, C., & Aslanides, A. (2020). From poem and song to cultural diplomacy: Challenges and opportunities for place branding and tourism promotion. *Place Branding and Public Diplomacy*, *16*(4), 304–315.

Liu, A., Wall, G., & Westlake, J. (2000). Marketing through frequent flyer programmes: The example of China airlines. *Tourism Economics*, *6*(3), 233–249.

Maydell, E. (2020). The visual representation of indigenous cultural identities in Australian and New Zealand tourism campaigns. *Visual Communication Quarterly*, *27*(4), 183–195.

Minardi, A., Afriantari, R., & Hasanah, N. U. (2021). Indonesian tourism diplomacy to India. *Indonesian Tourism Diplomacy to India*, *1*(1), 1–13.

Miño, P. (2023). Power imbalances and contested notions of the nation: Latin American nation branding through the lens of the cultural-economic model of public relations. *Journal of Public Relations Research*, *35*(5–6), 307–320.

Nickerson, C. (2022). English for specific business purposes in the United Arab emirates. *World Englishes*, *41*(4), 532–544.

Olivares, J. V. (2023). Alliances as a coopetitive strategy of the airlines: The case of Iberia (1980–2020). In P. Fernández Pérez & E. San Román (Eds.), *Collective entrepreneurship in the contemporary european services industries: A long term approach* (pp. 77–93). Emerald Publishing Limited.

Oliver, A. (2016). Travelling responsibly, but further to go: Australia's new consular diplomacy. *Australian Journal of International Affairs*, *70*(6), 681–694.

Pareja-Eastaway, M., Chapain, C., & Mugnano, S. (2013). Successes and failures in city branding policies In S. Musterd & Z. Kovacs (Ed.), *Place-making and policies for competitive cities* (pp. 149–171). Wiley-Blackwell.

Pop, N. A., Baba, C. A., Anysz, R. N., & Tohanean, D. (2020). National branding strategy and its effects on business and tourism. *Proceedings of the International Conference on Business Excellence*, *14*(1), 1005–1013.

Steinhilber, S. (2008). *Strategic alliances: Three ways to make them work*. Harvard Business Press.

Stephens Balakrishnan, M. (2008). Dubai–A star in the east: A case study in strategic destination branding. *Journal of Place Management and Development*, *1*(1), 62–91.

Sun, S., Tong, K. T., & Law, R. (2017). Chinese hotel guest perception of international chain hotels under the same hotel brand in different travel destinations: The cases of intercontinental and Sheraton. *Journal of Vacation Marketing*, *23*(2), 172–188.

Therkelsen, A., & Gram, M. (2010). Branding Europe–between nations, regions and continents. *Scandinavian Journal of Hospitality and Tourism*, *10*(2), 107–128.

Therkelsen, A., & Halkier, H. (2008). Contemplating place branding umbrellas. The case of coordinated national tourism and business promotion in Denmark. *Scandinavian Journal of Hospitality and Tourism*, *8*(2), 159–175.

Tijani, A., Majeed, M., Ofori, K. S., & Abubakari, A. (2024). Country branding research: A decade's systematic review. *Cogent Business & Management*, *11*(1), 1–10.

Tudor, A. C. (2022). From London to Dubai-171 years of national branding through world expos (1851–2022). *Europolity-Continuity and Change in European Governance*, *16*(1), 129–152.

Watts, R., & Parks, Z. (2018). *Development of Tourism and Travel Industry*. Scientific e-Resources.

Webster, C., Musyck, B., Orphanides, S., & Jacobson, D. (2014). Working on the other side. Cooperative tour organizers and uncooperative hoteliers: Evidence from greek cypriot tourism professionals. In N. Kumral & Ö. Önder (Eds.), *Tourism, regional development and public policy* (pp. 45–68). Routledge.

White, C., & Kolesnicov, I. (2015). Nation branding in a transitional democracy: The role of corporate diplomacy in promoting national identity. *Place Branding and Public Diplomacy*, *11*, 324–337.

Chapter 7

Building Back Stronger: Tourism Diplomacy in Addressing and Recovering From Global Crises

Abstract

Tourism diplomacy emerges as a critical mechanism in addressing and recovering from global crises, driving economic revival, environmental restoration, and sociopolitical resilience. By leveraging tourism as a catalyst for postcrisis economic recovery, it creates opportunities for job generation and international aid, illustrated through case studies of successful interventions. Integrating sustainable tourism fosters environmental recovery, with eco-tourism and conservation initiatives pivotal in restoring natural ecosystems. Collaborative international efforts further enhance the impact of tourism on environmental sustainability in postcrisis scenarios. Tourism diplomacy facilitates preparedness, risk management, and communication strategies in response to health crises, as demonstrated by recovery efforts following pandemics such as COVID-19. Strengthening health infrastructure through global tourism partnerships underscores its strategic value in health crisis management. In postconflict recovery, tourism diplomacy supports peacebuilding, cultural exchange, and promoting safe travel, contributing to social cohesion and reconciliation. Case studies highlight the transformative potential of tourism in revitalizing conflict-affected regions, showcasing its role as a tool for sustainable recovery and global solidarity. This comprehensive exploration provides insights into the multifaceted contributions of tourism diplomacy in navigating and overcoming global crises while emphasizing the importance of innovative and inclusive strategies for building resilience in the tourism sector.

Keywords: Tourism diplomacy; postcrisis recovery; sustainable tourism; health crisis management; postpandemic tourism

Tourism Diplomacy, 135–157

Copyright © 2025 Mahmut Demir and Şirvan Şen Demir
Published under exclusive licence by Emerald Publishing Limited

doi:10.1108/978-1-83708-676-420251007

1. Introduction

Tourism diplomacy has become a vital aspect of crisis management and recovery. The industry is significantly impacted by global crises yet equally capable of fostering resilience and renewal (Demir & Demir, 2024). From natural disasters and pandemics to political upheavals, crises can disrupt tourism at both local and international levels (Fig. 12). However, these challenges also offer unique opportunities for tourism diplomacy to play a transformative role, helping destinations rebuild.

Tourism diplomacy fosters international cooperation, communication, and resilience in global crisis management. In times of crisis, tourism acts as a conduit for cross-border support, enabling diplomatic efforts to create platforms for relief, recovery, and future preparedness (AlKhaldi et al., 2021; Senbeto et al., 2024). Governments, international organizations, and tourism bodies collaborate to deliver aid, resources, and expertise that promote recovery in crisis-affected regions. As some researchers emphasized (e.g., Anagnostou, 2022; Demir & Demir, 2024; Karsokiene & Giedraitis, 2023), tourism diplomacy helps rebuild confidence among

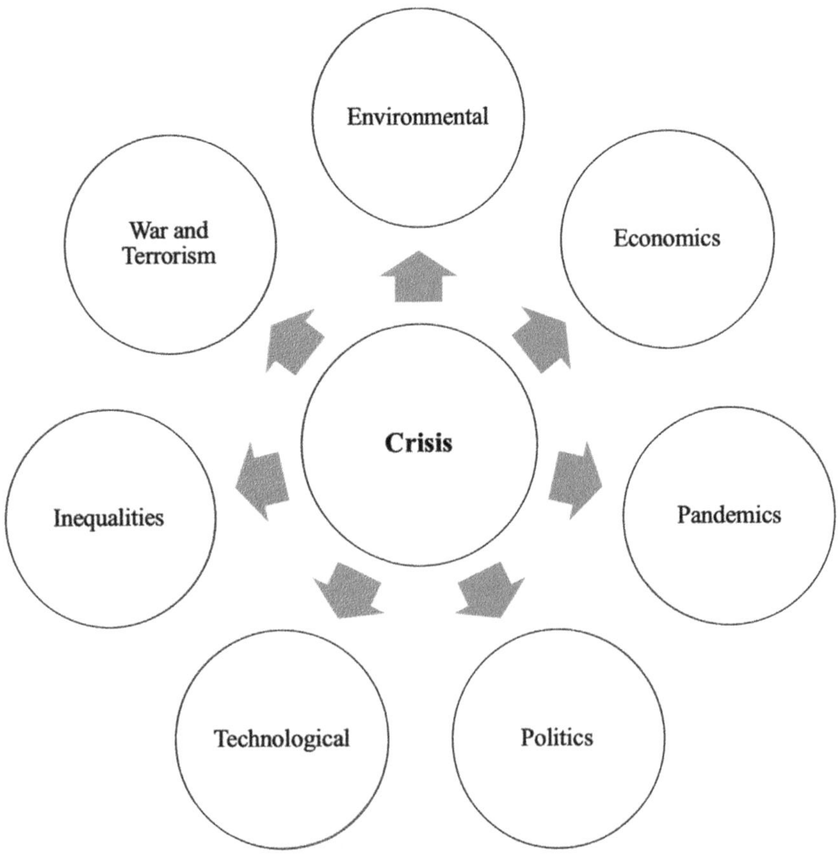

Fig. 12. Crisis Recovery Through Tourism Diplomacy.

travelers by creating unified health and safety protocols, marketing campaigns, and restoration projects. In this way, tourism diplomacy not only aids in economic stabilization but also in re-establishing a sense of normalcy and promoting long-term resilience in affected communities.

Historically, tourism has demonstrated its capacity to contribute to recovery following crises, from supporting war-torn economies to aiding in the aftermath of natural disasters. During the COVID-19 pandemic, the role of tourism in crisis response evolved significantly as the industry adapted to unprecedented disruptions, emphasizing health protocols and technological innovation (Demir et al., 2020). This shift marked a new era in which tourism became a strategic sector in global recovery, balancing public health priorities with economic and social needs. As crises become increasingly complex and frequent, the importance of tourism in crisis response continues to grow, with stakeholders recognizing the industry's potential to promote stability, resilience, and international solidarity (Karsokiene & Giedraitis, 2023; Mansfeld, 2006).

The recovery process in tourism diplomacy is shaped by diverse stakeholders who each play essential roles in fostering resilience and rebuilding trust (Anagnostou, 2022; Beirman, 2020). Key players include government agencies, international organizations like the World Tourism Organization (UNWTO), private sector entities, and local communities. Governments often provide strategic direction and funding, while international bodies facilitate collaboration and share best practices. The private sector, including airlines, hotels, and tour operators, contributes expertise, innovation, and resources essential for recovery efforts. As direct beneficiaries, local communities are involved in grassroots recovery initiatives, ensuring that tourism diplomacy efforts align with their needs and cultural values. Together, these stakeholders form a comprehensive network that enables tourism diplomacy to address crises and support sustainable recovery effectively.

2. Economic Recovery Through Tourism Diplomacy

Tourism diplomacy is instrumental in catalyzing economic revival after global crises. By bridging public and private sectors, tourism diplomacy enables targeted strategies that stimulate economies, restore jobs, and rebuild communities in regions severely impacted by disruptions such as natural disasters, pandemics, and economic downturns. Tourism's multifaceted impact on various sectors – from hospitality and transportation to agriculture and retail – makes it a critical pillar for economic recovery.

2.1 Role of Tourism in Postcrisis Economic Revival and International Aid

Tourism is one of the most potent sectors for economic recovery following a crisis due to its capacity to generate substantial revenue, attract foreign exchange, and provide employment. Tourism diplomacy facilitates cross-border cooperation, mobilizing resources for affected destinations and reinforcing the importance of international aid in restoring tourism-dependent economies (Beirman, 2020; Singh et al., 2022).

Through coordinated efforts, international organizations, governments, and private sectors collaborate to rebuild infrastructure, restore tourism services, and re-establish these regions as viable destinations.

In the aftermath of a crisis, international aid toward tourism can take many forms, from financial assistance to technical support for local businesses and infrastructure (Magnin & Nenovsky, 2022; Negassa, 2024). For example, the United Nations World Tourism Organization (UNWTO) has significantly directed funds, expertise, and marketing resources to aid countries in re-establishing their tourism sectors. This aid is typically contingent upon collaborative efforts with local governments to ensure that resources are effectively utilized to rebuild infrastructure, provide essential services, and re-open borders safely and responsibly. Furthermore, tourism diplomacy can facilitate policy frameworks that allow for flexible immigration, visa, and taxation policies – factors that can attract international tourists and boost economic activity in the recovery phase.

International economic aid also emphasizes sustainable tourism development, encouraging destination areas to build resilience (e.g., Boromisa & Raditya Ležaić, 2014; Qobo, 2022; Rana, 2013). Sustainability-driven aid initiatives protect the environment and cultural heritage and establish long-term economic stability, reducing the vulnerability of tourism-dependent economies to future crises. By incorporating sustainable tourism practices, affected areas can foster resilience while regaining the trust of international travelers and stakeholders, creating a foundation for more stable and enduring economic growth.

2.2 Utilizing Tourism for Economic Recovery and Job Creation

Tourism's potential to generate employment is one of its most valuable contributions to postcrisis economic recovery (Bouzanis, 2009; Jing, 2020). Tourism diplomacy strategies often include programs that prioritize job creation, skills development, and local workforce support. By rapidly stimulating job creation, tourism helps mitigate the economic shock felt by communities reliant on the industry and provides stable livelihoods, reducing poverty and contributing to social stability. The diversity of employment generated by tourism – from hospitality and travel services to food production and artisan crafts – creates opportunities for various skill levels, supporting broad economic inclusion.

Tourism diplomacy promotes collaborative public–private initiatives to drive economic recovery (Haq & Medhekar, 2019; Lozano, 2019). These partnerships encourage businesses and government bodies to create job opportunities that align with sustainable tourism goals, such as eco-tourism and community-based tourism, which enhance the resilience of local economies. By investing in skill development and training, tourism diplomacy enables communities to cultivate expertise in areas such as digital marketing, sustainable tourism management, and multilingual communication – skills that not only contribute to immediate recovery but also equip communities to adapt to changing market demands.

Digital transformation has become a significant aspect of tourism's economic recovery, with online platforms facilitating remote bookings, virtual experiences, and e-commerce for local products (Demir & Demir, 2024). This digital shift offers both direct and indirect employment opportunities, helping communities re-establish connections with global travelers and providing a source of income to regions that may remain otherwise inaccessible postcrisis. In addition, digital tourism diplomacy has opened up possibilities for remote work in the tourism sector itself, where content creation, customer service, and digital marketing can be managed from any location, allowing for economic continuity even in times of restricted travel.

2.3 Case Studies: Postcrisis Economic Recovery Through Tourism

2.3.1 Case Study 1: Japan's Tourism Recovery After the 2011 Tōhoku Earthquake and Tsunami

Following the 2011 Tōhoku earthquake and tsunami, Japan's tourism sector faced unprecedented challenges, with a sharp decline in international arrivals and damaged infrastructure across key regions. To address these challenges, Japan implemented a tourism diplomacy strategy focused on restoring confidence among international visitors and promoting regions less affected by the disaster. The government introduced policies that encouraged international collaboration and secured financial aid to rebuild damaged areas, especially the popular destinations in the Tōhoku region (Nagai et al., 2020; Wu & Shimizu, 2020). One of the critical components of Japan's recovery plan was the "Cool Japan" initiative, which promoted Japanese culture, technology, and gastronomy internationally, mainly through pop culture and heritage tourism. This initiative emphasized Japan's unique cultural identity and resilience, effectively rebuilding its image on a global stage. The Japanese government also invested in transportation infrastructure, such as the Shinkansen (bullet train) lines to Tōhoku, improving accessibility and encouraging tourist dispersal. By targeting critical international markets and adapting diplomatic initiatives to cultural appeal, Japan successfully re-established itself as a leading tourist destination, promoting regional recovery and demonstrating tourism's capacity for economic and social revitalization (Nakamura, 2013).

2.3.2 Case Study 2: Greece's Recovery From the Economic Recession of the 2010s

After a severe economic recession, Greece relied heavily on tourism as a primary engine for economic recovery. Tourism diplomacy became a focal point for Greece, with concerted efforts to market the country's unique historical and cultural assets while attracting foreign investment and creating jobs. Recognizing the importance of tourism to its economy, the Greek government reduced barriers to investment in tourism infrastructure, streamlined visa policies, and offered incentives for hotel and resort development (Siani-Davies & Siani-Davies, 2017; Sklias & Tzifakis, 2012). Greece's tourism diplomacy strategy included collaborations with international travel platforms, influencers, and cultural organizations, expanding its reach and positioning the country as a desirable destination for diverse travelers (Siani-Davies & Siani-Davies, 2017; Sklias & Tzifakis, 2012). The Greek National Tourism Organization (GNTO) launched campaigns highlighting Greece's rich heritage, pristine beaches, and authentic cultural experiences. Furthermore, the government promoted lesser-known regions to attract tourism to rural areas and reduce the strain on popular destinations like Athens and Santorini. Through these strategic branding and investment initiatives, Greece not only revived its economy but also diversified its tourism offerings, enhancing the resilience of its tourism sector in the face of future economic challenges.

2.3.3 Case Study 3: Puerto Rico's Recovery After Hurricane Maria (2017)

In 2017, Hurricane Maria devastated Puerto Rico, disrupting its tourism industry and inflicting severe economic damage. Tourism diplomacy was central to Puerto Rico's recovery strategy, with the government partnering with international agencies and private sectors to restore tourism infrastructure and rebrand the island's image. Recognizing the importance of visitor confidence, Puerto Rico implemented robust health and safety protocols, upgraded accommodation facilities, and initiated marketing campaigns focused on the island's natural beauty and resilience (Garriga-López, 2019; Griffith, 2020). Puerto Rico's "Rebuild and Renew" campaign showcased the island as both a resilient destination and a socially responsible choice for travelers, promoting volunteer tourism (voluntourism) as part of the recovery (Bonilla, 2020; Lele, 2019). This innovative approach allowed visitors to contribute to rebuilding efforts directly, supporting local communities while enjoying a transformative travel experience. By integrating sustainable tourism practices, Puerto Rico positioned itself as a leader in resilient tourism, attracting visitors who value both travel and social impact. This focus on sustainability and community involvement helped in short-term recovery and contributed to Puerto Rico's long-term tourism appeal.

3. Environmental Recovery and Sustainable Tourism Practices

Tourism's rapid growth has had both positive and negative environmental impacts, particularly in regions heavily dependent on natural landscapes and biodiversity. When crises, such as natural disasters or pandemics, disrupt tourism, these regions often face environmental degradation due to neglected conservation efforts or increased vulnerability to ecological decline. Sustainable tourism practices and environmental restoration have become critical priorities in post-crisis recovery, providing a pathway to economic and environmental resilience.

3.1 Integrating Sustainability in Tourism as a Pathway to Environmental Recovery

Integrating sustainability into tourism is not ignored for fostering environmental resilience and long-term recovery postcrisis. Sustainable tourism involves minimizing ecological footprints, protecting natural habitats, and promoting practices that encourage biodiversity conservation. Tourism diplomacy enables international and local stakeholders to align on sustainable practices, promoting recovery strategies that protect both economic and ecological systems.

Sustainable tourism can mitigate the adverse effects of over-tourism and resource depletion, often intensifying during peak travel seasons or in crisis recovery. Tourism authorities can ensure recovery processes align with long-term environmental goals by implementing policies that encourage responsible resource use, waste management, and energy efficiency (Folmer et al., 2016; Tamargo et al., 2022). For instance, government policies incentivize green certifications, sustainable infrastructure, and eco-friendly accommodations and encourage businesses to adopt practices that conserve resources and minimize emissions. Furthermore, integrating sustainability into tourism management helps attract travelers who prioritize environmental responsibility, creating a market-driven incentive for sustainability.

In postcrisis contexts, sustainable tourism allows communities to rebuild in a way that emphasizes environmental stewardship. Initiatives like carbon offset programs and community-based conservation projects enable tourists to participate directly in preserving and restoring natural resources. In addition, by training local communities in sustainable practices, tourism diplomacy empowers residents to become stewards of their environments, ensuring the continuity of conservation efforts and enhancing the resilience of regional economies (Garriga-López, 2019; Miño, 2023).

3.2 Eco-Tourism and Conservation Efforts in Postcrisis Settings

Eco-tourism, which promotes responsible travel to natural areas while supporting conservation efforts and benefiting local communities, plays a crucial role in environmental recovery. In postcrisis settings, eco-tourism rehabilitates damaged ecosystems, promotes biodiversity, and rebuilds local livelihoods. Tourism diplomacy can help facilitate these efforts by fostering international partnerships and garnering support for eco-tourism projects prioritizing conservation.

Eco-tourism initiatives often include activities like wildlife protection, habitat restoration, and educational programs that raise awareness about local biodiversity. These activities provide financial resources for conservation while encouraging travelers to engage in responsible tourism practices (Hutnyk, 2023; Okano-Heijmans, 2012). Additionally, eco-tourism can support crisis-affected communities by offering alternative income sources that reduce reliance on environmentally damaging industries, such as logging or unsustainable agriculture.

In crisis recovery, ecotourism helps rebuild local economies while fostering environmental resilience (Ibric et al., 2024; Karaman, 2015). Ecotourism minimizes the ecological footprint of recovery efforts by promoting eco-friendly accommodations, supporting the use of renewable energy, and advocating for local products and services. Moreover, ecotourism supports conservation by creating economic incentives for protecting natural habitats and endangered species. For example, protected wildlife areas can attract visitors who contribute to local economies while respecting the area's ecological integrity.

3.3 International Collaborations for Environmental Restoration Through Tourism

Tourism diplomacy is a critical platform for international collaboration on environmental restoration, especially in regions recovering from ecological crises. Cross-border partnerships allow countries to pool resources, share knowledge, and coordinate actions to rehabilitate natural habitats and mitigate environmental damage (Luo & Yun, 2023; Musavengane et al., 2022). Through international collaboration, tourism can foster environmental recovery that transcends national boundaries and aligns with global sustainability goals.

International organizations, such as the United Nations Environment Programme (UNEP) and the International Union for Conservation of Nature (IUCN), partner with governments and tourism bodies to support environmental restoration initiatives. These partnerships often focus on promoting biodiversity, protecting endangered ecosystems, and implementing sustainable tourism practices that mitigate environmental impact. For example, the UNEP collaborates with countries on ecotourism projects that restore wetlands, coral reefs, and forests, all essential for maintaining biodiversity and supporting climate resilience.

Collaborations between the public and private sectors also enhance environmental recovery efforts. Nongovernmental organizations, tourism companies, and conservation groups often collaborate to restore ecosystems while promoting sustainable tourism (Garriga-López, 2019; Okano-Heijmans, 2012). Public–private partnerships can fund conservation projects, establish eco-friendly infrastructure, and offer educational programs encouraging tourists to engage responsibly with natural environments. Additionally, these collaborations often support the development of green certification systems that promote eco-friendly tourism practices, enabling tourists to choose environmentally responsible travel options.

By facilitating these collaborations, tourism diplomacy helps establish a unified approach to environmental recovery (Sahoo et al., 2024; Tamargo et al., 2022). Countries can share successful strategies, pool resources, and strengthen their commitments to sustainability. Furthermore, collaborative environmental restoration efforts contribute to the global image of destinations as responsible and eco-conscious, attracting environmentally minded travelers and fostering international goodwill.

3.4 Case Studies: Restoration of Natural Ecosystems Through Responsible Tourism

3.4.1 Case Study 1: Costa Rica's Conservation Efforts Through Eco-Tourism

Costa Rica is widely regarded as a model for environmental recovery and sustainable tourism (Hohl, 2013; Levy & Hawkins, 2009). Following deforestation and biodiversity loss in the 20th century, the country adopted eco-tourism as a primary economic strategy. Costa Rica's government introduced policies prioritizing environmental protection, resulting in a network of national parks and protected areas covering over a quarter of its land area. Tourism diplomacy efforts focused on promoting Costa Rica's natural beauty and biodiversity, attracting visitors who value environmental conservation. Ecotourism has contributed to the restoration of Costa Rica's forests, supported wildlife conservation, and helped the country become a leader in renewable energy usage. By involving local communities in tourism initiatives, Costa Rica has provided economic opportunities that discourage deforestation and encourage sustainable practices. The country's emphasis on responsible tourism has also established it as an internationally recognized ecotourism destination, demonstrating the economic and environmental benefits of sustainable practices (Hohl, 2013).

3.4.2 Case Study 2: The Great Barrier Reef's Recovery Efforts Through Tourism Partnerships

The Great Barrier Reef, one of the world's most diverse ecosystems, has faced severe bleaching events due to climate change. In response, Australian tourism and environmental organizations have collaborated on restoration projects that involve responsible tourism practices. Through partnerships with marine biologists, government agencies, and tourism operators, initiatives like coral planting and reef monitoring have been implemented to protect and rehabilitate the reef's damaged areas (Coghlan et al., 2017; McGaurr & Lester, 2018). Tourism is vital in funding these conservation efforts, as visitors contribute directly to environmental restoration through eco-tourism fees and conservation donations. Education programs provided by tour operators raise awareness about the importance of reef conservation, encouraging visitors to participate in activities that support the reef's recovery. These efforts underscore the role of tourism diplomacy in fostering international cooperation for environmental preservation, demonstrating how collaborative restoration initiatives can enhance both ecological resilience and tourism appeal.

3.4.3 Case Study 3: Nepal's Postearthquake Recovery and Sustainable Mountain Tourism

In 2015, Nepal experienced a devastating earthquake that affected human communities and natural landscapes, particularly in mountainous areas popular with trekkers. Tourism diplomacy efforts focused on rebuilding Nepal's tourism sector by promoting sustainable mountain tourism and emphasizing the country's commitment to environmental stewardship. International partnerships with conservation organizations and eco-tourism operators have supported trail restoration, wildlife protection, and reforestation projects (Beirman et al., 2018; Ketter, 2016). Sustainable tourism initiatives have promoted waste reduction on trekking routes, sustainable lodging, and support for local artisans and guides. By integrating sustainability into mountain tourism, Nepal has attracted eco-conscious travelers who contribute to both economic and environmental recovery. The collaboration between local and international organizations has strengthened Nepal's image as a responsible tourism destination, demonstrating the potential for sustainable tourism to aid in crisis recovery while preserving natural environments (Paudel & Le Billon, 2020).

3.4.4 Case Study 4: Philippines' Boracay Island Rehabilitation and Eco-Tourism Transformation

Boracay Island in the Philippines faced a crisis of environmental degradation due to over-tourism, which resulted in severe water pollution and habitat loss. In 2018, the Philippine government temporarily closed the island to implement a comprehensive rehabilitation program. The rehabilitation focused on water treatment, waste management, and the restoration of coastal ecosystems (Rudiany et al., 2023). Tourism diplomacy efforts supported Boracay's transition to an eco-tourism model, emphasizing sustainable visitor practices and responsible business operations. Reopening the island with new regulations, such as visitor caps and strict environmental guidelines, helped protect Boracay's natural beauty and ensured a more sustainable tourism experience (Rudiany et al., 2023). The rehabilitation of Boracay serves as a case study of the effectiveness of responsible tourism for environmental recovery, illustrating how government intervention, tourism diplomacy, and sustainable practices can transform a destination's ecological and economic trajectory.

4. Health Crises and Tourism Diplomacy's Response

Health crises, such as pandemics and epidemics, significantly impact the global tourism sector, causing disruptions to travel, severe economic losses, and shifts in consumer behavior. Tourism diplomacy plays a crucial role in both addressing these health crises and enabling the sector's recovery by fostering international cooperation, promoting effective risk communication, and strengthening health infrastructure (Fig. 13).

4.1 Tourism's Role in Health Crisis Preparedness and Response

Due to its interconnectedness and frequent movement of people across borders, the tourism sector is inherently vulnerable to health crises. As such, tourism diplomacy has a pivotal role in fostering health crisis preparedness and developing rapid-response mechanisms to minimize disruptions. Preparing for health crises within tourism involves multi-level collaboration among governments, international health organizations, and industry stakeholders to establish protocols that protect travelers, employees, and host communities (Demir et al., 2020).

Proactive measures in tourism crisis preparedness include formulating guidelines for sanitation, implementing screening procedures at points of entry, and providing adequate training for tourism staff to handle health emergencies. For instance, the World Health Organization (WHO) and the UNWTO often

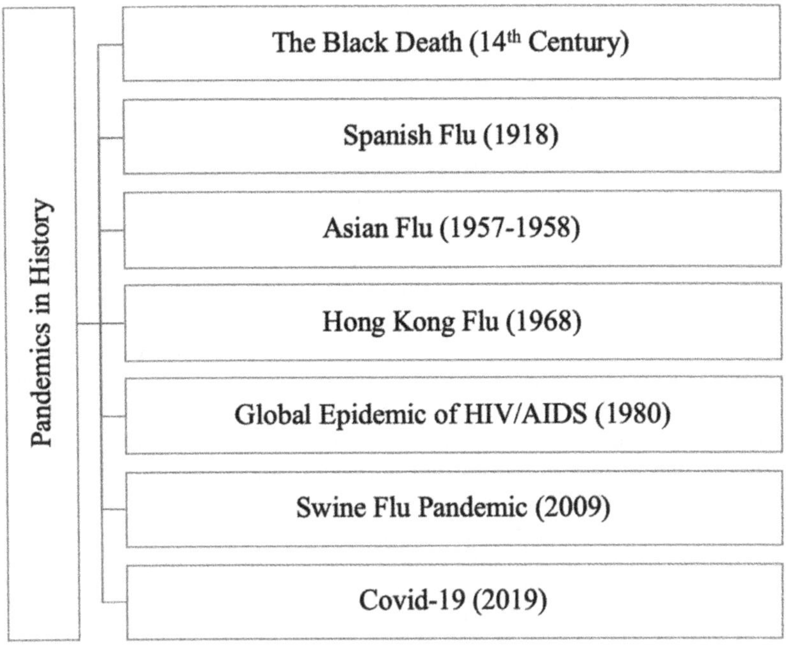

Fig. 13. Seven of the Worst Pandemics in History.

collaborate on health protocols that tourism operators can adopt to limit disease transmission. National tourism boards promote safe travel practices, distribute resources for crisis response, and ensure the necessary infrastructure is in place to support affected communities.

Tourism diplomacy is also integral in advocating for travel advisories and clear communication channels among governments. Coordinating health crisis responses at international airports, developing isolation and treatment facilities, and enforcing rapid response plans help minimize the spread of diseases. Tourism's role in preparedness is underscored by its ability to contribute to resilience through health education campaigns, on-site testing, and health certifications, which reassure travelers and support public health measures (AlKhaldi et al., 2021; Zhu et al., 2022).

4.2 Managing and Communicating Health Risks in the Tourism Sector

Clear, accurate, and timely communication is essential in managing health risks in the tourism industry. Tourists require reliable information about safety measures, travel restrictions, and health risks during health crises in destination regions. As stated by some researchers (e.g., Anderson, 2018; Demir et al., 2021; Kobierecka, 2023), tourism diplomacy supports this need by facilitating coordinated messaging across borders and leveraging digital platforms to reach global audiences. Effective health risk communication begins with international organizations and tourism authorities developing a consistent message (Demir et al., 2021). For example, the UNWTO, in collaboration with national tourism boards, issues guidance and updates on risk levels, advisories, and safety protocols. Risk communication strategies include clear information on hygiene practices, local health regulations, and contingency plans in case of illness during travel. By emphasizing transparent communication, tourism authorities can mitigate fears, encourage responsible travel behavior, and foster trust among travelers.

Social media, official websites, and collaboration with embassies are instrumental in disseminating real-time health information and travel advisories. These channels help counter misinformation, which is particularly challenging in health crises due to the prevalence of online speculation and rumor. A robust communication plan includes steps to educate both travelers and local populations on infection prevention measures, aligning tourism stakeholders with public health goals. Tourism operators and authorities must be adept at implementing health screenings, enforcing social distancing measures, and promoting personal protective equipment (PPE) in managing health risks. Tourism facilities, such as hotels, airlines, and attractions, must adopt rigorous sanitation practices to reassure guests. The collaborative efforts between tourism entities, health organizations, and government bodies illustrate the importance of tourism diplomacy in promoting consistent standards, supporting public health, and restoring confidence among potential travelers (Lee, 2023; Nabyl & Mulachela, 2021).

4.3 Case Study: Tourism Recovery Efforts Postpandemics

The COVID-19 pandemic offers valuable insights into tourism diplomacy's role in postpandemic recovery. As an unprecedented health crisis, COVID-19 caused widespread lockdowns, border closures, and a drastic decline in global tourism (Demir et al., 2021; Park et al., 2022). Recovery efforts involved strategically using tourism diplomacy to rebuild the sector, restore traveler confidence, and adapt to new safety protocols and health requirements.

Countries worldwide implemented various recovery measures tailored to the needs of their tourism sectors (Rozanah & Ishqila, 2024; Saha & Raghuvanshi, 2025). For example, European countries like Italy and Spain collaborated with the European Union to establish a typical health pass, the Digital Covid Certificate, which facilitated safe travel across borders by verifying vaccination and testing status. This standardized approach to health verification was instrumental in revitalizing tourism flows while ensuring safety.

The UNWTO, in collaboration with WHO and regional tourism boards, developed protocols that prioritized health and safety, including physical distancing, enhanced sanitation, and digital health checks (Demir et al., 2020; Park et al., 2022). National tourism bodies launched marketing campaigns, such as Japan's "Go To Travel" initiative, to stimulate domestic tourism while ensuring visitors followed health guidelines. These campaigns focused on promoting less crowded destinations to reduce the risk of viral transmission and support local economies.

Furthermore, recovery strategies included reimagining tourism products and services to appeal to a health-conscious market. Hotels, airlines, and other tourism operators began implementing flexible booking policies, contactless services, and virtual tours, catering to travelers' need for safety and flexibility. Tourism diplomacy's emphasis on collaboration allowed countries to share successful strategies and enhance mutual support, accelerating recovery across regions (Seyfi et al., 2023; Zhu et al., 2022).

4.4 Strengthening Health Infrastructure Through International Tourism Partnerships

Critical to responding to crises, health infrastructure benefits significantly from international tourism partnerships. Tourism diplomacy encourages collaboration between governments, tourism stakeholders, and health organizations to reinforce health systems in regions heavily dependent on tourism (Anderson, 2018; Demir et al., 2021; Rozanah & Ishqila, 2024). Strengthened health infrastructure supports crisis management, prevents the spread of disease, and builds resilience in destination communities. Partnerships with international organizations, such as the WHO, enable countries to access funding, resources, and technical support to enhance healthcare facilities (Kobierecka, 2023; Nabyl & Mulachela, 2021; Seyfi et al., 2023). For instance, during health crises, international tourism partnerships facilitate the establishment of temporary health facilities, providing medical supplies, and training healthcare workers. These partnerships also extend to sharing best practices, such as protocols for sanitizing accommodations, implementing quarantine procedures, and preparing for potential outbreaks among tourists.

Tourism diplomacy also promotes the role of private sector entities, including hotels, airlines, and cruise lines, in supporting health infrastructure (Demir et al., 2021; Saha & Raghuvanshi, 2025; Zhu et al., 2022). Private companies can contribute financially and logistically to the construction of medical facilities, provision of PPE, and vaccination distribution in tourism-dependent communities. Corporate social responsibility initiatives within tourism aim to improve health outcomes, particularly in under-resourced regions that lack adequate healthcare systems. For example, some international hotel chains provided isolation accommodations and logistical support to health workers during the COVID-19 pandemic. These collaborative efforts highlight how tourism diplomacy can bridge gaps in health infrastructure, ensuring that destinations are equipped to handle future health crises. By prioritizing health infrastructure development, tourism can strengthen the resilience of both the industry and the communities that rely on it, safeguarding both public health and the sustainability of tourism destinations.

5. Conflict Zones and Tourism Diplomacy

The relationship between conflict zones and tourism diplomacy is complex, with tourism often positioned as a tool for peacebuilding and postconflict recovery. In regions affected by war, terrorism, or other forms of conflict, tourism diplomacy can serve as a pathway to restore international perceptions, attract investment, and foster a sense of normalcy. By promoting cross-cultural understanding and solidarity, tourism diplomacy can counter the stigma associated with conflict zones, highlighting resilience and cultural richness instead. Governments and international organizations play a critical role in these initiatives, utilizing tourism diplomacy to rebuild the image of conflict-impacted destinations and encourage global support. Additionally, public–private partnerships can mobilize resources for tourism projects, enhance infrastructure, and create safe, controlled environments for tourists. Though challenges remain in managing safety and perceptions, tourism diplomacy in conflict zones can promote peace, improve local economies, and foster international cooperation by reframing the narrative from conflict to cultural resilience and unity.

5.1 The Role of Tourism Diplomacy in Postconflict Recovery

Tourism diplomacy contributes to postconflict recovery by fostering economic revitalization and social stability in regions emerging from conflict. In postconflict settings, the tourism sector offers significant potential to stimulate local economies through job creation, foreign exchange earnings, and infrastructure development, providing a foundation for long-term stability. Tourism diplomacy acts as a bridge between these regions and the international community, helping to rebuild not only the physical spaces that attract tourists but also the image and reputation of these destinations on the global stage (Carbone, 2017; Westermann-Behaylo et al., 2015).

Governments, international organizations, and NGOs engage in tourism diplomacy to reshape the narrative surrounding former conflict zones, highlighting cultural heritage and resilience (Çokişler & Çokişler, 2023; Trogisch & Fletcher, 2022). These efforts help counteract the lingering negative perceptions associated with conflict, which can deter tourists and investors alike. Tourism diplomacy also fosters partnerships with foreign governments, private enterprises, and media outlets to support sustainable tourism initiatives and attract foreign investments in postconflict regions. Furthermore, tourism diplomacy is an entry point for establishing peacebuilding mechanisms, offering opportunities for intercultural understanding and reconciliation among local and international communities.

Establishing collaborative policies is essential for the effectiveness of tourism diplomacy in postconflict recovery (Gelbman & Schweitzer, 2022). For instance, bilateral and multilateral agreements on tourism can improve regional cooperation and security measures, while financial and logistical support can aid the rebuilding of damaged infrastructure. Tourism diplomacy can be a diplomatic tool to attract essential funds and resources for rebuilding. It also supports initiatives like training programs that empower local communities to manage tourism responsibly, encouraging self-reliance and ownership of their economic recovery.

5.2 Peacebuilding and Cultural Exchange Through Tourism

Tourism fosters peacebuilding and cultural exchange in postconflict zones by creating platforms for meaningful interactions between international visitors and local communities (Haq & Medhekar, 2019; Strömbom, 2019). These exchanges allow former adversaries to engage in nonadversarial, cross-cultural encounters, gradually dismantling stereotypes and building mutual understanding. Such interactions can be critical in addressing underlying societal divisions that fuel conflict, fostering long-term social cohesion. Cultural movements facilitated through tourism provide tourists an insight into postconflict societies' historical, cultural, and social contexts (Higgins-Desbiolles et al., 2022; Levy & Hawkins, 2009). This form of "soft diplomacy" enables host communities to share their narratives and values with the global audience, which can lead to more outstanding international support for local peacebuilding efforts. Organizations like the UNWTO and other cultural institutions promote these exchanges by organizing heritage tours, local events, and intercultural workshops emphasizing peace and solidarity.

Beyond fostering goodwill, tourism also recovers economic resilience, which is a critical factor in preventing the recurrence of conflict (Scott, 2012; Strömbom, 2019; Trogisch & Fletcher, 2022). Through tourism, communities affected by conflict can diversify their income sources, reducing their reliance on potentially divisive resources and enhancing their resilience. By investing in cultural and heritage tourism initiatives, local governments can showcase the resilience of their communities and encourage positive narratives that shift focus from conflict to recovery. Over time, tourism can transform the image of a former conflict zone, making it a symbol of resilience and unity rather than division.

5.3 Case Studies: Tourism Recovery Efforts in Former Conflict Zones

Several case studies illustrate the transformative impact of tourism diplomacy in conflict-affected areas. Examples from regions like Rwanda, Bosnia and Herzegovina, and Cambodia highlight the success and challenges of tourism diplomacy in postconflict recovery.

Rwanda: Following the 1994 genocide, Rwanda faced significant challenges in rebuilding its tourism industry (Breed, 2009; Marijnen, 2022). Tourism diplomacy became central to Rwanda's recovery strategy, emphasizing national parks, cultural heritage, and wildlife conservation. Rwanda's government actively promoted the country's natural beauty and cultural history to reshape its international image, and the resulting influx of tourists has provided essential revenue to aid development efforts. Rwanda's focus on gorilla tourism and eco-friendly policies has attracted global attention and contributed to its transformation into a popular destination in Africa. Establishing the "Kwita Izina" gorilla naming ceremony, which brings together local communities, government officials, and international guests, highlights Rwanda's use of tourism diplomacy to foster community engagement and global collaboration.

Bosnia and Herzegovina: After the Yugoslav Wars in the 1990s, Bosnia and Herzegovina used tourism for economic and cultural recovery (Kelly & Baker, 2012; Williams, 2003). The country has marketed its historic sites and natural scenes to encourage international tourism, promoting places like Sarajevo, Mostar, and the historic Stari Most Bridge. Efforts by the government and international partners have helped restore these sites, attracting tourists and generating revenue for local communities. The Sarajevo Film Festival, established to celebrate peace and creativity after the war, is an example of how Bosnia and Herzegovina have integrated tourism diplomacy into their recovery efforts by encouraging intercultural dialogue and international interest.

Cambodia: Cambodia's Angkor Wat complex shows how cultural heritage can aid postconflict recovery through tourism (Putri & Muhyidin, 2019; Waisová, 2017). After years of internal conflict and the Khmer Rouge regime, Cambodia's government partnered with UNESCO to restore and promote Angkor Wat as a world heritage site. The site now attracts millions of visitors annually, providing economic stability and drawing international attention to Cambodia's cultural heritage. By prioritizing Angkor Wat's preservation and including local communities in tourism initiatives, Cambodia has positioned itself as a global destination, creating a positive postconflict narrative through tourism diplomacy.

5.4 Strategies for Promoting Safe Travel to Postconflict Destinations

Promoting safe travel to postconflict destinations requires a multifaceted approach, combining security measures, effective communication, and destination management strategies. First and foremost, ensuring traveler safety is essential to overcoming the stigma of conflict and attracting tourists. Governments and tourism boards must work closely with security agencies to develop stringent safety protocols that reassure tourists and investors. Enhanced airport and transit security, clear communication regarding safety protocols, and transparent updates on security situations in affected regions are fundamental for building traveler confidence (Carbone, 2017; Gelbman & Schweitzer, 2022).

Clear and strategic communication is required to reassure potential visitors (Higgins-Desbiolles et al., 2022; Trogisch & Fletcher, 2022). Digital media campaigns can showcase positive aspects of the destination, such as unique cultural offerings, natural attractions, and local traditions while avoiding references to past conflicts. Social media platforms and travel websites allow postconflict regions to share real-time updates and engage with potential visitors directly. Influencer partnerships and collaboration with travel bloggers can create a positive narrative around the destination, as personal endorsements tend to resonate with international audiences. For example, the "Visit Rwanda" campaign leveraged partnerships with international organizations, including sponsorships with popular sports teams, to build a positive image that has helped counteract lingering perceptions of past conflict.

Collaboration with international organizations, like the United Nations and the UNWTO, can enhance destination credibility. These organizations often offer guidelines for developing resilient tourism frameworks, crisis response mechanisms, and best practices for promoting postconflict tourism (Haq & Medhekar, 2019; Martin et al., 2011). Additionally, postconflict destinations can benefit from establishing public–private partnerships with tourism operators, airlines, and international hospitality chains, creating synergies that support local development and tourism growth.

Destination management organizations (DMOs) in postconflict areas can also implement initiatives that promote responsible and respectful tourism. These may include community-based tourism models that engage residents in the tourism industry, offering them ownership and economic benefits. Responsible tourism practices emphasizing respect for cultural heritage and local traditions help ensure that tourism development aligns with community values. DMOs further encourage sustainable tourism practices, such as eco-friendly accommodations and conservation-focused tourism activities, which resonate with modern tourists' interests and contribute to preserving natural and cultural resources (Çokişler & Çokişler, 2023; Strömbom, 2019).

6. Conclusions

Tourism diplomacy has emerged as a multifaceted tool for recovery, resilience, and peacebuilding in a world where crises have become increasingly frequent and diverse – from natural disasters and economic recessions to health crises and conflicts. One of the most immediate impacts of crises is the disruption of local economies, particularly in tourism-reliant regions. The affected areas can receive international aid and support through tourism diplomacy, fostering postcrisis economic revival. Tourism's capacity to generate income and employment is unparalleled, and initiatives that promote tourism are essential for restoring livelihoods in regions hit by crises. Examining case studies, from natural disaster recovery to economic recession, has highlighted the potential for tourism to act as a driver of regional stability. Tourism diplomacy facilitates partnerships between governments, international organizations, and private sectors, ensuring coordinated economic support that reaches the people who need it most. Tourism diplomacy paves the way for sustainable, long-term economic recovery through targeted investment, job creation, and the revitalization of tourism infrastructure.

Tourism diplomacy also plays a critical role in advancing environmental recovery. Integrating sustainability into tourism efforts not only aligns with global environmental goals but also creates a framework through which damaged ecosystems can regenerate. By promoting conservation efforts and supporting eco-friendly tourism practices, tourism diplomacy facilitates international collaborations that strengthen the resilience of natural habitats. These partnerships not only restore the environment but also educate travelers and local communities on the importance of preserving natural resources.

The COVID-19 pandemic served as a wake-up call for the tourism industry, revealing not only vulnerabilities but also opportunities for strengthening global health systems through tourism diplomacy. Measures have underscored how tourism can support health crisis preparedness through improved health protocols, risk management, and communication strategies. In times of health crises, effective tourism diplomacy prioritizes the safety of both travelers and local populations, ensuring accurate, transparent communication about risks and precautions. As demonstrated by postpandemic recovery initiatives, partnerships with health organizations and governments have become a cornerstone of recovery efforts. Moreover, tourism-driven funding for health infrastructure can provide crucial resources to communities that would otherwise struggle to maintain resilience during a health crisis. Developing more robust health measures, combined with the industry's adaptation to new safety standards, ensures that tourism survives crises and becomes a channel for health resilience in affected regions.

In conflict-affected regions, tourism diplomacy serves as a tool for peacebuilding, offering a means for former adversaries to engage in cultural exchange, mutual understanding, and economic cooperation. When approached with sensitivity and awareness of local contexts, tourism can contribute to healing and reconciliation, helping societies rebuild trust and social cohesion. As seen in regions that have recovered from conflict, tourism diplomacy promotes safe travel by collaborating with governments to establish protocols prioritizing traveler and community safety. By attracting international tourists to former conflict zones, tourism diplomacy not only reintegrates these regions into the global economy but also fosters a narrative of hope and progress. Tourism-driven cultural exchanges and educational programs further enhance peacebuilding efforts, demonstrating the transformative power of tourism as a platform for dialogue and cooperation.

Looking ahead, it is clear that tourism diplomacy's role in crisis response and recovery will only grow in importance. Global crises are becoming increasingly interconnected, affecting multiple aspects of society simultaneously. A multifaceted approach to tourism diplomacy – one that integrates economic, environmental, health, and social dimensions – is essential to address these challenges. Collaborative international frameworks will be necessary to build resilience against future crises. Public–private partnerships, transnational agreements, and community-based initiatives should work in tandem to maximize the benefits of tourism diplomacy. Furthermore, tourism diplomacy must continue to prioritize sustainable practices and equitable growth. A sustainable tourism approach addresses environmental concerns and ensures that local communities benefit directly from tourism revenues. Including diverse stakeholders in tourism diplomacy, from local governments to international organizations, will foster a more inclusive and resilient global tourism industry.

References

AlKhaldi, M., James, N., Chattu, V. K., Ahmed, S., Meghari, H., Kaiser, K., IJsselmuiden, C., & Tanner, M. (2021). Rethinking and strengthening the global health diplomacy through triangulated nexus between policy makers, scientists and the community in light of COVID-19 global crisis. *Global Health Research and Policy*, *6*, 1–6.

Anagnostou, Y. (2022). Diaspora public diplomacy at a time of homeland crisis: The philotimo nation as global distinction. In O. Anastasakis, M. Pratsinakis, F. Kalantzi, & A. Kamaras (Eds.), *Diaspora engagement in times of severe economic crisis: Greece and beyond* (pp. 243–265). Springer International Publishing.

Anderson, E. L. (2018). African health diplomacy: Obscuring power and leveraging dependency through shadow diplomacy. *International Relations*, *32*(2), 194–217.

Beirman, D. (2020). *Restoring tourism destinations in crisis: A strategic marketing approach*. Routledge.

Beirman, D., Upadhayaya, P. K., Pradhananga, P., & Darcy, S. (2018). Nepal tourism in the aftermath of the April/May 2015 earthquake and aftershocks: Repercussions, recovery and the rise of new tourism sectors. *Tourism Recreation Research*, *43*(4), 544–554.

Bonilla, Y. (2020). The coloniality of disaster: Race, empire, and the temporal logics of emergency in Puerto Rico, USA. *Political Geography*, *78*, 1–11.

Boromisa, A. M., & Raditya Ležaić, A. (2014). Croatian commercial diplomacy–stepping stone toward economic recovery? *International Journal of Diplomacy and Economy*, *2*(3), 172–184.

Bouzanis, J. (2009). The economic face of public diplomacy: International business promotion and tourism. In E. H. Potter (Ed.), *Branding Canada: Projecting Canada's soft power through public diplomacy* (pp. 173–193). McGill-Queen's University Press.

Breed, A. (2009). *Theatre for reconciliation in post-genocide Rwanda*. The University of Manchester.

Carbone, F. (2017). International tourism and cultural diplomacy: A new conceptual approach towards global mutual understanding and peace through tourism. *Tourism: An International Interdisciplinary Journal*, *65*(1), 61–74.

Coghlan, A., McLennan, C. L., & Moyle, B. (2017). Contested images, place meaning and potential tourists' responses to an iconic nature-based attraction 'at risk': The case of the Great Barrier Reef. *Tourism Recreation Research*, *42*(3), 299–315.

Çokişler, D. E., & Çokişler, N. (2023). A conceptual overview of the relationship between tourism and peace in terms of international relations theories. *Current Issues in Tourism*, *26*(5), 708–717.

Demir, M., & Demir, Ş.Ş. (2024). Is the global technological outage a caution for the service industries? Evidence from the tourism industry. *Current Issues in Tourism*, 1–21. https://doi.org/10.1080/13683500.2024.2408581

Demir, M., Demir, Ş. Ş., Dalgıç, A., & Ergen, F. D. (2021). Impact of COVID-19 pandemic on the tourism industry: An evaluation from the hotel managers' perspective. *Journal of Tourism Theory and Research*, *7*(1), 44–57. https://doi.org/10.24288/jttr.857610

Demir, M., Günaydın, Y., & Demir, Ş. Ş. (2020). Koronavirüs (Covid-19) salgınının Türkiye'de turizm üzerindeki öncülleri, etkileri ve sonuçlarının değerlendirilmesi. *International Journal of Social Sciences and Education Research*, *6*(1), 80–107.

Folmer, A., Revier, H., & Cupido, T. (2016). Sustainable tourism development and the world heritage status of the Wadden Sea: The case of Terschelling. *Research in Hospitality Management*, *6*(1), 45–50.

Garriga-López, A. (2019). Puerto Rico: The future in question. *Shima*, *13*(2), 174–192.

Gelbman, A., & Schweitzer, R. (2022). Tourism in protected areas and transboundary parks for peace. In D. J. Timothy & A. Gelbman (Eds.), *Routledge handbook of borders and tourism* (pp. 366–378). Routledge.

Griffith, D. (2020). Environmental change and human migration: Stylized facts from Puerto Rico and Honduras. *Coastal Management*, *48*(5), 398–417.

Haq, F., & Medhekar, A. (2019). Is spiritual tourism a peace vehicle for social transformation and economic prosperity in India and Pakistan? In *Marketing peace for social transformation and global prosperity* (pp. 189–211). IGI Global.

Higgins-Desbiolles, F., Blanchard, L. A., & Urbain, Y. (2022). Peace through tourism: Critical reflections on the intersections between peace, justice, sustainable development and tourism. *Journal of Sustainable Tourism*, *30*(2–3), 335–351.

Hohl, A. (2013). Ecotourism as an instrument to conserve biodiversity. In C. A. Tisdell (Ed.), *Handbook of tourism economics: Analysis, new applications and case studies* (pp. 813–843).

Hutnyk, J. (2023). Studying tourism means going to have a look for yourself: Co-research, vulnerabilities and opportunities after the pandemic. *Tourism Recreation Research*, *48*(4), 582–592.

Ibric, A., Bostenaru Dan, M., & Crăciun, C. (2024). Adapting street profile design by using nature-based solutions in new neighbourhoods and the retrofit of buildings. *Buildings*, *14*(7), 1–10.

Jing, L. (2020). Post-pandemic cooperation between China and Central and Eastern Europe. *China Quarterly of International Strategic Studies*, *6*(02), 165–180.

Karaman, Z. T. (2015). Corporate social responsibilities of stakeholders in terms of secure tourism at disasters and sustainable tourism governance. *Journal of Tourism Theory and Research*, *3*(2), 66–78.

Karsokiene, R., & Giedraitis, A. (2023). Systematic post crisis tourism supply chain transformation towards resilience in the context of tour operators. *European Journal of Studies in Management & Business*, *28*, 17–38.

Kelly, M., & Baker, C. (2012). *Interpreting the peace: Peace operations, conflict and language in Bosnia-Herzegovina*. Springer.

Ketter, E. (2016). Destination image restoration on facebook: The case study of Nepal's Gurkha Earthquake. *Journal of Hospitality and Tourism Management*, *28*, 66–72.

Kobierecka, A. (2023). International olympic committee struggle against the COVID-19 pandemic: Health diplomacy of non-state actors. *Athenaeum Polskie Studia Politologiczne*, *79*(1), 215–239.

Lee, S. T. (2023). Vaccine diplomacy: Nation branding and China's COVID-19 soft power play. *Place Branding and Public Diplomacy*, *19*(1), 64–71.

Lele, A. A. (2019). Puerto Rico Post-Hurricane Maria: Reconstruction and the pathway to self-determination. *William & Mary Journal of Race, Gender, and Social Justice*, *26*, 715–722.

Levy, S. E., & Hawkins, D. E. (2009). Peace through tourism: Commerce based principles and practices. *Journal of Business Ethics*, *89*, 569–585.

Lozano, P. L. (2019). Ready to assemble: A new economic diplomacy for Mexico. *Revista Mexicana de Política Exterior*, (117), 69–84.

Luo, Z., & Yun, L. (2023). Investigating risks and strategies in adopting green tourism practices in developing economy. *Environmental Science and Pollution Research, 30*(59), 123710–123728.

Magnin, E., & Nenovsky, N. (2022). Dependent monetary regimes in the Balkans. *Economic Alternatives*, (2), 171–200.

Mansfeld, Y. (2006). The role of security information in tourism crisis management: The missing link. In Y. Mansfeld & A. Pizam (Eds.), *Tourism, security and safety* (pp. 271–290). Routledge.

Marijnen, E. (2022). Eco-war tourism: Affective geographies, colonial durabilities and the militarization of conservation. *Security Dialogue*, *53*(6), 550–566.

Martin, A., Rutagarama, E., Cascão, A., Gray, M., & Chhotray, V. (2011). Understanding the co-existence of conflict and cooperation: Transboundary ecosystem management in the Virunga Massif. *Journal of Peace Research*, *48*(5), 621–635.

McGaurr, L., & Lester, L. (2018). See it before it's too late? Last-chance travel lists and climate change. *Climate Change and the Media*, *2*, 123–140.

Miño, P. (2023). Power imbalances and contested notions of the nation: Latin American nation branding through the lens of the cultural-economic model of public relations. *Journal of Public Relations Research*, *35*(5–6), 307–320.

Musavengane, R., Leonard, L., & Mureyani, S. (2022). Doing tourism in Southern Africa amid the coronavirus pandemic: Navigating political, socio-economic and environmental inequalities. *Development Southern Africa*, *39*(1), 3–19.

Nabyl, V., & Mulachela, A. (2021). COVID-19: Where public health and diplomacy converge. In H. Alhashimi, A. Fiallo, T.-S. Freckleton, M. A. Khalil, V. Mulachela, & J. Viera (Eds.), *The future of diplomacy after COVID-19* (pp. 16–35). Routledge.

Nagai, H., Sano, K., Ritchie, B. W., & Yoshino, T. (2020). International tourists in Japan: Their increasing numbers and vulnerability to natural hazards. In R. Sharpley & K. Kato (Eds.), *Tourism development in Japan* (pp. 239–256). Routledge.

Nakamura, T. (2013). Japan's new public diplomacy: Coolness in foreign policy objectives. *Media and Society*, *5*(1), 1–23.

Negassa, S. B. (2024). Tourism diplomacy: Fostering economic development through global connectivity. In A. B. Basnur (Ed.), *Tourism: For global connectivity and economic development* (pp. 68–75). Paramedia Komunikatama.

Okano-Heijmans, M. (2012). Japan's new economic diplomacy: Changing tactics or strategy? *Asia-Pacific Review*, *19*(1), 62–87.

Park, E., Kim, W. H., & Kim, S. B. (2022). How does COVID-19 differ from previous crises? A comparative study of health-related crisis research in the tourism and hospitality context. *International Journal of Hospitality Management*, *103*, 1–11.

Paudel, D., & Le Billon, P. (2020). Geo-logics of power: Disaster capitalism, Himalayan materialities, and the geopolitical economy of reconstruction in post-earthquake Nepal. *Geopolitics*, *25*(4), 838–866.

Putri, I. M., & Muhyidin, A. (2019). Cambodian and Thai Political actors interest in Preah Vihear temple border conflict in 2008–2011. *Jurnal Politik*, *4*(2), 14–22.

Qobo, M. (2022). *The political economy of China–US relations*. Springer International Publishing.

Rana, K. S. (2013). Economic diplomacy: What might best serve a developing country? *International Journal of Diplomacy and Economy*, *1*(3–4), 232–247.

Rozanah, A., & Ishqila, N. A. (2024). The influence of public diplomacy in G20 2022 summit in Indonesia's post-pandemic tourism and ecotourism recovery efforts. *Journal of Social Political Sciences*, *5*(1), 45–56.

Rudiany, N. P., Isnarti, R., Ramadhan, I., & Kusumawardhana, I. (2023). Aligning "energy culture" as part of sustainable tourism ideas. In *IOP conference series: Earth and environmental science* (Vol. 1199, No. 1, pp. 1–10). IOP Publishing.

Saha, R., & Raghuvanshi, L. (2025). Intercultural communication in tourism during COVID-19 pandemic: Analyzing audience appeal of Indian tourism campaign through social media. In S. S. Ghosh, D. Roy, T. Putatunda, & N. Ray (Eds.), *Language and cross-cultural communication in travel and tourism* (pp. 49–67). Apple Academic Press.

Sahoo, M., Mohanty, P. P., Kaushik, S., Islam, M. K., & Rourt, L. (2024). Ecotourism or ecological concerns? Tracing the impact of economic policy uncertainty and natural resources on tourism-driven ecological footprints. *Environmental Science and Pollution Research*, 1–17.

Scott, J. (2012). Tourism, civil society and peace in Cyprus. *Annals of Tourism Research*, *39*(4), 2114–2132.

Senbeto, D. L., Mamo, Y., & Seyfi, S. (2024). Light in the middle of the tunnel? A sentimental analysis of tourist responses to ongoing crisis. *Current Issues in Tourism*, *27*(6), 838–846.

Seyfi, S., Hall, C. M., & Shabani, B. (2023). COVID-19 and international travel restrictions: The geopolitics of health and tourism. *Tourism Geographies*, *25*(1), 357–373.

Siani-Davies, P., & Siani-Davies, M. (2017). *Crisis in greece*. Oxford University Press.

Singh, S., Nicely, A., Day, J., & Cai, L. A. (2022). Marketing messages for post-pandemic destination recovery-A Delphi study. *Journal of Destination Marketing & Management*, *23*, 1–11.

Sklias, P., & Tzifakis, N. (2012). Beyond nemesis and salvation: A reorientation of the debate on the Greek economic crisis. In P. Sklias & N. Tzifakis (Eds.), *Greece's horizons: Reflecting on the country's assets and capabilities* (pp. 1–7). Springer Berlin Heidelberg.

Strömbom, L. (2019). Exploring prospects for agonistic encounters in conflict zones: Investigating dual narrative tourism in Israel/Palestine. *Alternatives*, *44*(2–4), 75–93.

Tamargo, V., Pál, Á., & Szabóné Erdélyi, É. (2022). Sustainable tourism policy in practice: A comparative case study of Argentina and Costa Rica. *Prosperitas*, *9*(1–2), 1–11.

Trogisch, L., & Fletcher, R. (2022). Fortress tourism: Exploring dynamics of tourism, security and peace around the Virunga transboundary conservation area. In F. Higgins-Desbiolles, L. A. Blanchard, & Y. Urbain (Eds.), *Peace through tourism* (pp. 21–42). Routledge.

Waisová, Š (2017). *The Thai-Cambodian conflict and environmental cooperation*. Lexington Sooks.

Westermann-Behaylo, M. K., Rehbein, K., & Fort, T. (2015). Enhancing the concept of corporate diplomacy: Encompassing political corporate social responsibility, international relations, and peace through commerce. *Academy of Management Perspectives*, *29*(4), 387–404.

Williams, G. H. (2003). *Post conflict reconstruction: On the critical path to long-term peace*. US Army War College.

Wu, L., & Shimizu, T. (2020). Analyzing dynamic change of tourism destination image under the occurrence of a natural disaster: Evidence from Japan. *Current Issues in Tourism*, *23*(16), 2042–2058.

Zhu, J., Siriphon, A., Airey, D., & Mei-Lan, J. (2022). Chinese tourism diplomacy: A Chinese–style modernity review. *Anatolia*, *33*(4), 550–563.

Chapter 8

Technology and Innovation in Tourism Diplomacy

Abstract

The integration of technology and innovation is revolutionizing tourism diplomacy, offering unprecedented opportunities for engagement, collaboration, and influence on a global scale. This section examines the evolving role of tourism diplomacy in a digital world, highlighting how digital platforms act as catalysts for fostering cultural exchange, economic partnerships, and international understanding. Key contributions of digital tools such as social media, virtual and augmented reality, Artificial Intelligence, and data analytics are explored, emphasizing their potential to create immersive experiences, enhance strategic decision-making, and promote inclusivity through content personalization. The transformative impact of digitalization extends to strategic developments in tourism diplomacy, including utilizing blockchain for transparency, the Internet of Things (IoT) for connected travel experiences, and the ethical implications of sustainable innovation. Emerging phenomena like digital nomadism, remote work culture, and space tourism are also discussed as future frontiers of tourism diplomacy. This analysis underscores the importance of leveraging digital advancements responsibly to strengthen global tourism diplomacy by addressing challenges such as data privacy, technological disparities, and cultural sensitivities. Through diverse case studies and practical insights, this section provides a comprehensive framework for understanding the intersection of technology, innovation, and diplomacy in the tourism sector.

Keywords: Digital tourism diplomacy; virtual and augmented reality; blockchain in tourism; sustainable innovation; digital nomadism

Tourism Diplomacy, 159–174

Copyright © 2025 Mahmut Demir and Şirvan Şen Demir

Published under exclusive licence by Emerald Publishing Limited
doi:10.1108/978-1-83708-676-420251008

1. Introduction

As countries and international organizations strive to foster mutual understanding and cultural exchange through tourism, digital tools and innovative strategies have reshaped diplomacy within this sector. By leveraging technology, nations can communicate more effectively, connect with global audiences, and practically enhance their cultural presence. Traditional diplomatic practices, once characterized by onsite exchanges and formal protocols, are now complemented – and in some cases, replaced – by digital channels that offer immediate and widespread outreach. Social media platforms, online video-sharing services, and digital advertising have all become essential in tourism diplomacy, allowing countries and their organizations to craft appealing narratives and reach audiences beyond borders (Beşirova, 2024; Demir & Demir, 2024).

Digital tools, ranging from social media to virtual reality (VR), have become invaluable resources in the toolkit of tourism diplomacy. These technologies offer immersive and interactive experiences, enabling people worldwide to gain insights into other nations' history, culture, and traditions without leaving their homes (Demir et al., 2023; Gerlitz et al., 2021). For instance, virtual tours of cultural landmarks, interactive apps for language learning, and augmented reality (AR) applications showcasing historical sites are just a few examples of how digital tools shape tourism diplomacy (Demir & Demir, 2024). By making cultural experiences more accessible and engaging, these tools support the broader objectives of tourism diplomacy by breaking down geographical and cultural barriers.

As some researchers state (e.g., Carayannis, 2013; Gerlitz et al., 2021; Zugasti, 2019), digital transformation reshapes industries globally, and tourism diplomacy strategies have also evolved to incorporate new technologies. Nations adopt data-driven approaches to understand better and engage with tourists, customizing experiences to suit diverse interests and preferences. Machine learning algorithms, for example, allow tourism boards to analyze visitor data, track cultural trends, and refine their marketing approaches. Moreover, digital transformation enables streamlined coordination between government bodies and private tourism sectors, facilitating the implementation of cohesive and adaptive strategies.

Kalbaska et al. (2017) and Zugasti (2019) emphasized that looking toward the future, emerging technologies hold promise for further transforming tourism diplomacy. Innovations such as Artificial Intelligence (AI), blockchain for secure digital transactions, and the Internet of Things (IoT) for personalized travel experiences pave the way for new cultural exchange and diplomatic engagement dimensions (Demir & Demir, 2024; Yaşar et al., 2024). Additionally, the rise of digital nomadism, smart tourism ecosystems, and space tourism present new avenues for diplomacy, inviting countries to explore and adapt to unprecedented scenarios.

2. Tourism Diplomacy in a Digital World

Digitalization has fundamentally reshaped many aspects of modern diplomacy, including the specialized realm of tourism diplomacy. As global connectivity accelerates, tourism diplomacy now operates within a distinctly digital framework, leveraging digital tools and platforms to engage international audiences, strengthen bilateral relations, and promote cultural understanding (Arabiun et al., 2023; Demir & Demir, 2024). Digital technologies have become instrumental in not only widening the reach of tourism initiatives (Yaşar et al., 2024) but also enriching the content and accessibility of diplomatic efforts, thereby enhancing the role of tourism as a soft power tool in international relations (Zhanibek et al., 2022).

2.1 The Evolving Role of Tourism Diplomacy in the Digital Era

Historically, tourism diplomacy has relied on traditional diplomatic practices, where face-to-face interactions, official delegations, and cultural exchanges were central to promoting a nation's culture, heritage, and values (Ayodele, 2021; Kalbaska et al., 2017). As a soft power strategy, tourism seeks to shape perceptions and build international goodwill through people-to-people interactions and firsthand cultural experiences. However, in the digital era, such interactions are no longer confined to physical travel or in-person exchanges (Demir et al., 2023). Digital channels such as social media, online content platforms, and virtual tourism experiences now enable nations to engage with global audiences directly and immediately, providing opportunities for real-time communication and interactive cultural exchanges that were previously unavailable (Beşirova, 2024).

Digital tourism diplomacy leverages technology to bypass physical limitations, making cultural narratives and experiences accessible to people regardless of location (Silva et al., 2023; Zugasti, 2019). This shift holds significant implications for both tourism diplomacy practitioners and target audiences. On the one hand, governments and tourism boards can now craft and disseminate narratives that reach millions instantly, often at a fraction of the cost associated with traditional tourism campaigns. On the other hand, audiences worldwide gain access to diverse cultures and national identities, often without the necessity of travel. This expanded accessibility enhances the ability of tourism diplomacy to foster cross-cultural understanding, even among those who might not otherwise engage with foreign cultures directly (Demir & Demir, 2024).

2.2 Digital Platforms as Catalysts for Tourism Diplomacy

Social media platforms, such as Instagram, Facebook, YouTube, and TikTok, have become central to tourism diplomacy in the digital age. Through these platforms, countries showcase their cultural heritage, landscapes, and unique traditions to global audiences in engaging, visually appealing ways (Beşirova, 2024). For instance, social media campaigns can highlight a country's cultural festivals, historical sites, and culinary experiences, creating an immersive narrative that fosters interest and encourages visitation. These platforms also allow for two-way interaction, where tourists can provide feedback, share their experiences, and engage with local culture, thus creating a dynamic exchange that strengthens diplomatic ties at the individual level.

Moreover, digital tourism diplomacy on social media offers the unique advantage of targeted outreach. Advanced algorithms and data analytics enable tourism agencies to segment audiences and tailor content based on demographics, interests, and engagement patterns. This precision allows for more effective promotion, where countries can connect with audiences more likely to be receptive to cultural tourism, thus maximizing the impact of their efforts (Beşirova, 2024; Demir et al., 2023). For example, targeted advertisements can attract visitors interested in historical architecture, cuisine, or outdoor adventure, ensuring that each demographic receives relevant and appealing content.

2.3 The Broader Impact of Digital Tourism Diplomacy

Beyond individual campaigns and experiences, digital tourism diplomacy plays a strategic role in shaping international relations. By participating in global digital networks, countries not only promote tourism but also enhance their geopolitical positioning (Carayannis, 2013; Silva et al., 2023). Nations can align their tourism diplomacy strategies with broader foreign policy objectives, using cultural attractions and tourism campaigns to reinforce international partnerships, improve their global image, and counter negative perceptions. For instance, in regions where diplomatic tensions may be high, digital tourism diplomacy offers a less politicized platform for cultural exchange and engagement, creating avenues for dialogue that may otherwise be inaccessible.

Digital tourism diplomacy can also serve as a tool for national branding, where countries leverage their unique cultural assets to differentiate themselves in the global arena (Ayodele, 2021; Carayannis, 2013). Japan, for instance, utilizes digital platforms to promote both traditional elements, such as tea ceremonies and cherry blossom festivals, and modern cultural assets like anime and high-tech innovation, presenting a multifaceted national identity. Similarly, smaller nations can use digital tourism diplomacy to increase visibility and attract international attention, positioning themselves as unique travel destinations. This aspect of tourism diplomacy is particularly relevant in a competitive global tourism market, where nations constantly seek to attract foreign visitors and boost their tourism economy.

3. The Contribution of Digital Tools to Tourism Diplomacy

Digital tools have impacted how countries interact with international audiences. By facilitating communication, increasing accessibility, and enriching cultural exchange, digital tools have strengthened tourism diplomacy's role in promoting national identity and fostering mutual understanding. As tourism diplomacy becomes increasingly digital, tools such as social media, VR, AR, AI, data analytics, etc., offer invaluable resources that enhance its reach, effectiveness, and adaptability.

3.1 Social Media Platforms: Expanding the Reach of Tourism Diplomacy

Social media platforms are indispensable in modern tourism diplomacy, providing robust cultural exchange and promotion tools. Platforms like Instagram, Facebook, X, TikTok, YouTube, etc., allow countries to connect directly with global audiences and showcase their unique attractions, cultural heritage, and values (Beşirova, 2024; Seccardini & Desmoulins, 2023). Through curated content that highlights landmarks, festivals, local traditions, and natural beauty, countries can create narratives that resonate with audiences and inspire travel interest. Social media platforms also facilitate two-way communication, allowing foreign audiences to engage, comment, and share their experiences, fostering a more interactive and inclusive approach to diplomacy.

A notable example of social media's contribution to tourism diplomacy is Instagram's use by national tourism boards to attract potential visitors through visually engaging content (Demir & Demir, 2024). Countries such as Türkiye, New Zealand, Japan, and Italy use Instagram to share high-quality images and videos portraying their landscapes' beauty, distinctiveness, and cultural heritage. This visual storytelling creates an emotional connection with audiences, inspiring wanderlust and interest in the cultural aspects of these destinations. Moreover, as some researchers explain (e.g., Jiang, 2017; Negassa, 2024; Ranteallo & Andilolo, 2017), the user-generated content tourists share amplifies these narratives, as visitors' personal experiences contribute to a country's digital reputation and authenticity.

Additionally, social media platforms allow for targeted marketing, where algorithms and data analytics enable tourism boards to customize content for specific demographics (Beşirova, 2024; Grincheva, 2013; Saliu, 2022). For instance, younger audiences may be drawn to unique, adventure-focused activities, while older audiences may be more interested in historical and cultural experiences. This targeted approach maximizes the effectiveness of tourism diplomacy campaigns by delivering relevant and appealing content to each audience segment.

3.2 Virtual and Augmented Reality: Enabling Immersive Cultural Experiences

VR and AR technologies have redefined how audiences experience foreign cultures, offering immersive and interactive experiences that bring distant places closer (Cheer et al., 2021; Yfantis & Ntalianis, 2022). These tools allow individuals to explore sites of cultural significance, natural wonders, and historical landmarks without physically traveling (Ergen, 2020). Through VR and AR, tourism diplomacy can engage people who may be unable or unwilling to travel but still wish to experience another culture. This approach widens access to cultural exchange, enabling a deeper understanding and appreciation of other nations and their identities.

Countries increasingly incorporate VR into their tourism diplomacy strategies, offering virtual tours of iconic sites and cultural institutions (De Luca et al., 2022; Popescu et al., 2020). For instance, VR tours of UNESCO World Heritage sites, national museums, and architectural landmarks allow users to explore these destinations in 360-degree detail. For example, a virtual tour of the Louvre in Paris lets viewers navigate galleries and view famous artworks up close, fostering interest and appreciation for French culture and art. These experiences provide an immersive way for foreign audiences to connect with the host nation, fostering a sense of familiarity and curiosity that can ultimately lead to physical travel.

AR, conversely, offers interactive cultural experiences by overlaying digital information on the physical world (Grincheva, 2024; Negassa, 2024). For example, visitors at historical sites can use AR-enabled apps to view reconstructions of ancient architecture or access information on significant historical events and figures. This combination of physical and digital interaction creates an enriched, informative experience that enhances cultural appreciation. By blending education and entertainment, AR tools support the broader goals of tourism diplomacy, helping to make cultural experiences more engaging and accessible (Fig. 14).

3.3 AI and Data Analytics: Informing Strategy and Enhancing Engagement

AI and data analytics offer sophisticated methods for understanding and engaging with international audiences, providing insights that support strategic decision-making in tourism diplomacy (Achary & Albuquerque, 2024; Visvizi et al., 2023). AI-powered tools can analyze vast amounts of data to reveal patterns in travel behavior, preferences, and interests, allowing tourism boards to tailor their outreach efforts more effectively. By leveraging data analytics, tourism diplomacy practitioners can identify which cultural narratives resonate most with target audiences, enabling them to design campaigns that align with audience expectations and preferences (Grincheva, 2024; Nag & Mishra, 2024).

AI tools also enable automated and personalized engagement, enhancing the overall experience for potential tourists (Negassa, 2024; Pawar & Singh, 2023). Chatbots, for example, are widely used by tourism agencies to provide real-time

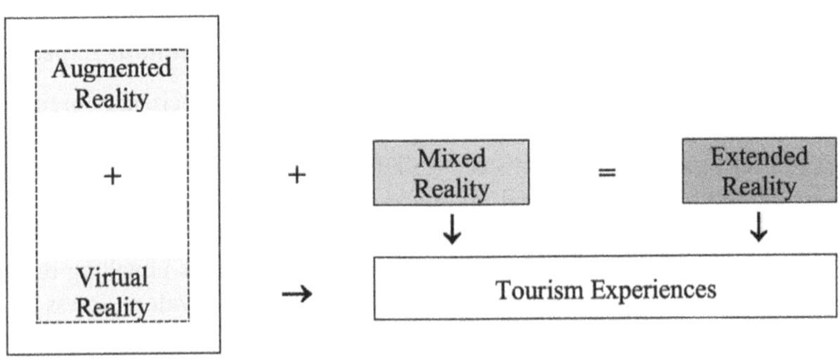

Fig. 14. Virtual and Augmented Reality for Enabling Tourism Experiences.

information, answer frequently asked questions, and recommend activities or sites based on user preferences. This personalized interaction fosters a connection with the destination, increasing the likelihood of a visit. Additionally, AI-driven recommendation systems can suggest itineraries based on a user's interests, encouraging a deeper exploration of a country's cultural offerings. For instance, a visitor interested in culinary tourism might receive tailored recommendations for local food markets, cooking classes, and traditional dining experiences, all of which contribute to a more enriching and memorable visit.

Through predictive analytics, AI also aids tourism boards in anticipating trends and preparing for future developments. For example, during peak travel seasons, AI can forecast tourist inflows and help manage resources to ensure a smooth and enjoyable experience for visitors. By aligning operational strategies with anticipated trends, tourism diplomacy efforts can be made more efficient and effective, enhancing the country's image as a welcoming and well-prepared destination (Demir & Demir, 2023).

3.4 Content Personalization and Cultural Sensitivity: Building Trust and Inclusivity

Digital tools also allow content personalization and cultural sensitivity, two critical factors in tourism diplomacy that build trust and inclusivity (Chowdhury et al., 2024; Jin, 2024). Personalization enables tourism boards to create customized experiences that align with individual preferences and cultural backgrounds, fostering a sense of connection with the destination. For example, a tourism campaign targeted at Asian audiences may highlight aspects of cultural heritage that resonate more strongly, such as family-oriented activities, historical connections, or spiritual sites. Tourism diplomacy efforts can foster greater inclusivity by tailoring content to reflect cultural values and preferences, making foreign audiences feel understood and valued.

Cultural sensitivity is also enhanced through digital tools that provide insights into local customs, etiquette, and values (Grincheva, 2024; Sigala, 2020). Digital resources such as cultural etiquette apps, language translation tools, and informative content on social media help tourists understand the social norms and practices of the host country. This awareness encourages respectful interactions and minimizes cultural misunderstandings, contributing to a positive experience for both tourists and locals (Negassa, 2024; Recuero-Virto & Arróspide, 2024). When a country demonstrates respect for visitors' cultural backgrounds while promoting its own, it creates a reciprocal relationship that strengthens diplomatic ties and builds trust.

3.5 Challenges and Opportunities in Using Digital Tools for Tourism Diplomacy

While digital tools offer significant advantages for tourism diplomacy, they also present challenges that must be navigated carefully (Cheer et al., 2021; Sigala, 2020; Visvizi et al., 2023). Privacy concerns, cybersecurity threats, and the potential for cultural misrepresentation are risks associated with digital tourism diplomacy. For instance, social media campaigns that rely on user-generated content may inadvertently spread stereotypes or oversimplified cultural narratives, damaging a country's image. Therefore, tourism boards must exercise caution in curating content that accurately reflects their culture and values, ensuring that digital tools are used responsibly and ethically.

On the other hand, the continued development of digital tools presents vast opportunities for innovation and growth in tourism diplomacy (Grincheva, 2013; Nag & Mishra, 2024; Saliu, 2022). Emerging technologies such as blockchain for secure transactions, the IoT for personalized experiences, and AI advancements for predictive analytics all promise to further enhance the effectiveness of tourism diplomacy. By investing in these technologies, countries can stay at the forefront of digital engagement and maintain competitive advantages in the global tourism market.

4. Shaping Tourism Diplomacy Strategies With Digital Transformation

In the era of rapid technological advancement, digital transformation has redefined the scope and strategy of tourism diplomacy, enabling countries to engage with global audiences through innovative digital means. By integrating digital technologies, countries can enhance their cultural outreach, showcase their identities, and build stronger international relationships. This transformation is not merely about incorporating technology but about fundamentally reshaping tourism diplomacy strategies to align with global audiences' digital behaviors and expectations. This digitalization goes beyond traditional forms of tourism promotion, involving new technologies that enable real-time engagement, data-driven decision-making, and immersive experiences that enhance cultural exchange. Trends such as AI, the IoT, blockchain, virtual and augmented reality, and predictive analytics are leading the way, offering powerful tools for tourism diplomats. Digital transformation in tourism diplomacy encompasses various tools and approaches, including digital platforms for cultural exchange, data analytics to inform policy, and interactive technologies to offer immersive experiences, all converging to create a more effective and adaptive framework for tourism diplomacy.

4.1 The Role of Digital Transformation in Modernizing Tourism Diplomacy

Digital transformation refers to integrating digital technologies into all aspects of operations and strategy, resulting in fundamental changes in how organizations and governments engage with their stakeholders (Chowdhury et al., 2024; Gerlitz et al., 2021). In tourism diplomacy, this transformation involves using digital platforms, AI, VR, social media, and data-driven insights to enhance how countries communicate, promote cultural understanding, and influence perceptions globally (Ergen, 2020). Digital transformation enables tourism diplomats to act dynamically, tailoring strategies to specific target audiences' preferences, interests, and behaviors. For example, countries can now respond quickly to social trends, leveraging digital platforms to reach audiences in real-time with personalized content that resonates with their cultural interests.

The shift toward two-way communication is a significant component of digital transformation in tourism diplomacy (Demir et al., 2023). Traditional tourism diplomacy often relied on one-sided promotional campaigns, with limited interaction between countries and their target audiences. However, digital transformation facilitates interactive communication, creating a platform where audiences can actively participate, provide feedback, and engage in dialogue (De Luca et al., 2022; Silva et al., 2023). This transformation enables tourism diplomacy efforts to be more inclusive and representative, fostering a sense of connection and mutual understanding.

4.2 The IoT and Connected Experiences

The IoT is reshaping various industries by connecting devices, platforms, and people in real-time networks, allowing interactive and immersive experiences (Demir & Demir, 2023, 2024). For tourism diplomacy, IoT technologies open new avenues for connecting with tourists before, during, and after their travel experience, creating a cohesive and comprehensive interaction. For example, smart cities and smart tourism initiatives offer potential benefits in tourism diplomacy by enabling governments to enhance the visitor experience through real-time information, interactive guides, and location-based recommendations.

One significant application of IoT in tourism diplomacy is the development of "smart" cultural sites and tourist attractions. By equipping cultural sites with IoT devices, countries can provide visitors with rich information about a site's cultural, historical, or environmental significance through mobile notifications or interactive installations (Cardoso & Ruiz, 2021; Lee, 2020). These smart interactions enrich the visitor experience and convey cultural values and narratives in engaging and accessible ways. Furthermore, IoT can support eco-friendly tourism initiatives, which are becoming an increasingly important aspect of international tourism diplomacy (Lee, 2020; Salem, 2017). With sensors that track environmental impact, such as carbon footprints and water usage, IoT can offer tourists insights into their ecological impact while suggesting sustainable travel practices. This aligns with the growing emphasis on sustainability within tourism diplomacy, helping countries project a responsible, environmentally conscious image that appeals to modern travelers who prioritize sustainable tourism.

4.3 Blockchain Technology for Trust and Transparency

Blockchain technology, which has garnered attention primarily in finance, is emerging as a tool for establishing transparency, security, and trust – essential values in tourism diplomacy. Blockchain offers a decentralized and secure method for recording transactions and information, making it a powerful tool for managing data in tourism-related services (Demir & Demir, 2023). The transparency enabled by blockchain helps build credibility, an essential asset in diplomacy where trust is paramount.

In tourism diplomacy, blockchain's capacity for secure data management is particularly relevant in visa processing, health documentation, and traveler identity verification (Achary & Albuquerque, 2024; Whitaker et al., 2021). Countries can streamline these processes using blockchain, making travel more accessible and efficient. For instance, blockchain could create a secure, easily verifiable system for health certificates, facilitating safe travel in response to pandemics or other health crises. This would be a significant advantage in post-COVID-19 tourism diplomacy, where health and safety are top priorities.

Blockchain can support eco-certification programs, allowing countries to verify and display their environmental standards transparently (Gričar et al., 2023; Hsu et al., 2024). This adds a layer of trust to sustainability claims, helping destinations differentiate themselves as environmentally responsible options. As travelers increasingly seek destinations with sustainable practices, blockchain can enhance the credibility of tourism diplomacy campaigns centered on environmental stewardship, creating a lasting, positive impact on a country's reputation.

4.4 Embracing Ethical and Sustainable Innovation in Tourism Diplomacy

As countries embrace technological innovation in tourism diplomacy, they must also navigate these technologies' ethical considerations and sustainability implications. Data privacy, cybersecurity, cultural sensitivity, and environmental sustainability are all crucial factors that must be addressed as digital tools continue to advance. Transparency in data usage and a commitment to protecting user privacy are fundamental to building trust in a digital age, where concerns about data misuse are prevalent (Demir & Demir, 2024). As tourism diplomats use technology to reach broader audiences, they must remain mindful of cultural differences, ensuring that digital content authentically represents and respects the promoted cultures. Embracing ethical standards in digital tourism diplomacy not only fosters positive international relations but also strengthens a country's reputation as a respectful and responsible global actor. Sustainability, too, must be at the forefront of innovation. With growing awareness of climate change and the environmental impact of tourism, tourism diplomacy campaigns prioritizing eco-friendly initiatives will resonate strongly with modern travelers.

4.5 Digital Nomadism and Remote Work Culture

The rise of digital nomadism and remote work culture is one of the most significant shifts in modern labor dynamics (Demaj et al., 2021; Jiwasiddi et al., 2024). This trend, fueled by technology and accelerated by the COVID-19 pandemic, has enabled professionals to work from anywhere with a stable internet connection. Digital nomads, often attracted to diverse cultural experiences and flexible lifestyles, embody a new category of travelers contributing to tourism diplomacy's evolution. By attracting digital nomads, nations have the opportunity to foster international interactions that lead to greater cultural exchange and potentially long-term economic benefits.

Countries can capitalize on digital nomadism by creating policies encouraging remote workers to stay and work within their borders. Many nations, including Portugal, Estonia, and Barbados, have introduced digital nomad visas, granting long-term stays to those working remotely. This influx of international remote workers contributes economically through local spending and bolsters the nation's image as a welcoming, globally connected destination. By creating environments that facilitate digital nomadism, countries are essentially engaging in tourism diplomacy, as the presence of international workers promotes cross-cultural interactions and enhances the global perception of the host country (Lord & Lord, 2017; Mikac & Kravaršćan, 2021).

Moreover, digital nomads often act as informal ambassadors, sharing their experiences through social media and digital platforms, thus promoting the destination to a broader audience (Jiwasiddi et al., 2024; Lord & Lord, 2017). This organic tourism promotion complements traditional tourism diplomacy by creating authentic, user-generated content that reflects a personal connection to the destination. Digital nomads' extended stays also enable deeper cultural immersion, which can help dismantle stereotypes, foster understanding, and build lasting bonds between the host nation and the nomad's home country. The potential for these digital ambassadors to shape global perceptions underscores the importance of embracing digital nomadism within tourism diplomacy strategies.

4.6 Space Tourism: The New Frontier for Tourism Diplomacy

Space tourism represents an unprecedented expansion of tourism beyond Earth's borders. Once considered a distant fantasy, the commercialization of space travel is becoming a reality, with companies like SpaceX, Blue Origin, and Virgin Galactic pioneering private space flights. Although still in its nascent stages, space tourism has the potential to redefine tourism diplomacy by offering a unique platform for international cooperation, exploration, and cultural exchange on a cosmic scale.

The idea of space tourism as a diplomatic tool introduces a new realm for collaboration and soft power (Brobst, 2024; Congden et al., 2024). Governments may collaborate with private space companies to promote their national achievements in space technology, positioning themselves as leaders in scientific innovation and exploration. Nations that establish themselves as pioneers in space tourism could enhance their global influence, as space travel captivates public imagination and fosters a shared human curiosity about the cosmos. Moreover, space tourism could strengthen relationships between countries through joint initiatives and partnerships that span research, safety regulations, and educational programs.

Space tourism's symbolic value as a unifying experience could also play an important role in diplomacy (Congden et al., 2024; Simonin, 2008). The "overview effect," a phenomenon experienced by astronauts viewing Earth from space, often leads to a profound shift in perspective, fostering a sense of interconnectedness and global responsibility. If space tourism becomes accessible to a broader demographic, it could promote similar shifts in perspective among civilians, encouraging a renewed focus on unity and environmental stewardship (Karimipour & Abdi, 2015; Polkowska, 2021). This experiential shift has the potential to influence international relations as space tourists return to Earth with a heightened awareness of global interconnectedness and may advocate for policies that support international cooperation, environmental preservation, and peace. In this sense, space tourism could be a powerful mechanism for fostering diplomatic ties and mutual understanding between nations.

5. Conclusions

Tourism diplomacy in a digital world represents an evolved approach to international engagement, where technology enhances diplomatic efforts' scope, reach, and efficacy. Digital platforms, virtual experiences, and targeted outreach enable countries to connect with diverse audiences, break down barriers to cultural understanding, and create lasting international connections. The contribution of digital tools to tourism diplomacy is profound and far-reaching, allowing nations to engage with global audiences in new and meaningful ways. Countries can more effectively present their cultural heritage, shape perceptions, and foster cross-cultural understanding through AI, the IoT, blockchain, social media, VR, AR, and data analytics. These tools not only extend the reach of tourism diplomacy but also enrich the quality of cultural exchange, making it more accessible, personalized, and inclusive.

The future of tourism diplomacy lies in the strategic integration of digital innovation and emerging technologies. These trends reflect a transformative period for tourism diplomacy, from digital nomadism and space tourism to enhancing traditional tourism tools through AI, blockchain, and immersive technologies (Demir & Demir, 2024). By embracing these innovations, countries can foster international connections, promote cultural understanding, and build a positive global image, ultimately reinforcing tourism as a powerful instrument of diplomacy. As countries continue to leverage technological advancements, they must also navigate challenges related to data privacy, ethical considerations, and sustainability to ensure that tourism diplomacy remains an inclusive, positive force. Moving forward, tourism diplomacy will depend on a balanced approach that combines cutting-edge innovation with a commitment to responsible practices, fostering a global environment where tourism serves as a gateway to discovery and a bridge to understanding and peace.

Digitalizing tourism diplomacy also involves optimizing online resources, such as government tourism websites, often the first point of contact for international visitors. Countries can enhance visitor engagement by providing comprehensive, user-friendly platforms with interactive features, making a positive first impression, and strengthening diplomatic outreach. Adopting digital tools in tourism diplomacy extends to creating personalized and inclusive travel experiences. Tourism actors can identify specific market segments through data collection and analysis, allowing for tailored campaigns that resonate with different cultural backgrounds and personal interests. This targeted approach makes outreach more efficient and enables countries to position themselves as inclusive, welcoming destinations, thereby enhancing their reputation on the international stage.

Innovation in mobile technology and app development has also made it possible for tourists to experience destinations in new ways (Beşirova, 2024). Many countries now offer mobile apps with personalized itineraries, real-time translation, and AR guides. These tools provide convenience and enhance the visitor experience by catering to their specific needs and preferences, creating a positive impression of the host country. By providing tourists with innovative resources that simplify their travel experience, countries build goodwill and foster positive associations, which can extend to diplomatic relations.

Blockchain technology further exemplifies the potential of innovation in tourism diplomacy. Its applications in secure, transparent transactions make it a valuable tool for managing travel logistics, from identity verification to health records and visa processing. Blockchain enables governments to ensure security, privacy, and trust in international travel processes, which is especially relevant given heightened health and safety concerns. This emphasis on security and transparency can reinforce a country's reputation as a responsible and reliable travel destination, adding a layer of trust that enhances its diplomatic appeal.

References

Achary, A., & Albuquerque, D. D. (2024). Artificial intelligence in the tourism and hospitality industry. In V. K. Shukla, A. Verma, & J. P. G. Lacap (Eds.), *Artificial intelligence for smart technology in the hospitality and tourism industry* (pp. 105–117). Apple Academic Press.

Arabiun, A., Hosseini, E., Mahmoodi, K., & Mohsen, B. (2023). An investigation of the socio-cultural impacts of the digital transformation in developed, developing, and middle: Africa and Asia pacific. In M. Joshi, M. Brahmi, L. Aldieri, & C. P. Vinci (Eds.), *Exploring business ecosystems and innovation capacity building in global economics* (pp. 112–130). IGI Global.

Ayodele, O. (2021). The digital transformation of diplomacy: Implications for the African union and continental diplomacy. *South African Journal of International Affairs*, *28*(3), 379–401.

Beşirova, S. (2024). Effect of sponsored social media advertisements and word-of-mouth communication on consumer purchasing behavior in tourism: A case study of Facebook. *Journal of Tourism Theory and Research*, *10*(1), 23–31.

Brobst, J. A. (2024). Legal strategies to preserve the natural and cultural heritage of space. In B. B. Sandeepa (Ed.), *Space tourism* (pp. 133–152). Routledge India.

Carayannis, E. G. (2013). Innovation diplomacy as driver of democracy, innovation and development: The case of Greece. In E. G. Carayannis (Ed.), *The innovation union in Europe* (pp. 123–143). Edward Elgar Publishing.

Cardoso, I. B. F., & Ruiz, T. C. D. (2021). Smart tourism destinations - A case study of Seoul, South Korea. *Applied Tourism*, *6*(1), 36–44.

Cheer, J. M., Lapointe, D., Mostafanezhad, M., & Jamal, T. (2021). Global tourism in crisis: Conceptual frameworks for research and practice. *Journal of Tourism Futures*, *7*(3), 278–294.

Chowdhury, A. T., Newaz, M., Saha, P., Pedersen, S., Khan, M. S., & Chowdhury, M. E. (2024). Use of artificial intelligence in the surveillance of seasonal respiratory infections. In *Surveillance, prevention, and control of infectious diseases: An AI perspective* (pp. 219–237). Springer Nature.

Congden, S. W., Bertels, H. M., Desplaces, D., & Drew, T. (2024). Space tourism: An industry with a future? *CAS Journal*, 1–11.

De Luca, V., Marcantonio, G., Barba, M. C., & De Paolis, L. T. (2022). A virtual tour for the promotion of tourism of the city of Bari. *Information*, *13*(7), 339–349.

Demaj, E., Hasimja, A., & Rahimi, A. (2021). Digital nomadism as a new flexible working approach: Making Tirana the next European hotspot for digital nomads. In *The flexible workplace: Coworking and other modern workplace transformations* (pp. 231–257). Springer International Publishing.

Demir, Ş. Ş., & Demir, M. (2023). Professionals' perspectives on ChatGPT in the tourism industry: Does it inspire awe or concern? *Journal of Tourism Theory and Research*, *9*(2), 61–77.

Demir, M., & Demir, Ş. Ş. (2024). Digital technologies and applications in tourist guidance: The dilemma between adopting innovations and career concerns. *Journal of Human Resources in Hospitality & Tourism*, 1–25.

Demir, M., Yaşar, E., & Demir, Ş. Ş. (2023). Digital transformation and human resources planning: The mediating role of innovation. *Journal of Hospitality and Tourism Technology*, *14*(1), 21–36.

Ergen, F. D. (2020). Artırılmış ve sanal gerçeklik teknolojilerinin Isparta ilinin kültürel miras alanlarında uygulanabilirliği üzerine bir literatür taraması. *Journal of Tourism Theory and Research*, *6*(1), 62–74.

Gerlitz, L., Meyer, C., & Prause, G. (2021). Marketing and branding strategy for the South Baltic Sea Region: Reinforcing regional innovation in SMEs through cross-border collaboration models in the age of transformation. *Entrepreneurship and Sustainability Issues*, (4), 467–478.

Gričar, S., Šugar, V., Baldigara, T., & Folgieri, R. (2023). Potential integration of metaverse, non-fungible tokens and sentiment analysis in quantitative tourism economic analysis. *Journal of Risk and Financial Management*, *17*(1), 15–24.

Grincheva, N. (2024). The future of cultural diplomacy. In Y. Jung, N. Vakharia, & M. Vecco (Eds.), *The Oxford handbook of arts and cultural management* (pp. 183–202). Oxford University Press.

Grincheva, N. (2013). Cultural diplomacy 2.0: Challenges and opportunities in museum international practices. *Museum & Society*, *11*(1), 39–49.

Hsu, C. T., Lin, Y. C., Yao, K. C., & Ma, P. C. (2024). A study on the performance of B&B operations is conducted in sustainable tourism. *Sustainability*, *16*(18), 1–12.

Jiang, Y. (2017). *Social media and e-diplomacy in China*. Palgrave Macmillan.

Jin, D. Y. (2024). The rise of digital platforms as a soft power apparatus in the New Korean Wave era. *Communication and the Public*, *9*(2), 161–177.

Jiwasiddi, A., Schlagwein, D., Cahalane, M., Cecez-Kecmanovic, D., Leong, C., & Ractham, P. (2024). Digital nomadism as a new part of the visitor economy: The case of the "digital nomad capital" Chiang Mai, Thailand. *Information Systems Journal*, *34*(5), 1493–1535.

Kalbaska, N., Janowski, T., Estevez, E., & Cantoni, L. (2017). When digital government matters for tourism: A stakeholder analysis. *Information Technology & Tourism*, *17*, 315–333.

Karimipour, Y. L., & Abdi, A. (2015). The impact of geopolitical tourism on convergence of space political units (Case Study: Iran-Azarbayejan). *Journal of Tourism Hospitality Research*, *4*(1), 59–75.

Lee, K. C. (2020). Neglected agents: Elucidating Chinese social actors' role in Thai-Sino smart city diplomacy. *International Journal of China Studies*, *11*(1), 1–9.

Lord, G. D., & Lord, B. (2017). *Manual of digital museum planning*. Rowman & Littlefield.

Mikac, R., & Kravaršćan, K. (2021). Croatian tourism sector and crisis management-a case study related to the COVID-19 pandemic. *Tourism: An International Interdisciplinary Journal*, *69*(4), 611–629.

Nag, A., & Mishra, S. (2024). Sustainable competitive advantage in heritage tourism: Leveraging cultural legacy in a data-driven world. In R. P. Singh Kaurav & V. Mishra (Eds.), *Review of technologies and disruptive business strategies* (Vol. 3, pp. 137–162). Emerald Publishing Limited.

Negassa, S. B. (2024). Tourism diplomacy: Fostering economic development through global connectivity. In A. B. Basnur (Ed.), *Tourism: For global connectivity and economic development* (pp. 68–75). Paramedia Komunikatama.

Pawar, R., & Singh, I. (2023). *The virtual vanguards: Exploring the evolution of digital diplomacy*. Pencil.

Polkowska, M. (2021). Space tourism challenges. *Review European & Comparative Law*, *45*, 153–182.

Popescu, D., Dragomir, D., Comes, R., Popescu, S., Dragomir, M., & Neamțu, C. (2020). *Enhancing management and marketing in cultural heritage by using new technologies. The best romanian management studies 2017–2018* (Vol. 21). Trivent Publishing.

Ranteallo, I. C., & Andilolo, I. R. (2017). Food representation and media: Experiencing culinary tourism through foodgasm and foodporn. In A. Saufi, I. Andilolo, N. Othman, & A. Lew (Eds.), *Balancing development and sustainability in tourism destinations: Proceedings of the tourism outlook conference 2015* (pp. 117–127). Springer.

Recuero-Virto, N., & Arróspide, C. V. (2024). Culinary destination enchantment: The strategic interplay of local gastronomy in regional tourism development. *International Journal of Gastronomy and Food Science*, *36*, 1–11.

Salem, F. (2017). Social media and the internet of things towards data-driven policymaking in the Arab world: Potential, limits and concerns. In *The arab social media report*. MBR School of Government. https://ssrn.com/abstract=2911832

Saliu, H. (2022). Rethinking media diplomacy and public diplomacy towards a new concept: Digital media diplomacy. *On-line Journal Modelling the New Europe*, (39), 4–24.

Seccardini, G., & Desmoulins, L. (2023). Flawed public diplomacy: When Croatia Instagram Riviera narrative destination branding ignores dark tourism amateurs. *Journal of Communication Management*, *27*(2), 277–292.

Sigala, M. (2020). Tourism and COVID-19: Impacts and implications for advancing and resetting industry and research. *Journal of Business Research*, *117*, 312–321.

Silva, M. J., Durão, M., & De Lemos, F. F. (2023). Leading digital transformation in tourism and hospitality. In J. Marques & R. P. Marques (Eds.), *Digital transformation of the hotel industry: Theories, practices, and global challenges* (pp. 247–262). Springer International Publishing.

Simonin, B. L. (2008). Nation branding and public diplomacy: Challenges and opportunities. *Fletcher Forum of World Affairs*, *32*(3), 19–27.

Visvizi, A., Troisi, O., & Grimaldi, M. (2023). *Big data and decision-making: Applications and uses in the public and private sector*. Emerald Publishing Limited.

Whitaker, A., Bracegirdle, A., De Menil, S., Gitlitz, M. A., & Saltos, L. (2021). Art, antiquities, and blockchain: New approaches to the restitution of cultural heritage. *International Journal of Cultural Policy*, *27*(3), 312–329.

Yaşar, E., Demir, M., & Cobanoglu, C. (2024). Big data analytic capabilities, intrapreneurship, and service innovation behaviors: A moderated mediation model. *Service Industries Journal*, 1–25.

Yfantis, V., & Ntalianis, K. (2022). Exploring the potential adoption of metaverse in government. In I. J. Jacob, S. Kolandapalayam Shanmugam, & I. Izonin (Eds.), *Data intelligence and cognitive informatics: Proceedings of ICDICI 2022* (pp. 815–824). Springer Nature Singapore.

Zhanibek, A., Abazov, R., & Khazbulatov, A. (2022). Digital transformation of a country's image: The case of the Astana international finance centre in Kazakhstan. *Virtual Economics*, *5*(2), 71–94.

Zugasti, J. E. S. (2019). Casa México: Promotion, innovation and cultural diplomacy in south by Southwest (SXSW). *Revista Mexicana de Política Exterior*, (117), 85–98.

Chapter 9

Sustainable Environmental Management Through Tourism Diplomacy: Strategic Issues for Global Cooperation

Abstract

Tourism diplomacy in advancing sustainable environmental management has a critical role in fostering global cooperation. It underscores tourism's dual capacity as both a contributor to and a solution for environmental challenges, particularly in addressing climate change and carbon emissions. Key focus areas include the diplomatic potential of tourism in promoting carbon reduction strategies, protecting biodiversity and natural heritage, and managing pollution and waste. It further explores the impact of tourism on water resources and transboundary air and marine pollution, emphasizing the necessity of strategic frameworks for sustainable resource management. Challenges such as achieving global consensus, balancing economic interests with environmental priorities, and overcoming operational barriers are discussed alongside emerging opportunities for collaboration. By leveraging tourism diplomacy as a tool for international cooperation, the chapter highlights pathways for aligning environmental objectives with broader sustainability goals, offering insights into innovative strategies and diplomatic interventions. Through an integrated approach, this study contributes to understanding how tourism diplomacy can drive actionable solutions to environmental issues, ensuring a more sustainable future for global tourism.

Keywords: Sustainable tourism diplomacy; carbon emissions reduction; biodiversity conservation; pollution management; water resource sustainability

Tourism Diplomacy, 175–199

Copyright © 2025 Mahmut Demir and Şirvan Şen Demir
Published under exclusive licence by Emerald Publishing Limited

doi:10.1108/978-1-83708-676-420251009

1. Introduction

In an era of unprecedented environmental challenges, sustainable environmental management has become crucial to global governance, particularly within tourism. As one of the largest and fastest-growing sectors worldwide, tourism significantly impacts the environment, often triggering climate change, loss of biodiversity, pollution, and the depletion of water resources. These issues are not confined to national borders, necessitating a cooperative approach through tourism diplomacy to ensure the sustainability of natural resources and the preservation of cultural and natural heritage. Tourism increases carbon emissions through transportation modes such as aviation and cruise travel (De Jong et al., 2019). The industry's growing carbon footprint exacerbates global warming, posing risks to vulnerable ecosystems and communities reliant on tourism. International cooperation is essential to develop and implement policies that promote sustainable travel options, incentivize low-carbon technologies, and encourage eco-conscious behavior among travelers.

The protection of biodiversity and natural heritage is intrinsically linked to sustainable tourism. Tourism activities can lead to habitat degradation, species extinction, and the erosion of cultural heritage, particularly in high-traffic areas (Ishwaran, 2004). Promoting biodiversity conservation through tourism diplomacy can facilitate the establishment of international agreements and frameworks aimed at protecting endangered species and preserving UNESCO World Heritage sites. Such efforts not only safeguard natural ecosystems but also enhance the cultural and aesthetic value that attracts tourists to these regions.

Tourism is also a significant source of pollution, particularly in waste generation and resource depletion. Single-use plastics and inadequate waste management pose severe environmental threats, especially in popular tourist destinations. Effective tourism diplomacy can drive initiatives that promote zero-waste tourism practices, enhance recycling efforts, and establish international protocols to reduce pollution (Luo & Yun, 2023). Countries can protect their natural environments by fostering collaborative solutions to waste management while ensuring sustainable tourism growth.

Tourism can pressure water resources in water-scarce regions, leading to competition with local communities and ecosystems. Sustainable water management strategies are critical to balancing the needs of tourism and local populations (Koff et al., 2020). Tourism diplomacy can facilitate the development of international agreements focused on reducing water consumption and promoting efficient water use in the tourism sector, particularly in areas facing significant water scarcity.

Air and marine pollution from tourism activities, such as cruise and air travel, often have transboundary effects that threaten ecosystems beyond national borders (Yoon, 2006). Addressing these challenges requires robust international collaboration to develop regulations and best practices to minimize pollution. Tourism diplomacy can play a pivotal role in fostering partnerships and coordinating efforts to combat transboundary pollution, ensuring a healthier environment for current and future generations (Fig. 15).

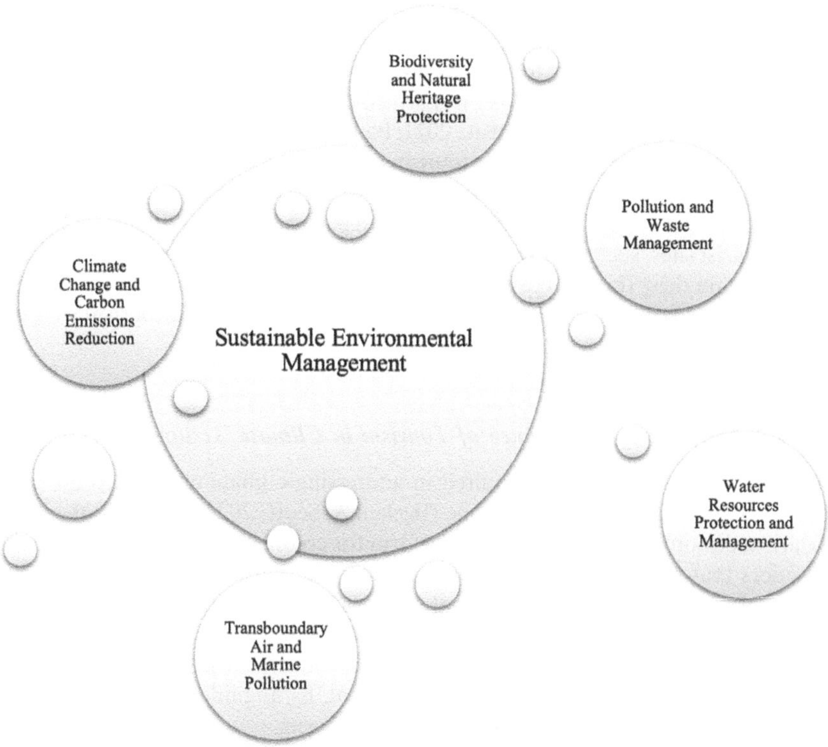

Fig. 15. Global Cooperation for Environmental Issues.

2. Climate Change and Carbon Emissions Reduction in Sustainable Tourism Diplomacy

Tourism is a global industry with complex environmental impacts, contributing to local economies while posing significant environmental challenges. One of the most critical issues is tourism's role in exacerbating climate change, primarily through greenhouse gas (GHG) emissions from air and land transportation. As climate change intensifies, it threatens natural environments, biodiversity, and weather stability – essential to tourism's sustainability. This predicament highlights the need for a diplomatic approach to encouraging international cooperation in reducing carbon emissions within the tourism industry. Countries can work together to address tourism's environmental impact and encourage a shift toward sustainable travel models by using tourism diplomacy to promote eco-friendly policies and practices.

2.1 Tourism and Carbon Emissions

Tourism accounts for a substantial share of global carbon emissions, primarily from transportation. According to the United Nations World Tourism Organization (UNWTO), tourism contributes approximately 8% of global carbon emissions, with air travel alone responsible for nearly 40% of this footprint. Land transportation – especially private vehicles and diesel-fueled buses – also contributes significantly. These emissions are linked to various adverse effects, including global warming, sea-level rise, and biodiversity loss, jeopardizing the natural assets that make many destinations attractive (Higham et al., 2021; Platts et al., 2023). The impact of climate change on tourism is cyclical: while tourism activities accelerate climate change, the resulting environmental degradation diminishes tourism's long-term viability (Apriliani & Dina, 2024; Zhang et al., 2024). In particular, climate change threatens iconic tourist sites, such as coral reefs, beaches, and alpine ecosystems. Destinations dependent on these fragile ecosystems face both economic losses and environmental challenges, underlining the need for collective action to reduce tourism's carbon footprint.

2.2 The Diplomatic Importance of Tourism in Climate Action

International cooperation is required in addressing climate change, as no single country can mitigate its effects alone (Becken & Scott, 2024; Wilby et al., 2023). Tourism diplomacy offers a unique platform for countries to promote sustainable practices that reduce carbon emissions collectively. Through tourism diplomacy, countries can negotiate international policies that prioritize the reduction of tourism-related carbon emissions and foster commitments to sustainable tourism practices. Moreover, tourism diplomacy can catalyze the implementation of global frameworks, such as the Paris Agreement, by aligning the tourism sector's goals with national and international climate targets.

Countries with robust tourism industries can be pivotal in promoting eco-friendly transportation solutions and other sustainable initiatives. Tourism diplomacy facilitates cross-border partnerships that foster innovation in sustainable transportation, encourage the use of renewable energy, and support carbon offset initiatives in tourism (Hamida, 2024; Scott et al., 2016). For example, agreements could incentivize airlines to adopt more fuel-efficient fleets or promote alternative transport forms, such as high-speed rail networks, for regional travel. The diplomatic importance of these efforts lies in their potential to set a global standard for sustainable tourism and demonstrate a commitment to reducing the industry's environmental footprint.

2.3 Strategies for Carbon Emissions Reduction Through Tourism Diplomacy

Promoting Sustainable Transportation Alternatives: Encouraging environmentally friendly transportation is a key strategy for reducing tourism's carbon footprint (Manfredi Sánchez & Seoane Pérez, 2021; McGaurr & Lester, 2018). Tourism diplomacy can foster regional agreements supporting the development and promotion of alternative transportation systems, such as high-speed rail and electric buses, which offer lower emissions than traditional air and land travel. Countries with well-established high-speed rail networks, such as Japan and many European nations, could share knowledge and technology with countries aiming to implement similar systems. Bilateral or multilateral agreements can facilitate joint infrastructure projects, such as international rail networks, to offer alternatives to short-haul flights.

Encouraging Carbon Offset Programs and Sustainable Practices: Carbon offsetting mitigates tourism-related emissions. Tourism diplomacy can significantly standardize industry carbon offset practices, enabling tourists and businesses to engage in carbon-neutral travel. Diplomatic initiatives promote cross-national partnerships to invest in developing countries' reforestation projects, renewable energy, and carbon offset programs (Negassa, 2024; Platts et al., 2023). Additionally, tourism diplomacy can push for certification programs that recognize hotels, airlines, and tour operators for reducing their carbon footprints. By promoting recognized certifications internationally, countries can raise awareness among tourists about eco-friendly options and encourage more responsible travel choices.

Developing Sustainable Tourism Policies and Frameworks: Tourism diplomacy supports the development of global and regional policies that set carbon reduction targets for the tourism industry to ensure a coordinated approach (Apriliani & Dina, 2024; Becken & Scott, 2024). Diplomatic platforms like the UNWTO or the International Civil Aviation Organization (ICAO) can be central in facilitating discussions on tourism's environmental impact (Demir, 2017). Through diplomatic engagement, countries could agree on standardized frameworks that integrate carbon emission targets, environmental protections, and sustainable tourism practices. These policies could also incentivize companies to implement sustainable practices, aligning tourism with broader national and international environmental goals.

Advocating for Climate Education and Awareness among Tourists: Education and awareness are not ignored when changing travel behaviors. Tourism diplomacy can drive global campaigns to raise awareness about tourism's environmental impact and promote responsible travel practices. Initiatives like the "Travel for Climate Action" campaign could educate tourists on reducing their carbon footprint by choosing eco-friendly accommodations, reducing plastic use, and supporting local sustainable tourism businesses. Diplomatically endorsed programs help reshape tourist expectations, making eco-conscious choices a normative aspect of travel (Manfredi Sánchez & Seoane Pérez, 2021; Negassa, 2024).

2.4 Challenges in Achieving Global Cooperation

Despite tourism diplomacy's potential to promote sustainable practices, achieving consensus on carbon emission reduction presents several challenges (Higham et al., 2021; Negassa, 2024; Wilby et al., 2023). Economic dependence on tourism can make countries reluctant to impose restrictions that may deter tourists. Developing countries, in particular, often prioritize tourism for economic growth and job creation, which may complicate commitments to stringent environmental policies. Additionally, varying levels of technological development affect countries' ability to invest in sustainable transportation infrastructure and eco-friendly tourism alternatives.

Balancing the diverse interests of countries with varying economic priorities requires careful negotiation and compromise. However, tourism diplomacy has served as a bridge, fostering understanding and collaboration between developed and developing countries (Platts et al., 2023; Scott et al., 2016). International funding mechanisms, such as climate finance, could be incorporated into diplomatic discussions to support sustainable tourism initiatives in lower-income nations. This approach can enhance global cooperation, ensuring that environmental goals do not come at the expense of economic development.

2.5 Opportunities for Future Collaboration

The ongoing development of digital technologies could reduce the demand for high-emission travel by providing alternative ways to experience destinations. Diplomatically backed partnerships could support the development of virtual tourism options, reducing air travel demand while promoting tourism. Another opportunity lies in the expansion of renewable energy sources for transportation. Tourism diplomacy can foster cooperation on clean energy innovation, encouraging the use of electric vehicles, biofuels, and other low-carbon alternatives within the tourism sector. By prioritizing sustainability in tourism recovery strategies, countries can address both climate change and economic resilience, fostering a tourism model that benefits both the environment and local communities.

3. Biodiversity and Natural Heritage Protection in Sustainable Tourism Diplomacy

Biodiversity and natural heritage are the bedrock of many tourist destinations, drawing visitors worldwide to experience unique ecosystems, wildlife, and cultural environments. However, tourism's growing footprint, especially in ecologically sensitive areas, poses a significant threat to biodiversity and natural habitats. As tourism activities intensify, the resulting pressures on flora, fauna, and their habitats can lead to environmental degradation and, in severe cases, permanent loss of biodiversity. This critical issue highlights the need for international cooperation in managing tourism's environmental impact and fostering diplomatic efforts that promote biodiversity conservation. Tourism diplomacy plays a strategic role by advancing global agreements, conservation policies, and collaborative projects that protect biodiversity while promoting sustainable tourism practices.

3.1 Tourism and Its Impact on Biodiversity

The expansion of tourism activities often coincides with increased environmental pressures on natural habitats (Adhikari & Dahal, 2019; Carter & Turnock, 2002).

Popular tourist sites, such as coral reefs, wildlife reserves, and heritage sites, can experience ecological stress from the influx of visitors. These impacts may include habitat disruption, pollution, waste generation, and the introduction of invasive species – all of which endanger the biodiversity that attracts tourists in the first place. In particular, constructing tourism infrastructure, such as hotels, roads, and recreational facilities, can result in habitat fragmentation, altering ecosystems and disrupting wildlife patterns.

Tourism's impact on biodiversity is especially concerning in biodiversity hotspots – regions with exceptional levels of endemic species also under threat. As tourism activities intensify in these areas, the ecological balance is often disturbed, leading to the loss of species and the degradation of ecosystems. Marine biodiversity is equally vulnerable, especially as coastal and marine tourism grows (Wang et al., 2023). Given tourism's environmental impact, a coordinated approach to biodiversity conservation is essential to minimize these adverse effects.

3.2 The Diplomatic Importance of Biodiversity Protection

Preserving biodiversity is a global challenge that requires cooperation across borders. Tourism diplomacy offers a valuable platform for fostering international agreements and conservation initiatives that protect biodiversity while promoting sustainable tourism. This approach helps protect biodiversity and ensures that natural assets remain viable for future generations of tourists. Tourism diplomacy plays a strategic role in advocating for international conservation efforts, such as protecting UNESCO World Heritage Sites, establishing transboundary conservation areas, and supporting marine protected areas (Hohl, 2013; Parnwell, 2010). Through collaborative initiatives, countries can strengthen their commitment to biodiversity conservation and address the shared challenges of managing high-traffic tourist sites. Furthermore, tourism diplomacy can foster partnerships between developed and developing countries, promoting knowledge-sharing and capacity-building to ensure that conservation practices are both practical and inclusive. This diplomatic emphasis on biodiversity protection underscores the importance of collective responsibility, highlighting the need for sustainable practices that balance tourism development with ecological preservation (Adhikari & Dahal, 2019; Hohl, 2013).

3.3 Strategies for Biodiversity and Natural Heritage Protection Through Tourism Diplomacy

Establishing and Expanding Protected Areas: Protected areas, including UNESCO World Heritage Sites, national parks, and marine reserves, are among the most effective tools for safeguarding biodiversity. Tourism diplomacy encourages international commitments to expand and enforce these protected zones, ensuring that tourism-related activities undisturbed critical habitats (Sofield & Li, 2013; Taylor, 2015). For instance, countries could collaborate on cross-border conservation areas, allowing wildlife to roam freely without disrupting international boundaries. By negotiating agreements that designate specific sites as conservation priorities, tourism diplomacy can help prevent habitat fragmentation and preserve biodiversity in high-traffic tourist regions. Tourism diplomacy supports the creation of buffer zones around protected areas, reducing tourism's ecological impact (Carter & Turnock, 2002; Wang et al., 2023). Buffer zones serve as transitional areas where sustainable tourism practices are encouraged, helping to relieve pressure on core conservation zones. Through diplomatic channels, countries can negotiate agreements on the shared management of these buffer zones, fostering a balanced approach to tourism that respects ecological boundaries.

Promoting Sustainable Tourism Practices and Certifications: Sustainable tourism practices minimize tourism's impact on biodiversity (Adhikari & Dahal, 2019; Wang et al., 2023). Tourism diplomacy can facilitate the development and promotion of eco-certifications that recognize and reward businesses and destinations committed to environmental stewardship. These certifications, such as the Global Sustainable Tourism Council (GSTC) certification, encourage hotels, tour operators, and other tourism stakeholders to adopt eco-friendly practices that protect biodiversity. By promoting these certifications through diplomatic channels, countries can set industry standards that promote responsible tourism and raise awareness among tourists about the importance of environmental conservation. Their ecological footprint is reflected in their visits to natural heritage sites (Carter & Turnock, 2002; Hohl, 2013). Such initiatives can promote responsible behaviors, such as respecting wildlife, staying on designated paths, and avoiding single-use plastics. Diplomatic efforts can also emphasize the importance of sustainable tourism education, ensuring that tourists understand their role in protecting biodiversity during their travels.

Supporting Marine Protected Areas (MPAs) and Coastal Conservation: Marine tourism remarkably impacts coastal biodiversity, affecting coral reefs, fish populations, and aquatic ecosystems. Tourism diplomacy promotes establishing and expanding MPAs, which protect marine habitats from overfishing, pollution, and other tourism-related threats. By advocating for MPAs, tourism diplomacy encourages countries to preserve marine biodiversity while promoting sustainable tourism practices in coastal regions (Hohl, 2013; Parnwell, 2010). Diplomatic initiatives also encourage collaboration between nations with shared coastlines, fostering joint efforts to protect marine ecosystems and enforce sustainable practices. Cross-border partnerships could involve agreements on fishing quotas, pollution controls, and marine tourism regulations that minimize ecological disturbances. For example, countries with shared coral reefs could collaborate on reef restoration projects, ensuring the longevity of these critical habitats for both marine life and tourism.

Encouraging Community Involvement in Conservation Efforts: Local communities are essential to biodiversity conservation, as they often profoundly connect to their natural surroundings. Tourism diplomacy can promote community-based conservation initiatives, empowering local populations to actively manage tourism's environmental impact (Parnwell, 2010; Sofield & Li, 2013). By involving communities in conservation efforts, countries can ensure that tourism development aligns with local needs and cultural values, fostering a sense of ownership and responsibility for biodiversity protection. Diplomatically facilitated initiatives include capacity-building programs that provide local communities with the skills and resources to manage sustainable tourism enterprises. Tourism diplomacy reduces the pressure on natural resources while generating economic opportunities by supporting eco-tourism ventures owned and operated by local populations. Additionally, tourism diplomacy can promote indigenous knowledge-sharing, incorporating traditional practices that support biodiversity conservation into modern tourism strategies.

3.4 Challenges to Global Biodiversity Conservation Through Tourism

Achieving practical international cooperation on biodiversity conservation presents several challenges (Carter & Turnock, 2002; Hohl, 2013; Wang et al., 2023). One of the main obstacles is the economic reliance on tourism, particularly in developing countries where tourism is a primary source of income. Balancing the need for economic growth with environmental preservation can create tensions, as some countries may prioritize short-term tourism revenue over long-term conservation goals. Additionally, differences in environmental policies and enforcement capabilities can hinder collaborative conservation efforts, as some countries lack the resources to implement and monitor conservation measures effectively.

Another challenge is ensuring equitable access to conservation funding. Developing countries often depend on international assistance to fund conservation initiatives, which can create disparities in conservation outcomes. Tourism diplomacy can address these challenges by promoting climate finance and conservation grants that support biodiversity protection in low-income countries. Tourism diplomacy can also help level the playing field by advocating for fair resource allocation, ensuring that all nations can actively contribute to global biodiversity conservation.

3.5 Opportunities for Future Collaboration

Tourism diplomacy offers significant opportunities for future collaboration in biodiversity conservation (Hohl, 2013; Taylor, 2015). The rapid advancement of technology provides innovative solutions for monitoring and managing tourism's impact on natural habitats. Countries can share data on biodiversity hotspots through diplomatic channels, track real-time environmental changes, and implement data-driven conservation strategies. Collaborative research on eco-tourism models and environmental protection technologies can also enhance the tourism industry's sustainability, offering scalable solutions that reduce tourism's ecological footprint. Another opportunity lies in integrating biodiversity conservation into international tourism recovery plans postpandemic. Tourism diplomacy can strategically ensure that recovery initiatives prioritize sustainability, promoting biodiversity-friendly practices as the industry rebuilds. This approach can foster a tourism model that supports economic growth and preserves natural assets, creating a balanced path for tourism and environmental conservation.

4. Pollution and Waste Management in Sustainable Tourism Diplomacy

Pollution and waste management are among the most pressing environmental challenges in the tourism industry as global tourism expands. In popular tourist destinations, the accumulation of waste, particularly from single-use materials, has led to significant environmental degradation. From polluted beaches to disrupted ecosystems, tourism-related waste has far-reaching consequences for natural habitats, marine environments, and the communities that rely on these ecosystems. Therefore, waste management is not merely a local issue but a global concern that necessitates international cooperation. Tourism diplomacy is a strategic approach to tackling pollution and promoting sustainable waste management practices worldwide. By fostering international protocols, zero-waste initiatives, and eco-friendly policies, tourism diplomacy can help reduce the environmental impact of tourism and cultivate a culture of sustainability.

Tourism, Pollution, and the Global Waste Crisis: Tourism generates substantial waste, especially in high-traffic destinations where tourists rely on single-use items for convenience. Plastic water bottles, food packaging, and disposable cutlery are among the most common pollutants in these areas, contributing to the global waste crisis. The environmental impact is particularly severe in coastal and island destinations, where tourism-related waste often ends up in the oceans, harming marine life and contaminating ecosystems (Agamuthu et al., 2019; Wu, 2022). Additionally, inadequate waste management infrastructure in many popular destinations exacerbates the problem, as local systems struggle to process the influx of waste generated by tourists. The environmental impact of tourism-related waste extends beyond local ecosystems, affecting global biodiversity and causing microplastic pollution. Microplastics, originating from the breakdown of plastic waste, have infiltrated food chains and ecosystems worldwide, posing health risks to wildlife and humans. As waste pollution escalates, the need for coordinated efforts to manage waste sustainably becomes more urgent (Duraku & Nasufi, 2023; Teczke et al., 2022). Tourism diplomacy can be critical in addressing these issues by fostering international collaboration and promoting policies that prioritize pollution reduction and sustainable waste management.

The Diplomatic Importance of Pollution and Waste Management: The challenge of pollution and waste management in tourism transcends national boundaries, highlighting the need for a collaborative, diplomatic approach (Fuller et al., 2022; Talukder & Hoque, 2025). Tourism diplomacy provides a platform for nations to collectively address tourism's environmental impact, fostering cooperation to reduce waste and promote sustainable practices. This diplomatic approach aligns with the United Nations' Sustainable Development Goals (SDGs), particularly those focused on responsible consumption, production, and life below water. Through tourism diplomacy, countries can work together to establish international protocols, share best practices, and support zero-waste tourism initiatives that minimize the industry's environmental footprint. Tourism diplomacy can encourage destinations to adopt effective and sustainable waste management strategies by advancing global waste reduction and pollution control agreements. Collaborative efforts also bridge the gap between developed and developing countries, ensuring all nations have the resources and knowledge to implement sustainable waste management practices (Hassan et al., 2024; Roumiani et al., 2023). In this way, tourism diplomacy underscores the importance of shared responsibility, recognizing that pollution is a global issue that requires a unified response.

4.1 Strategies for Pollution Reduction and Waste Management Through Tourism Diplomacy

Promoting International Protocols on Waste Reduction: Establishing international protocols for waste reduction is essential for managing tourism's environmental impact (Luo & Yun, 2023; Pata et al., 2024). Tourism diplomacy can support the development of global agreements that set standards for waste management, such as limiting the use of single-use items in tourist destinations. For instance, countries could negotiate agreements to ban plastic bags, straws, and other disposable items in tourism hotspots, encouraging travelers and providers to adopt sustainable alternatives. Tourism diplomacy can foster partnerships that facilitate waste reduction in cross-border destinations, such as shared natural parks or coastal regions. By aligning waste management standards and practices, neighboring countries can create cohesive environmental policies that protect shared ecosystems. This diplomatic approach promotes a holistic view of pollution management, recognizing that waste reduction efforts in one country can benefit ecosystems beyond its borders.

Supporting Zero-Waste Tourism Initiatives: Zero-waste tourism is a sustainable approach to eliminate waste generation by promoting reusable and eco-friendly alternatives (Fuller et al., 2022; Onyena et al., 2021). Tourism diplomacy can be pivotal in advocating for zero-waste initiatives and encouraging countries to adopt policies that minimize waste production in tourism. Diplomatic efforts could include promoting the use of refillable water stations, encouraging eco-friendly packaging, and supporting local businesses that prioritize sustainability. Tourism diplomacy can also help raise awareness of zero-waste practices among tourists, fostering a culture of sustainability within the industry. It can also inspire tourists to reduce their environmental impact by promoting international campaigns that educate travelers on responsible waste management. For instance, countries could collaborate on initiatives encouraging tourists to bring reusable water bottles, avoid single-use plastics, and dispose of waste responsibly. Such initiatives help shift public perceptions of tourism, positioning sustainability as a central value in the travel experience.

Enhancing Recycling and Waste Management Infrastructure: Effective waste management requires robust infrastructure, including recycling facilities and waste collection systems (Roumiani et al., 2023; Wu, 2022). Tourism diplomacy can support the development of waste management infrastructure in countries that lack the resources to handle large volumes of tourism-related waste. By fostering international partnerships, tourism diplomacy can provide technical assistance, funding, and expertise to help developing countries build sustainable waste management systems. For instance, developed countries could offer support through recycling technology or waste processing facilities, helping tourist destinations improve their waste management capabilities. Through diplomatic initiatives, countries can also share best practices in waste management, offering guidance on implementing recycling programs, managing organic waste, and promoting circular economy principles. Such partnerships enhance the resilience of tourism-dependent communities, ensuring that they can manage waste sustainably even as tourism numbers increase.

Encouraging Eco-Friendly Tourism Accommodations and Services: Tourism diplomacy can promote eco-friendly standards for accommodations and tourism services, encouraging businesses to reduce waste and adopt sustainable practices. By supporting green certification programs, tourism diplomacy can incentivize hotels, restaurants, and tour operators to minimize waste and reduce their environmental footprint. Certifications such as Green Key, EarthCheck, and other eco-labels encourage businesses to adopt waste reduction strategies, such as composting organic waste, eliminating single-use plastics, and implementing recycling programs.

Diplomatic initiatives could promote the adoption of these certifications globally, making them a standard in the tourism industry (Talukder & Hoque, 2025; Teczke et al., 2022). Furthermore, tourism diplomacy can support international campaigns that raise travelers' awareness about the benefits of choosing eco-certified accommodations. By highlighting eco-friendly tourism options, tourism diplomacy fosters consumer demand for sustainable practices, creating a market incentive for businesses to prioritize waste reduction.

Implementing Environmental Education and Awareness Campaigns: Education is a powerful tool in changing behaviors and reducing waste. Tourism diplomacy can support environmental education campaigns that target tourists and local communities, raising awareness about the impact of waste pollution on ecosystems (Duraku & Nasufi, 2023; Hassan et al., 2024). Diplomatic efforts can encourage countries to implement awareness programs in popular tourist areas, educating visitors on responsible waste disposal and protecting natural environments. Tourism diplomacy promotes global initiatives such as International Coastal Clean-up Day, World Environment Day, and other events that engage tourists and locals in environmental conservation activities. These initiatives help instill a sense of responsibility among travelers, fostering a culture of sustainability that extends beyond their vacation experience. By promoting awareness campaigns on a global scale, tourism diplomacy contributes to a collective understanding of waste management as a shared responsibility.

4.2 Challenges to Achieving Sustainable Waste Management in Tourism

Sustainable waste management in tourism faces several challenges, particularly in balancing economic growth with environmental preservation (Luo & Yun, 2023; Teczke et al., 2022). Developing countries, which often depend heavily on tourism revenue, may prioritize tourism development over environmental considerations, leading to inadequate waste management systems. The lack of standardized waste management policies and practices across countries makes implementing cohesive pollution reduction strategies challenging. While some nations have advanced recycling systems, others struggle to process even basic waste, resulting in significant environmental disparities. Another challenge lies in consumer behavior, as many tourists are unaware of the environmental impact of their actions. Addressing these challenges requires a collaborative approach that fosters a global culture of sustainability and encourages responsible travel behavior (Teczke et al., 2022; Wu, 2022). Tourism diplomacy can help bridge these gaps by promoting international cooperation and fostering a shared commitment to pollution reduction.

4.3 Opportunities for Future Collaboration in Pollution and Waste Management

Despite these challenges, tourism diplomacy offers significant opportunities for future collaboration in pollution reduction and waste management. As technology advances, new opportunities exist to integrate smart waste management systems in tourism destinations (Demir & Demir, 2024). For example, data-driven approaches to waste collection and sorting can enhance the efficiency of waste management systems, reducing pollution and supporting recycling efforts. Countries can improve their waste management practices by sharing technological innovations through diplomatic channels and minimizing tourism's environmental impact (Agamuthu et al., 2019; Pata et al., 2024; Talukder & Hoque, 2025). Another opportunity lies in integrating waste management into tourism recovery plans postpandemic (Teczke et al., 2022). Tourism diplomacy can encourage nations to rebuild their tourism industries with a focus on sustainability, prioritizing eco-friendly practices and reducing reliance on single-use plastics. Through international collaboration, countries can foster a tourism model that balances economic recovery with environmental responsibility, creating a more sustainable future for the industry.

5. Water Resources Protection and Management in Sustainable Tourism Diplomacy

Water resources, including tourism, are essential for sustaining life, ecosystems, and economic activities. However, tourism places significant pressure on these water resources, especially in areas with limited natural supplies. The water demands of hotels, resorts, golf courses, and recreational facilities can reduce availability for local communities and ecosystems, potentially leading to conflicts over water usage. As global tourism increases, addressing water scarcity becomes more urgent. This requires sustainable management and protection strategies to balance tourism demands with those of local populations and natural habitats. Tourism diplomacy serves as a platform to address this challenge by promoting international cooperation on sustainable water use policies and encouraging collaborative efforts to safeguard these resources. Through tourism diplomacy, countries can negotiate and implement agreements that improve water conservation, establish standards for sustainable water management in tourism, and promote policies prioritizing water efficiency. By encouraging responsible tourism practices, tourism diplomacy helps preserve water resources for future generations, benefiting both the tourism industry and the communities dependent on these vital resources.

5.1 The Impact of Tourism on Water Resources

Tourism activities, especially those involving high-consumption amenities, significantly demand water resources. Luxury accommodations, swimming pools, water parks, and golf courses often require large amounts of water, while the influx of tourists can strain local water supplies. In arid regions, where water resources are already limited, the extra demand from tourism worsens water scarcity, leading to conflicts between residents, agricultural needs, and tourism providers (Jacobs, 2002; Karimipour & Abdi, 2015). For instance, hotels may prioritize water access for guests in areas with high tourism demand, restricting water availability for local communities. Ecosystems can suffer from reduced water levels, affecting wildlife and vegetation essential for biodiversity and ecological balance.

Beyond direct consumption, tourism also causes water pollution, impacting water quality in surface and groundwater sources (Koff et al., 2020; Nirwandy & Awang, 2014). Untreated wastewater from tourism facilities, chemicals from swimming pools, and runoff from recreational areas can introduce contaminants into natural water sources, harming aquatic ecosystems and reducing the availability of clean water. Addressing these issues requires coordinated action to manage water use responsibly, minimize pollution, and promote sustainable practices across the tourism sector.

5.2 Diplomatic Importance of Water Resource Management in Tourism

Water scarcity is a global challenge that requires international collaboration, particularly as climate change continues to alter precipitation patterns and reduce water availability in certain regions (Vij et al., 2020; Wirsing & Jasparro, 2007). Tourism diplomacy provides a framework for countries to address shared water challenges, encouraging cooperation on water conservation policies and sustainable resource management practices. Through diplomatic efforts, countries can develop international agreements that prioritize water efficiency, establish guidelines for sustainable water use, and promote water conservation initiatives in tourism. These agreements align with the United Nations Sustainable Development Goals (SDGs), particularly SDG 6 (Clean Water and Sanitation), which seeks to ensure water availability and sustainable management for all.

Tourism diplomacy also highlights the shared responsibility of nations to protect water resources and emphasizes the need for sustainable tourism practices (Karimipour & Abdi, 2015; Zhang & Li, 2020). By fostering collaboration among countries with shared water basins or transboundary rivers, tourism diplomacy can help protect these resources from overexploitation and pollution. Moreover, diplomatic initiatives can encourage information-sharing on water-saving technologies, water management strategies, and best practices for reducing water consumption in tourism. Such collaborations promote a holistic approach to water resource management, recognizing that protecting water resources benefits the tourism industry and local communities (Fig. 16).

5.3 Strategies for Sustainable Water Resource Management Through Tourism Diplomacy

Promoting Water Conservation Agreements in Tourism: Tourism diplomacy supports the development of international agreements that promote water conservation in tourism destinations (Wirsing & Jasparro, 2007; Woldemaryam, 2020). For example, countries could negotiate protocols to reduce water consumption in high-traffic tourist areas, particularly water-scarce regions. These agreements could set water efficiency targets for tourism facilities, encourage

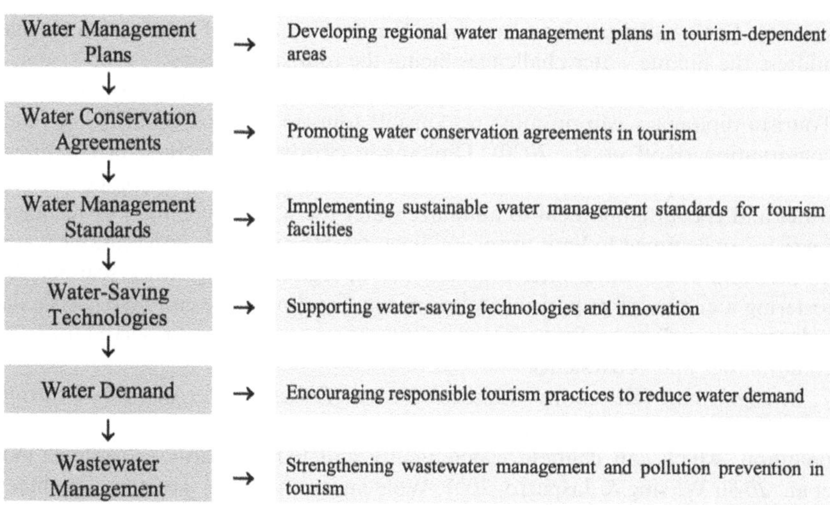

Fig. 16. Strategies for Sustainable Water Resource Management Through Tourism Diplomacy.

water-saving technologies, and establish guidelines for sustainable water use. Additionally, diplomatic efforts could encourage cross-border collaboration in regions with shared water resources, such as rivers or lakes that span multiple countries. By aligning water management strategies, neighboring countries can ensure that tourism does not deplete or degrade shared water resources.

Implementing Sustainable Water Management Standards for Tourism Facilities: Establishing sustainable water management standards is essential for reducing the tourism industry's impact on water resources (Koff et al., 2020; Xie et al., 2018). Tourism diplomacy can promote the adoption of internationally recognized water use standards, which could be integrated into certification programs for sustainable tourism. These standards may include requirements for water-efficient appliances, rainwater harvesting systems, and greywater recycling in hotels and resorts. Additionally, diplomatic efforts can encourage hotels and tourism operators to conduct regular water audits to identify areas where water consumption can be reduced. By promoting these standards globally, tourism diplomacy can help ensure that water efficiency becomes a core aspect of sustainable tourism.

Supporting Water-Saving Technologies and Innovation: Advancements in water-saving technologies offer promising solutions to reduce water consumption in tourism (Nirwandy & Awang, 2014; Zhang & Li, 2020). Tourism diplomacy can facilitate knowledge sharing about innovative water-saving technologies, such as low-flow showerheads, efficient irrigation systems, and desalination processes for water-scarce regions. By sharing expertise and resources, countries can support adopting these technologies in tourism facilities, reducing the industry's reliance on freshwater resources. Furthermore, diplomatic initiatives can promote research collaborations focused on water conservation innovations, encouraging countries to invest in technologies that enhance water efficiency and resilience to scarcity. Such collaborations can drive the development of new solutions that address the unique water challenges facing the tourism industry.

Encouraging Responsible Tourism Practices to Reduce Water Demand: Tourism diplomacy can promote responsible tourism practices prioritizing water conservation (Koff et al., 2020). Diplomatic efforts may include international awareness campaigns educating tourists about the importance of conserving water and encouraging them to minimize water use while traveling. For instance, tourists can be urged to limit towel and linen washing in hotels, use reusable water bottles, and avoid water-intensive activities in regions facing water scarcity. By fostering a culture of responsible tourism, tourism diplomacy can help reduce the industry's overall water footprint, ensuring water resources are preserved for local communities and ecosystems.

Strengthening Wastewater Management and Pollution Prevention in Tourism: Effective wastewater management is critical for protecting water resources from pollution, which can degrade water quality and harm aquatic ecosystems (Vij et al., 2020; Wirsing & Jasparro, 2007; Woldemaryam, 2020). Tourism diplomacy can support international efforts to improve wastewater treatment and reduce pollution from tourism facilities. For instance, diplomatic initiatives could promote the adoption of wastewater treatment technologies that remove contaminants before discharge into natural water bodies. Additionally, tourism diplomacy can encourage countries to implement policies that restrict the use of harmful chemicals in tourism activities, such as fertilizers and pesticides used in landscaping. By addressing wastewater management and pollution prevention, tourism diplomacy helps protect the quality of water resources, ensuring that they remain viable for both tourism and local communities.

Developing Regional Water Management Plans in Tourism-Dependent Areas: Tourism diplomacy can facilitate the creation of regional water management plans in tourism-dependent areas, particularly in regions facing water scarcity. These plans could involve collaboration among local governments, tourism providers, and international organizations to develop sustainable water management strategies that balance tourism needs with community water requirements. Regional water management plans could include policies for equitable water allocation, incentives for water-saving measures, and guidelines for preserving local water sources. By fostering collaboration at the regional level, tourism diplomacy can help ensure that water resources are managed sustainably, benefiting both the tourism industry and local populations.

5.4 Challenges to Sustainable Water Management in Tourism

Sustainable water management in tourism presents several challenges (Jacobs, 2002; Nirwandy & Awang, 2014; Zhang & Li, 2020). These include the water needs of different tourism activities and the economic pressures promoting water-intensive development. In regions where tourism significantly boosts the economy, local governments often prioritize tourism development over water conservation, resulting in insufficient water-use regulations. Moreover, the tourism industry frequently lacks incentives to reduce water consumption, as water costs are usually lower than the revenue generated by tourism. Addressing these challenges requires a multi-faceted approach that balances economic growth with sustainable resource management. Another challenge is the countries' water management infrastructure and technology disparity (Wirsing & Jasparro, 2007; Xie et al., 2018). While developed nations often have access to advanced water-saving technologies, many developing countries lack the resources to invest in these solutions. Tourism diplomacy can help bridge these disparities by promoting technology transfer and supporting capacity-building initiatives, allowing all countries to implement sustainable water management practices.

5.5 Opportunities for Future Collaboration in Water Resource Management

Despite these challenges, tourism diplomacy offers significant opportunities for future collaboration in managing water resources (Koff et al., 2020; Vij et al., 2020; Xie et al., 2018). As climate change worsens water scarcity in many regions, the need for sustainable water use in tourism will become more critical. Tourism diplomacy can be crucial in addressing this issue by fostering partnerships that prioritize water conservation and support resilient water management practices. For instance, countries could collaborate on projects promoting rainwater harvesting, restoring natural water sources, and developing drought-resistant landscaping at tourism facilities. Another opportunity lies in integrating water resource management into the broader framework of sustainable tourism. Tourism diplomacy can help shift the focus of tourism development toward environmental sustainability, encouraging the industry to adopt water-efficient practices as part of its commitment to responsible tourism. By promoting a culture of sustainability, tourism diplomacy can help ensure that water resources are preserved for both the tourism industry and the communities that depend on them.

6. Transboundary Air and Marine Pollution in Sustainable Tourism Diplomacy

As global tourism grows, so does its environmental impact, especially regarding air and marine pollution. Activities like cruise travel, heavy reliance on aviation, and coastal recreation significantly contribute to air and marine pollution, which can spread across borders and impact ecosystems and communities far from the source. Tourism diplomacy offers a crucial platform for fostering global cooperation to tackle the challenges of transboundary air and marine pollution. Through international negotiations, countries can collaborate to develop and implement policies that reduce emissions from tourism, establish regulations to limit pollutants, and encourage sustainable practices. Partnerships with international aviation and maritime organizations are essential for advancing regulatory frameworks and promoting the adoption of environmentally responsible tourism models. This collaborative approach not only helps reduce pollution but also supports broader sustainable development goals, benefiting both the tourism industry and the environment.

6.1 Impact of Tourism on Air and Marine Pollution

Air Pollution From Tourism Activities: Tourism, especially aviation and cruise travel, is a significant source of air pollution (Demir, 2017; Egelston, 2022). Aircraft emit large quantities of GHGs, nitrogen oxides, and particulates at high altitudes, contributing to climate change and affecting air quality. Similarly, cruise ships are known for their high fuel consumption and emissions, releasing sulfur oxides (SOx), nitrogen oxides (NOx), and particulate matter that degrade air quality both at sea and in port cities (Bin Amin et al., 2024; Otsuka, 2018). Cruise ships often use bunker fuel, one of the most polluting fuel types. This fuel has a high sulfur content and produces harmful emissions that contribute to acid rain and human respiratory issues. The cumulative effect of these pollutants can have serious health and environmental impacts, particularly in port cities where emissions are concentrated.

Marine Pollution From Cruise Tourism: Cruise ships are also a significant source of marine pollution, directly discharging large quantities of wastewater, sewage, and solid waste into the ocean (Dow, 1999; Tolba, 2008). Bilge water, which accumulates at the bottom of ships and contains oil, chemicals, and other contaminants, is often discharged into the sea without adequate treatment. Additionally, cruise ships generate vast amounts of gray water (water from sinks, showers, and kitchens) and black water (sewage), which can introduce pathogens, nutrients, and toxins into the marine environment. These discharges can devastate marine ecosystems, contributing to algal blooms, coral reef degradation, and the destruction of fish habitats. Furthermore, the sheer scale of waste produced by cruise ships can overwhelm waste management facilities in port cities, leading to additional environmental burdens.

Transboundary Effects of Pollution: One of the defining characteristics of air and marine pollution from tourism is its transboundary nature (Kim, 2007). Emissions from ships and airplanes can drift across borders, affecting air quality and ecosystems in neighboring countries. Marine pollutants, carried by currents, can spread across vast distances, impacting marine life and coastal communities far from the pollution's source. This interconnectedness means that pollution generated by tourism activities in one country can have far-reaching consequences, underscoring the need for international cooperation in addressing these issues (Haas, 1989; Manos, 1991). Transboundary pollution presents unique regulatory challenges, as it requires countries to consider the impacts of their tourism industries on other nations and collaborate on solutions that protect shared environmental resources (Kim, 2007).

6.2 The Role of Tourism Diplomacy in Addressing Transboundary Pollution

Tourism diplomacy is essential in addressing the transboundary nature of air and marine pollution. Through diplomatic channels, countries can work together to establish international regulations, promote sustainable practices, and encourage accountability in the tourism sector. Collaborative efforts can lead to the development of uniform standards for emissions, waste management, and environmental protections, ensuring that tourism activities are managed sustainably and responsibly.

Developing International Regulations for Emission Control: Tourism diplomacy facilitates the development of international agreements to control emissions from tourism-related activities, such as aviation and maritime transport (Hashimoto, 1999; VanDeveer, 2013). For example, countries could negotiate binding emissions reduction targets for cruise ships and airplanes, limiting sulfur and nitrogen oxides, particulate matter, and GHG emissions. Tourism diplomacy can support the expansion of emission control areas (ECAs) in international waters, which mandate cleaner fuels and emissions reduction technologies within designated zones. By establishing these regulatory frameworks, countries can reduce the environmental impact of tourism and protect air quality on a global scale.

Collaboration With the International Maritime Organization (IMO): The International Maritime Organization (IMO) plays a central role in regulating pollution from ships, including cruise ships, through its International Convention for the Prevention of Pollution from Ships (MARPOL) (Manos, 1991; Otsuka, 2018). Tourism diplomacy can enhance collaboration with the IMO to promote the adoption of MARPOL standards among cruise operators and encourage cleaner technologies, such as exhaust gas cleaning systems (scrubbers) and liquefied natural gas (LNG) as alternative fuels. By working with the IMO, countries can advocate for stricter regulations on marine pollution and support the establishment of specific areas where the discharge of pollutants is heavily restricted. Furthermore, diplomatic efforts can help countries align their national policies with IMO guidelines, ensuring consistent enforcement and accountability in reducing marine pollution from tourism.

Promoting Sustainable Tourism Practices: Tourism diplomacy can promote sustainable practices in the tourism industry, urging businesses to reduce their environmental impact. For example, diplomatic initiatives can advocate for eco-certification programs that reward tourism operators, including cruise lines, that follow high environmental standards. These programs motivate operators to implement sustainable waste management, lower emissions, and invest in cleaner technologies (Haas, 1989; Wettestad, 1999). Furthermore, tourism diplomacy can back awareness campaigns to educate tourists about the environmental effects of their travel choices, encouraging them to choose eco-friendly options and lessen their carbon footprint. By promoting sustainable tourism, diplomacy can guide the industry toward more responsible practices that mitigate transboundary pollution.

Establishing Waste Management Standards in Port Cities: Effective waste management is crucial for preventing marine pollution in port cities, which are important centers for cruise tourism (Bin Amin et al., 2024; Egelston, 2022). Through tourism diplomacy, countries can work together to establish waste management standards for ports, ensuring that facilities can handle the waste generated by cruise ships. Diplomatic efforts can also promote investment in waste treatment infrastructure, including systems for processing sewage, gray water, and solid waste. By providing adequate waste management facilities, port cities can reduce the risk of marine pollution and ensure that tourism does not compromise the health of coastal ecosystems.

Encouraging Technological Innovation to Reduce Pollution: Technological advances provide promising solutions to reduce air and marine pollution caused by tourism (Kim, 2007; Otsuka, 2018). Tourism diplomacy can support international research partnerships to develop and deploy cleaner technologies, such as electric or hybrid-powered cruise ships and energy-efficient aircraft. By fostering innovation, countries can accelerate the adoption of low-emission technologies in the tourism sector and lessen its environmental impact. Additionally, tourism diplomacy can promote knowledge-sharing initiatives that allow countries to learn from each other's experiences in implementing pollution-reduction technologies and strategies. This collaborative approach can help scale successful practices and encourage adopting environmentally friendly solutions.

6.3 Challenges and Opportunities for Tourism Diplomacy in Pollution Management

Tourism diplomacy has the potential to address transboundary pollution, but several challenges remain (Kim, 2007). Economic factors often affect decisions in the tourism sector since many countries rely on tourism for revenue (Demir, 2017). These countries may hesitate to enforce regulations that could raise costs or decrease visitor numbers. Moreover, enforcing international rules can be difficult, especially in regions with limited resources for monitoring and compliance. To overcome these challenges, a commitment to prioritizing environmental protection and a readiness to invest in sustainable practices are essential, even if this requires short-term economic adjustments.

However, these challenges also present opportunities for tourism diplomacy to create meaningful change (Manos, 1991; VanDeveer, 2013). As awareness of environmental issues grows, tourists' support for sustainable travel options increases, generating market incentives for tourism operators to adopt eco-friendly practices. Additionally, the rise of global environmental movements and the growing emphasis on corporate social responsibility exert more pressure on the tourism industry to address its environmental impact. By leveraging these trends, tourism diplomacy can foster a more sustainable future for the industry, encouraging countries and businesses to prioritize environmental stewardship.

7. Conclusions

Addressing tourism's role in climate change requires a collaborative approach that utilizes the strengths of tourism diplomacy. Through international cooperation, countries can establish policies and practices that lower the tourism industry's carbon footprint while ensuring its sustainability for future generations. Tourism diplomacy is a platform for global engagement, allowing countries to promote eco-friendly travel options, develop carbon reduction strategies, and raise awareness of responsible tourism practices. The international community can work toward a sustainable future that balances economic benefits with environmental stewardship by prioritizing carbon emissions reduction in tourism diplomacy. This joint effort mitigates climate change's impact on tourism destinations and reinforces the industry's role as a leader in sustainable development.

Protecting biodiversity and natural heritage is essential for ensuring tourism's sustainability and resilience against environmental challenges. Tourism diplomacy is critical to foster international cooperation and promote policies that prioritize biodiversity conservation. By supporting initiatives such as protected areas, sustainable tourism certifications, and community-based conservation, tourism diplomacy can help mitigate the impact of tourism on natural habitats and preserve the ecosystems that attract visitors worldwide. Achieving global cooperation in biodiversity protection requires commitment, compromise, and shared responsibility, highlighting the importance of tourism diplomacy in promoting a sustainable future for both tourism and the planet. Countries can safeguard their natural heritage for future generations through coordinated efforts while balancing tourism's economic benefits and environmental responsibilities.

Pollution and waste management are essential for sustainable tourism and require coordinated efforts to reduce tourism's environmental impact. Tourism diplomacy addresses these challenges by encouraging international agreements and promoting policies that minimize waste and support eco-friendly practices. Tourism diplomacy can alleviate tourism's environmental effects and safeguard the ecosystems that attract visitors by implementing waste reduction protocols, zero-waste initiatives, and improved recycling systems. Achieving global cooperation in waste management calls for a commitment to shared responsibility, underscoring the significance of tourism diplomacy in creating a sustainable future for the industry. Through collaborative efforts, countries can ensure that tourism remains thriving while protecting the natural environments that make it viable.

Protecting and managing water resources is essential for ensuring the sustainability of the tourism industry and the well-being of local communities. Tourism diplomacy provides a strategic avenue to address the challenges of water scarcity by fostering international cooperation on sustainable water use and promoting policies that prioritize conservation. Through initiatives such as water conservation agreements, sustainable management standards, and responsible tourism practices, tourism diplomacy can help reduce the industry's impact on water resources. By promoting a shared commitment to water stewardship, tourism diplomacy contributes to a more sustainable future for tourism, ensuring that water resources are preserved for generations to come.

Transboundary air and marine pollution from tourism activities, especially cruise tourism, poses significant environmental challenges that need coordinated international responses. Tourism diplomacy is essential for addressing these issues by helping develop regulations, promoting sustainable practices, and fostering collaboration with organizations like the IMO. Through diplomatic efforts, countries can work together to reduce the environmental footprint of the tourism industry, protect shared resources, and promote a sustainable future for global tourism. By adopting tourism diplomacy as a tool for environmental management, nations can ensure that tourism continues to thrive while preserving the planet's health for future generations.

References

Adhikari, M., & Dahal, K. (2019). Inquiry into the preservation of cultural and natural heritages in Nepal. *Nepal Law Review*, *28*(1–2), 382–401.

Agamuthu, P., Mehran, S. B., Norkhairah, A., & Norkhairiyah, A. (2019). Marine debris: A review of impacts and global initiatives. *Waste Management & Research*, *37*(10), 987–1002.

Apriliani, D., & Dina, D. (2024). Climate change diplomacy: Towards sustainable global cooperation. *Social Studies and Humanities Journal (SOSHUM)*, *1*(1), 31–42.

Becken, S., & Scott, D. (2024). Tourism and climate change stocktake: A call to action. *Journal of Sustainable Tourism*, *32*(9), 2018–2038.

Bin Amin, U., Khanum, S., & Naazer, M. A. (2024). The threats to coastal and marine tourism of Pakistan. *Journal of Tourism, Hospitality, and Services Industries Research (JTHS)*, *4*(01), 79–92.

Carter, F., & Turnock, D. (2002). *Environmental problems in East-Central Europe* (Vol. 16). Routledge.

Duraku, A., & Nasufi, I. A. (2023). EU integration of chapter 27 "environment and climate change" in Albania. *Academic Journal of Business, Administration, Law and Social Sciences*, *9*(3), 54–61.

De Jong, M., Hoppe, T., & Noori, N. (2019). City branding, sustainable urban development and the rentier state. How do Qatar, Abu Dhabi and Dubai present themselves in the age of post oil and global warming? *Energies*, *12*(9), 1–13.

Demir, M. (2017). *Seyahat Acentacılığı ve Tur Operatörlüğü: İlkeler ve Yönetim*. Detay Yayıncılık.

Demir, M., & Demir, Ş. Ş. (2024). Digital technologies and applications in tourist guidance: The dilemma between adopting innovations and career concerns. *Journal of Human Resources in Hospitality & Tourism*, 1–25.

Dow, K. (1999). Caught in the currents: Pollution, risk, and environmental change in Marine space. *The Professional Geographer*, *51*(3), 414–426.

Egelston, A. (2022). *Worth saving: International diplomacy to protect the environment*. Springer Nature.

Fuller, S., Ngata, T., Borrelle, S. B., & Farrelly, T. (2022). Plastics pollution as waste colonialism in Te Moananui. *Journal of Political Ecology*, *29*(1), 534–560.

Haas, P. M. (1989). Do regimes matter? Epistemic communities and Mediterranean pollution control. *International Organization*, *43*(3), 377–403.

Hamida, H. B. (2024). Cross-domain dynamics: How geopolitical and climate policy uncertainties shape tourism patterns in the United States. *Tourism Economics*, 1–14.

Hashimoto, A. (1999). Comparative evolutionary trends in environmental policy: Reflections on tourism development. *International Journal of Tourism Research*, *1*(3), 195–216.

Hassan, T. H., Almakhayitah, M. Y., & Saleh, M. I. (2024). Sustainable stewardship of Egypt's iconic heritage sites: Balancing heritage preservation, visitors' well-being, and environmental responsibility. *Heritage*, *7*(2), 737–757.

Higham, J., Font, X., & Wu, J. (2021). Code red for sustainable tourism. *Journal of Sustainable Tourism*, *30*(1), 1–13.

Hohl, A. (2013). Ecotourism as an instrument to conserve biodiversity. In C. A. Tisdell (Ed.), *Handbook of tourism economics: Analysis, new applications and case studies* (pp. 813–843). World Scientific Publishing Co. Pte. Ltd.

Ishwaran, N. (2004). International conservation diplomacy and the world heritage convention. *Journal of International Wildlife Law and Policy*, *7*(1–2), 43–56.

Jacobs, J. W. (2002). The mekong river commission: Transboundary water resources planning and regional security. *Geographical Journal*, *168*(4), 354–364.

Karimipour, Y. L., & Abdi, A. (2015). The impact of geopolitical tourism on convergence of space political units (Case Study: Iran-Azarbayejan). *Journal of Tourism Hospitality Research*, *4*(1), 59–75.

Kim, I. (2007). Environmental cooperation of Northeast Asia: Transboundary air pollution. *International Relations of the Asia-Pacific*, *7*(3), 439–462.

Koff, H., Maganda, C., & Kauffer, E. (2020). Transboundary water diplomacy among small states: A giant dilemma for Central American regionalism. *Water International*, *45*(4), 275–291.

Luo, Z., & Yun, L. (2023). Investigating risks and strategies in adopting green tourism practices in developing economy. *Environmental Science and Pollution Research, 30*(59), 123710–123728.

Manfredi Sánchez, J. L., & Seoane Pérez, F. (2021). Climate change begins at home: City diplomacy in the age of the anthropocene. In P. Surowiec & I. Manor (Eds.), *Public diplomacy and the politics of uncertainty* (pp. 57–81). Springer International Publishing.

Manos, A. (1991). An international programme for the protection of a semi-enclosed sea—The Mediterranean action plan. *Marine Pollution Bulletin, 23*, 489–496.

McGaurr, L., & Lester, L. (2018). See it before it's too late? Last-chance travel lists and climate change. *Climate Change and the Media, 2*, 123–140.

Negassa, S. B. (2024). Tourism diplomacy: Fostering economic development through global connectivity. In A. B. Basnur (Ed.), *Tourism: For global connectivity and economic development* (pp. 68–75). Paramedia Komunikatama.

Nirwandy, N., & Awang, A. A. (2014). Conceptualizing public diplomacy social convention culinary: Engaging gastro diplomacy warfare for economic branding. *Procedia-Social and Behavioral Sciences, 130*, 325–332.

Onyena, A. P., Aniche, D. C., Ogbolu, B. O., Rakib, M. R. J., Uddin, J., & Walker, T. R. (2021). Governance strategies for mitigating microplastic pollution in the marine environment: A review. *Microplastics, 1*(1), 15–46.

Otsuka, K. (2018). Shift in China's commitment to regional environmental governance in Northeast Asia? *Journal of Contemporary East Asia Studies, 7*(1), 16–34.

Parnwell, M. (2010). Tourism and natural heritage management in Vietnam and Thailand. *Heritage Tourism in Southeast Asia*, 236–263.

Pata, U. K., Pata, S. K., & Erdogan, S. (2024). Effects of waste generation on the load capacity factor: A novel waste management assessment for OECD countries. *Geological Journal*, 1–11.

Platts, E. J., Keifer, H. L., & Samuels, K. L. (2023). Carbon footprints of travel to world heritage sites: Communicating climate to potential tourists through a consumption-based life-cycle assessment. *Journal of Heritage Tourism, 18*(4), 407–426.

Roumiani, A., Shayan, H., Sharifinia, Z., & Moghadam, S. S. (2023). Estimation of ecological footprint based on tourism development indicators using neural networks and multivariate regression. *Environmental Science and Pollution Research, 30*(12), 33396–33418.

Scott, D., Hall, C. M., & Gössling, S. (2016). A report on the Paris Climate Change Agreement and its implications for tourism: Why we will always have Paris. *Journal of Sustainable Tourism, 24*(7), 933–948.

Sofield, T., & Li, S. (2013). Tourism governance and sustainable national development in China: A macro-level synthesis. In B. Bramwell & B. Lane (Eds.), *Tourism Governance* (pp. 91–124). Routledge.

Strouhal, M. (2020). CORSIA-Carbon offsetting and reduction scheme for international aviation. *MAD-Magazine of Aviation Development, 8*(1), 23–28.

Talukder, M. B., & Hoque, M. (2025). Cultural heritage tourism in Bangladesh: Balancing preservation and visitor experience. In A. Albattat, N. Azman, M. Valeri, Z. M. Talib, & P. K. Tyagi (Eds.), *Navigating intellectual property challenges in tourism* (pp. 83–110). IGI Global.

Taylor, P. (2015). Toward a national ocean policy in New Zealand. In B. Cicin-Sain, D. Vanderzwaag, & M. C. Balgos (Eds.), *Routledge handbook of national and regional ocean policies* (pp. 361–392). Routledge.

Teczke, M., Kaliyeva, T., Sembiyeva, L., Zhagyparova, A., Zholamanova, M., & Zhussupova, A. (2022). Silk roads routes. Sustainable tourism after COVID-19. *Journal of Environmental Management & Tourism*, *13*(4), 1192–1206.

Tolba, M. K. (2008). *Global environmental diplomacy: Negotiating environmental agreements for the world, 1973–1992*. MIT Press.

VanDeveer, S. D. (2013). Agenda setting at sea and in the air. In N. Kanie, S. Andresen, & P. M. Haas (Eds.), *Improving global environmental governance* (pp. 31–55). Routledge.

Vij, S., Warner, J., & Barua, A. (2020). Power in water diplomacy. *Water International*, *45*(4), 249–253.

Wang, X., Zhen, J., & Meng, Q. (2023). Natural Heritage Sites and Space Observations. In X. Wang, J. Zhen, & Q. Meng (Eds.), *Spatial observation of giant panda habitat: Techniques and methods* (pp. 1–26). Springer Nature Singapore.

Wettestad, J. (1999). More 'discursive diplomacy' than 'dashing design'? The convention on long-range transboundary air pollution (LRTAP). In J. Wettestad (Ed.), *Designing effective environmental regimes* (pp. 85–124). Edward Elgar Publishing.

Wilby, R. L., Orr, M., Depledge, D., Giulianotti, R., Havenith, G., Kenyon, J. A., Matthews, T. K. R., Mears, S. A., Mullan, D. J., & Taylor, L. (2023). The impacts of sport emissions on climate: Measurement, mitigation, and making a difference. *Annals of the New York Academy of Sciences*, *1519*(1), 20–33.

Wirsing, R. G., & Jasparro, C. (2007). River rivalry: Water disputes, resource insecurity and diplomatic deadlock in South Asia. *Water Policy*, *9*(3), 231–251.

Woldemaryam, E. (2020). Making the Nile River a point of cooperation between Ethiopia and Egypt: Building confidence through water diplomacy. *Budapest International Research and Critics Institute-Journal (BIRCI-Journal)*, *3*(3), 2494–2500.

Wu, H. H. (2022). A study on transnational regulatory governance for marine plastic debris: Trends, challenges, and prospect. *Marine Policy*, *136*, 1–12.

Xie, L., Zhang, Y., & Panda, J. P. (2018). Mismatched diplomacy: China–India water relations over the Ganges–Brahmaputra–Meghna river basin. *Journal of Contemporary China*, *27*(109), 32–46.

Yoon, E. (2006). South Korean environmental foreign policy. *Asia-Pacific Review*, *13*(2), 74–96.

Zhang, H., Ben, F., & Qin, M. (2024). Mineral resources, tourism, human capital, and carbon neutrality: A path towards balanced and sustainable development. *Resources Policy*, *90*, 1–16.

Zhang, H., & Li, M. (2020). China's water diplomacy in the Mekong: A paradigm shift and the role of Yunnan provincial government. *Water international*, *45*(4), 347–364.

Chapter 10

From Theory to Practice: Tourism Diplomacy

Abstract

This chapter delves into the transition from theoretical frameworks to practical applications within tourism diplomacy, highlighting its significance as a multidimensional tool for fostering international cooperation and understanding. It begins by outlining the theoretical underpinnings and core objectives of tourism diplomacy, emphasizing its potential to leverage tourism as a means of soft power. Drawing on case studies from various countries, the analysis explores how strategic initiatives in tourism diplomacy have promoted cultural exchange, economic development, and mutual understanding among nations. Specific attention is given to its role in enhancing national images, addressing global crises, and fostering peace and stability. The interplay between tourism diplomacy and environmental conservation is also examined, underscoring its importance in achieving Sustainable Development Goals. Contributions from international organizations are analyzed to reveal their influence on shaping tourism diplomacy practices and policies. Challenges such as geopolitical tensions, resource limitations, and the dynamic nature of global tourism are critically evaluated alongside future growth and innovation prospects. Through its comprehensive exploration of both theory and practice, the study provides actionable insights into how tourism diplomacy can serve as a transformative force in strengthening global relations and addressing complex international issues.

Keywords: Tourism diplomacy; soft power and cultural exchange; the economic impact of tourism; strategic diplomatic initiatives; environmental conservation in tourism

Tourism Diplomacy, 201–222

Copyright © 2025 Mahmut Demir and Şirvan Şen Demir
Published under exclusive licence by Emerald Publishing Limited

doi:10.1108/978-1-83708-676-420251010

1. Introduction

Tourism diplomacy, a multidisciplinary approach that bridges tourism and international relations, has emerged as a dynamic tool for fostering economic growth, cultural understanding, and geopolitical stability. Rooted in soft power, cultural exchange, and international cooperation theoretical frameworks, tourism diplomacy enables nations to enhance their global standing while addressing pressing socioeconomic and environmental challenges. As globalization continues to reshape the world, the strategic application of tourism diplomacy has become increasingly critical for promoting peace, sustainability, and mutual understanding among diverse communities.

The theoretical foundations of tourism diplomacy lie in its capacity to leverage the intangible assets of culture, heritage, and human connection to achieve tangible outcomes in diplomacy and international relations. By utilizing tourism as a platform for soft power, countries can project positive images of themselves, foster goodwill, and establish stronger ties with other nations. Tourism also serves as a conduit for cultural exchange, enabling individuals to experience the traditions, values, and lifestyles of others, thereby promoting mutual understanding and tolerance. Furthermore, tourism diplomacy encompasses the economic dimensions of tourism, emphasizing its potential to stimulate job creation, attract foreign investments, and strengthen bilateral and multilateral partnerships.

Across the globe, numerous countries have adopted innovative approaches to integrate tourism into their diplomatic strategies. For instance, Japan's "Cool Japan" initiative highlights the role of cultural exportation in enhancing national branding, while Spain's global promotion of its UNESCO World Heritage sites underscores the intersection of cultural conservation and international appeal. Similarly, small nations like Bhutan have leveraged niche tourism offerings such as high-value, low-impact tourism to preserve their cultural identity while engaging with the global community. These examples underscore the diverse ways in which tourism diplomacy can be tailored to a country's unique strengths and objectives.

In addition to promoting cultural exchange, tourism diplomacy has demonstrated its efficacy in addressing global crises and fostering peace. During periods of geopolitical tension, tourism initiatives have served as platforms for dialogue and reconciliation, as seen in the case of South Korea's efforts to promote inter-Korean tourism exchanges. Similarly, in postconflict settings, tourism has played a pivotal role in economic recovery and the rebuilding of social cohesion, as evidenced by efforts in Rwanda and the Balkans. Tourism diplomacy also extends to environmental conservation, where collaborative international efforts aim to protect shared natural resources and address climate change through sustainable tourism practices.

International organizations, such as the United Nations World Tourism Organization (UNWTO) and UNESCO, further amplify tourism diplomacy's impact. These institutions provide critical platforms for fostering multilateral cooperation and setting global standards for sustainable and inclusive tourism. Their initiatives facilitate cross-border collaboration and ensure that tourism diplomacy aligns with broader global objectives, such as the United Nations Sustainable Development Goals (SDGs).

However, tourism diplomacy is not without its challenges. Issues such as over-tourism, cultural commodification, and geopolitical instability can undermine its effectiveness and sustainability. The COVID-19 pandemic has further highlighted vulnerabilities within the tourism sector, necessitating innovative crisis management and resilience-building approaches. Addressing these challenges requires a forward-looking perspective incorporating technological advancements, ethical considerations, and inclusive policymaking.

As the field continues to evolve, tourism diplomacy's future lies in its ability to adapt to emerging global trends and priorities. Digital transformation, for instance, offers new avenues for enhancing tourism diplomacy through virtual tourism, social media engagement, and data-driven decision-making. Meanwhile, the growing emphasis on sustainability calls for strategies that balance economic growth with environmental preservation and social equity. Tourism diplomacy can remain vital for fostering global cooperation and understanding by embracing these developments.

This chapter explores the transition of tourism diplomacy from theoretical concepts to practical applications, drawing on case studies and strategic initiatives from around the world. It examines the multifaceted roles of tourism in enhancing national images, promoting peace, and addressing global challenges while also highlighting the contributions of international organizations and the opportunities presented by technological advancements. By providing a comprehensive overview of tourism diplomacy's objectives, practices, and future directions, the chapter aims to equip policymakers, practitioners, and scholars with insights into how tourism can continue to serve as a force for positive change in an interconnected world.

2. Theoretical Foundations and Objectives of Tourism Diplomacy

Tourism diplomacy can be understood within the broader context of public diplomacy, which refers to a nation's efforts to influence the foreign public and shape international perceptions through nonpolitical channels. Unlike traditional diplomacy, which is often state-centered and involves formal negotiations between diplomats, public diplomacy focuses on engaging directly with citizens of other countries. Tourism diplomacy leverages the tourism industry as a channel for public diplomacy, utilizing the mobility of people across borders to achieve foreign policy objectives.

Tourism diplomacy draws upon several international relations and sociology theories, such as soft power, social exchange, and nation branding theories. Soft power theory describes a country's ability to attract and co-opt rather than coerce (Nye, 1990). Tourism significantly generates soft power by fostering positive perceptions of a country among international visitors, who act as informal ambassadors upon returning home. The social exchange theory suggests that people form opinions about other groups or cultures based on social interactions (Cropanzano & Mitchell, 2005). Positive tourism experiences can improve people's perceptions of a host country and promote long-term relationships between nations. According to nation branding theory, nations, like corporations, can be branded to shape international

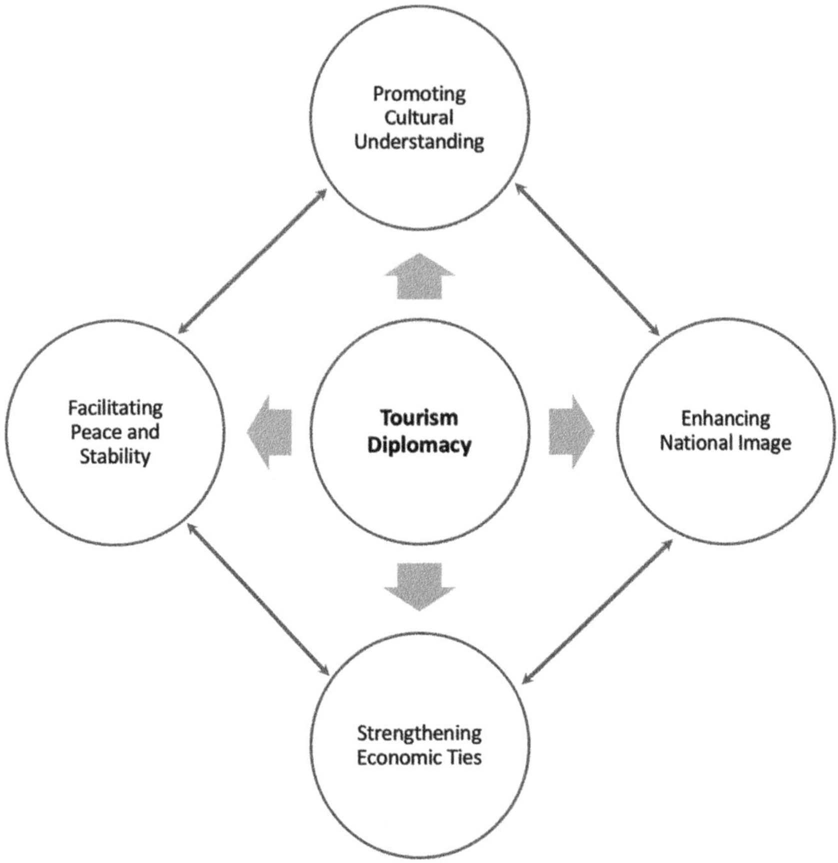

Fig. 17. The Core Objectives of the Tourism Diplomacy.

perceptions (Merkelsen & Rasmussen, 2016). Tourism is a crucial component of a country's brand, and tourism diplomacy helps create a favorable national image, attracting visitors and investments (Fig. 17).

Tourism diplomacy can be categorized into several core objectives, such as promoting cultural understanding, enhancing national image, strengthening economic ties, and facilitating peace and stability (Minardi et al., 2021; Negassa, 2024).

Promoting Cultural Understanding: Tourism diplomacy bridges cultural gaps by offering visitors immersive experiences in diverse societies. By experiencing a host country's history, culture, and values firsthand, visitors can better understand the local people and their way of life.

Enhancing National Image: Tourism diplomacy is a powerful tool for improving a country's global image. Nations facing negative stereotypes or political tensions can utilize tourism initiatives to showcase their positive attributes, emphasizing culture, hospitality, and economic opportunities.

Strengthening Economic Ties: Tourism generates significant economic benefits by creating jobs, stimulating local businesses, and fostering trade partnerships. By attracting foreign tourists, countries can enhance bilateral and multilateral economic relationships, contributing to their economies and improving diplomatic relations.

Facilitating Peace and Stability: Tourism diplomacy fosters connections among people, promoting peaceful coexistence and collaboration. It serves as a platform for reconciliation and mutual understanding in conflict-affected regions.

3. Examples From Countries on Tourism Diplomacy

The practical applications of tourism diplomacy vary based on the sociopolitical and economic goals of the country implementing it. From soft power to future directions, there are some examples of how tourism diplomacy is practiced around the world (Fig. 18).

Fig. 18. Examples From Countries on Tourism Diplomacy.

3.1 Tourism as a Tool for Soft Power

"Cool Japan" Initiatives: Japan's "Cool Japan" initiative is a strategic cultural diplomacy effort to promote Japanese culture globally through a unique fusion of its traditional heritage and contemporary innovations (Tamaki, 2019). Launched by the Japanese government, "Cool Japan" seeks to attract international tourists by highlighting the country's diverse cultural assets, including ancient arts, technological advancements, and globally popular media forms such as anime, manga, fashion, and cuisine. By presenting Japan as a modern, creative, and culturally rich destination, this initiative enhances Japan's soft power – its ability to influence others through attraction rather than coercion (Nakamura, 2013). Through "Cool Japan," Japan utilizes tourism as a diplomatic tool to shape global perceptions. The campaign showcases various aspects of Japanese life that resonate with international audiences, from historic shrines and tea ceremonies to cutting-edge robotics and digital entertainment (Nakamura, 2013; Tamaki, 2019). Anime and manga, in particular, have become cultural symbols that bridge cultures and introduce Japanese language, art, and values to international fans, creating emotional and cultural ties. This popular culture-driven diplomacy positions Japan as a nation that is not only rooted in tradition but also a leader in innovation. "Cool Japan" also contributes to Japan's economic growth by increasing inbound tourism and expanding the reach of Japanese products abroad. Japan fosters stronger international connections and enhances its cultural influence by encouraging cultural exports. Overall, "Cool Japan" exemplifies tourism diplomacy by using cultural assets to build Japan's positive, globally appealing image, strengthening its economic and diplomatic standing on the world stage.

Destinations of France by Atout France: France effectively utilizes its rich cultural assets, including historical landmarks, fashion, cuisine, and the arts, to reinforce its status as a global tourism powerhouse. The country's strategic focus on tourism diplomacy leverages its cultural heritage to cultivate international goodwill and influence. France's diverse offerings, from iconic landmarks like the Eiffel Tower and the Louvre Museum to its culinary excellence and haute couture, create a unique cultural appeal that attracts millions of visitors annually (Byrne, 2013; Yeoman et al., 2019). The French tourism agency Atout France plays a pivotal role in this process by organizing workshop events themed "Destinations of France" in various countries (Soyez, 2019). It actively promotes the country's heritage and lifestyle, creating immersive experiences that showcase the essence of French culture. By focusing on experiential tourism, Atout France improves the global perception of France, establishing it as a top destination for travelers seeking both luxury and authenticity. Through tourism diplomacy, France enhances its soft power by using cultural exports to build diplomatic ties and foster cross-cultural understanding (Yeoman et al., 2019). The country's tourism initiatives not only bring economic benefits but also support a broader strategy to increase its international influence. This strategy goes beyond simply promoting travel and tourism; it acts as a platform for cultural exchange and global engagement, deepening connections with other nations and solidifying France's position as a leader in culture and diplomacy on the international stage.

3.2 Cultural Exchange and Mutual Understanding

China's "Belt and Road Initiative": China's tourism diplomacy significantly strengthens its global influence, mainly through the "Belt and Road Initiative" (BRI). Launched in 2013, the BRI is an ambitious infrastructure and economic development project spanning Asia, Africa, and Europe (Quer & Andreu, 2023). Beyond its focus on trade and infrastructure, the initiative also incorporates tourism to deepen cultural exchange and build stronger bilateral ties with participating countries. By promoting tourism, China aims to enhance the international image of its culture and heritage, fostering mutual understanding and goodwill with neighboring nations, particularly in Asia and Africa. The BRI encourages tourism exchanges by developing tourism infrastructure, facilitating travel, and organizing cultural events that showcase Chinese history, traditions, and modern achievements (Li et al., 2020). For example, China has invested in transportation and hospitality facilities in countries along the BRI routes, making travel to China more accessible for foreign tourists. Furthermore, cultural programs and partnerships increase awareness of Chinese culture while offering visitors the chance to experience the country's rich diversity. This tourism diplomacy benefits participating countries by enhancing economic cooperation, creating opportunities for tourism-related industries, and stimulating local economies. Through the BRI, China aims to develop a network of interconnected nations, using tourism to build long-lasting relationships that promote peace, cultural understanding, and sustainable development (Li et al., 2020; Quer & Andreu, 2023). This approach aligns with China's broader soft power strategy, positioning the country as a key player in global diplomacy.

South Korea's "Korean Wave": South Korea's tourism diplomacy is closely intertwined with the global phenomenon known as the "Korean Wave" or "Hallyu" (Bae et al., 2017). This cultural movement encompasses the widespread popularity of K-pop, K-dramas, and Korean cuisine. It has played a pivotal role in positioning South Korea as a significant player in the global tourism industry, attracting millions of worldwide visitors. Through the success of K-pop and K-dramas, South Korea has garnered international attention, directly contributing to increased tourism (Kim, 2018). Fans of Korean entertainment seek to visit the country to experience the culture they have come to admire through these media. South Korea has launched various tourism initiatives, such as the "Imagine Your Korea" campaign, to capitalize on this. This program invites visitors to immerse themselves in Korean culture, offering tailored experiences highlighting the country's rich history, modern attractions, and unique traditions. By promoting cultural exchange, these efforts not only draw tourists to South Korea but also help to break down stereotypes and misconceptions about the country. The "Korean Wave" fosters a greater understanding of South Korea's values, traditions, and innovations, showcasing the country's dynamic and evolving identity to a global audience (Bae et al., 2017; Kim, 2018). Furthermore, tourism diplomacy through the "Korean Wave" supports South Korea's soft power strategy, enhancing its global standing by encouraging international engagement through cultural, economic, and diplomatic exchanges. As a result, South Korea effectively uses its cultural exports to improve its image and deepen its global relationships.

3.3 Economic Impact and Diplomatic Relations

Thailand's "ASEAN Tourism" Campaigns: Tourism is crucial to Thailand's economy, contributing significantly to the country's GDP. To capitalize on this, Thailand actively promotes tourism not only within its borders but also in collaboration with neighboring Association of Southeast Asian Nations (ASEAN) countries (Putri & Purnawarman, 2024). This regional approach fosters economic interdependence and cohesion, creating a shared tourism space that benefits all member states. Through joint initiatives and programs, Thailand works with other ASEAN nations to enhance the tourism infrastructure and promote the Southeast Asian region as a top global destination (Zhu et al., 2022). The countries involved can collectively attract more international tourists, improve global visibility, and boost economies. For example, regional campaigns such as "ASEAN Tourism" help highlight each member country's unique cultural, historical, and natural attractions while also promoting cross-border travel within the region. This regional collaboration also strengthens diplomatic ties within Southeast Asia, as the tourism sector becomes a platform for cooperation and mutual support. As Thailand leads efforts to enhance the tourism potential of the ASEAN region, it reinforces its position as a key player in Southeast Asia (Beirman, 2018; Zhu et al., 2022). Furthermore, Thailand's active role in promoting regional tourism diplomacy helps bolster its image on the global stage, fostering both economic growth and international goodwill. In this way, tourism diplomacy not only supports Thailand's economy but also contributes to broader regional stability and integration, enhancing its diplomatic relations and positioning the country as a leader in Southeast Asian affairs.

Turkey's "Safe Tourism Certification" Program: Turkey's tourism diplomacy is vital in enhancing its global standing, particularly as a bridge between Europe and Asia. One of the critical initiatives driving this strategy is the "Safe Tourism Certification" program, launched in response to the COVID-19 pandemic (Demir et al., 2020). This program aims to ensure the health and safety of tourists by establishing strict hygiene protocols in hotels, resorts, and other tourism-related services. By prioritizing safety, Turkey not only reassured international visitors but also contributed to the economic recovery of the tourism sector, which is essential after the global disruptions caused by the pandemic (Demir et al., 2021). Tourism from European Union (EU) countries and Russia is particularly significant to Turkey's economy, with millions of tourists visiting annually. These regions have long been vital sources of inbound tourism, and Turkey's diplomatic efforts are closely tied to fostering strong relations with both (Demir et al., 2023).

Through targeted promotional campaigns, Turkey works to strengthen its diplomatic and economic ties with EU countries and Russia, ensuring that its tourism sector remains attractive and accessible to these critical markets. The "Safe Tourism Certification" program also serves as a diplomatic tool. It showcases Turkey's commitment to maintaining high standards for foreign visitors and boosts its reputation as a safe and reliable travel destination. Turkey's tourism diplomacy drives economic growth by emphasizing the safety and well-being of international tourists. It is crucial in reinforcing its diplomatic ties with neighboring regions and global partners (Demir et al., 2020; Demir & Dalgıç, 2022).

3.4 Promoting Peace and Stability

Rwanda's Gorilla Trekking in Volcanoes National Park: Rwanda's tourism diplomacy has significantly reshaped the country's international image, especially after the 1994 genocide. By focusing on eco-tourism, Rwanda has established itself as a premier destination for sustainable and conservation-oriented travel, with gorilla trekking in Volcanoes National Park as the main attraction (Stewart et al., 2016). This effort has profoundly affected Rwanda's economy and reputation, drawing travelers from around the globe interested in nature and responsible tourism. Gorilla trekking, in particular, has allowed Rwanda to generate substantial revenue while supporting efforts to conserve its unique wildlife (Marijnen, 2022). These funds are reinvested into local communities and conservation initiatives, creating economic opportunities for Rwandans and encouraging environmental stewardship. By engaging local communities in tourism operations and sharing the economic benefits, Rwanda has cultivated a sense of ownership and pride among its citizens, contributing to its stability and development. Beyond economic gains, Rwanda's ecotourism has become a powerful diplomatic tool, reshaping the country's image on the global stage. Once associated with conflict, Rwanda is now recognized as a peaceful, forward-thinking nation committed to conservation and sustainable growth. This change in perception has strengthened Rwanda's diplomatic relationships with international partners and attracted support for further development projects. Through ecotourism, Rwanda illustrates how tourism diplomacy can drive economic recovery while fostering global goodwill, advancing environmental goals, and reshaping the country's narrative to emphasize peace, resilience, and ecological responsibility (Marijnen, 2022; Stewart et al., 2016).

Israel and Jordan's Cross-border Tourism in the Dead Sea: Israel and Jordan have used tourism diplomacy to build peaceful relations and promote economic development, focusing on the shared Dead Sea region. Despite their historical and political tensions, both countries see the economic and cultural benefits of encouraging cross-border tourism, especially around significant historical and religious sites. The joint initiatives highlight their shared heritage, with places like Petra, Jerash, Jerusalem, and the Dead Sea attracting visitors from around the world. Both nations invite tourists to explore the area's rich history and beautiful environments, making cross-border travel easier (Arieli, 2012; Talozi & Westheimer, 2020). This strategy not only improves each country's attractiveness as a destination but also fosters a better understanding and appreciation among tourists for the region's unique cultural dynamics. Cross-border tourism in the Dead Sea area benefits Israel and Jordan significantly economically (Talozi & Westheimer, 2020). It supports local businesses, creates jobs, and fosters regional development. This cooperation shows how tourism can bridge gaps between neighboring countries by emphasizing shared interests over political differences. Joint promotional campaigns and travel packages that include visits to sites in both countries illustrate tourism diplomacy, promoting peace through economic interdependence and a shared cultural heritage (Gelbman & Maoz, 2012; Hazbun, 2012). Thus, Israel and Jordan demonstrate how tourism diplomacy can overcome long-standing differences, creating avenues for dialogue, collaboration, and lasting regional stability while offering travelers enriching cross-cultural experiences.

3.5 Strategic Tourism Diplomacy Initiatives

India's "Incredible India" Campaign: The globally recognized "Incredible India" campaign exemplifies India's tourism diplomacy, aiming to change international perceptions and showcase the nation's vast cultural heritage, diverse environments, and rich spiritual traditions (Nair, 2021). Launched to attract global tourists, "Incredible India" has effectively positioned India as a welcoming, vibrant, and multifaceted destination. It highlights the country's ancient history, lively arts, and religious diversity. The campaign draws attention to critical aspects of Indian culture, including iconic landmarks like the Taj Mahal, historic cities like Jaipur, spiritual experiences in Varanasi, and wellness tourism rooted in practices like yoga and Ayurveda. By presenting India as both modern and traditional, "Incredible India" has significantly boosted tourism while emphasizing the country's unique cultural identity on the global stage (Saha & Raghuvanshi, 2025). Beyond its economic impact, this initiative has strengthened India's diplomatic relations, particularly with countries interested in cultural exchange, heritage tourism, and wellness tourism. As international travelers engage with India's diverse culture and spiritual offerings, they gain a deeper understanding and appreciation for the nation's values, fostering goodwill and positive perceptions abroad. Moreover, "Incredible India" supports India's soft power strategy by promoting cultural diplomacy. This outreach helps India build connections with other countries and enhances its global influence since people-to-people connections promote mutual respect and cooperation. Through the "Incredible India" campaign, tourism serves not only as a vehicle for economic growth but also as a means to strengthen international ties and enhance India's global image as a diverse, inclusive, and hospitable country (Isar, 2020; Nair, 2021).

Australia's "Tourism Australia" Campaign: Australia's tourism diplomacy is led by "Tourism Australia," a campaign highlighting the country's unique wildlife, stunning environments, and vibrant multicultural cities (Chitty, 2008). Featuring iconic attractions like the Great Barrier Reef and the Outback, along with thriving cities such as Sydney and Melbourne, the campaign emphasizes Australia's natural beauty and cultural diversity, attracting millions of tourists each year. "Tourism Australia" not only boosts the country's economy but also enhances diplomatic relationships, especially within the Asia-Pacific region (Fullerton & Kendrick, 2011). By portraying Australia as an inclusive and welcoming destination, the campaign strengthens bonds with neighboring Asian nations, from which a large share of Australia's inbound tourists originates. This outreach fosters mutual goodwill, as many visitors from these regions experience Australia's hospitality, inclusivity, and appreciation for diverse cultures firsthand. The campaign promotes environmental sustainability by focusing on conservation and responsible tourism, appealing to environmentally conscious travelers worldwide. This strategy aligns with Australia's image as a protector of unique ecosystems, from coastal reefs to native forests. Such a commitment to the environment enhances Australia's diplomatic appeal, especially as the world increasingly prioritizes sustainable travel and conservation. Through "Tourism Australia," the country uses its tourism assets for cultural diplomacy, creating lasting, positive impressions and deeper international connections (Maydell, 2020). Australia bolsters its reputation as a friendly, diverse, and environmentally responsible nation by showcasing its environments, wildlife, and inclusive society, strengthening diplomatic ties, and fostering goodwill across borders.

3.6 Crisis Management and Tourism Diplomacy

New Zealand's "Travel Bubble" Collaboration: New Zealand's tourism diplomacy was highlighted by its collaborative response to the COVID-19 pandemic, which created a "travel bubble." This arrangement allowed for safe, limited travel between New Zealand and Australia, enabling tourism to continue despite global lockdowns. The travel bubble was essential for sustaining the tourism industries in both nations and served as a testament to their solid diplomatic relationship (Draper & To, 2020). It allowed citizens from each country to visit one another without quarantine, demonstrating mutual trust and coordination. By maintaining some level of tourism during the pandemic, New Zealand and Australia supported their vital tourism sectors, helped local businesses survive, preserved jobs, and sustained tourism revenue despite the overall decline in international travel. The travel bubble emphasized New Zealand's reputation as a reliable partner, strengthening diplomatic ties with Australia and demonstrating its commitment to innovative solutions (Fusté-Forné & Michael, 2023). This initiative also showcased New Zealand's focus on safety and public health, enhancing its image as a safe travel destination and attracting future tourists once global travel resumed. The travel bubble was a notable example of tourism diplomacy, illustrating how cross-border collaboration bolsters economic resilience and fosters goodwill (Timothy, 2022). Through these strategic partnerships, New Zealand not only sustained its tourism sector but also deepened its diplomatic relationship with Australia, positioning itself as a proactive and dependable ally during crises.

Greece's "All You Want is Greece" Campaigns: In response to its economic crisis, Greece turned to tourism diplomacy as a critical strategy for recovery. To attract international visitors, it implemented targeted marketing and safety-focused policies. The "All You Want is Greece" campaign was central to this effort, highlighting the country's rich cultural heritage, beautiful environments, and renowned hospitality (Kokkinidis, 2022). This campaign positioned Greece as a top destination, appealing especially to travelers from Europe and beyond who sought safe, enjoyable experiences. It emphasized Greece's unique attractions, from ancient archaeological sites and historic cities to stunning islands and Mediterranean cuisine. By promoting these features, Greece aimed to generate much-needed revenue, helping to stabilize its economy and support local communities reliant on tourism. The initiative was well-received, showcasing Greece's proactive measures to ensure visitor safety, primarily through strong health protocols that reassured tourists amid the uncertainties of the postpandemic period. Beyond its economic advantages, Greece's tourism diplomacy has strengthened relationships with European Union (EU) countries and other international partners. By promoting Greece as a safe and appealing destination, the campaign improved the country's image as a trustworthy and resilient partner, fostering goodwill and encouraging repeat visits from European travelers (Krinis, 2022). This strategy also helped Greece solidify its status within the EU as a premier destination, enhancing broader regional cooperation in tourism. Through initiatives like "All You Want is Greece," Greece successfully utilized tourism diplomacy to boost economic recovery and reinforce its international connections, positioning itself as a welcoming, vibrant, and resilient nation.

3.7 The Role of International Organizations in Tourism Diplomacy

Italy's Collaboration With UNESCO: Italy has effectively used tourism diplomacy to enhance its international presence, particularly by promoting its UNESCO World Heritage sites (Clarke et al., 2020; Di Giovine, 2008). With support from UNESCO, Italy showcases its vast collection of cultural and historical treasures – from the ancient ruins of Rome and Pompeii to the Renaissance art in Florence and the canals of Venice. This strategy not only attracts millions of tourists each year but also bolsters Italy's diplomatic status by showing its commitment to global cultural preservation and environmental standards. Italy's partnership with UNESCO has strengthened its role as a vital advocate for heritage conservation. By aligning its tourism initiatives with UNESCO's values, Italy emphasizes preserving historical sites and protecting cultural diversity, which resonates with global audiences (Debarbieux et al., 2023). Italy's commitment to these principles appeals to international visitors interested in meaningful, responsible tourism, encouraging them to see Italy as a guardian of global heritage. Italy's focus on UNESCO sites promotes international partnerships and collaborative conservation projects, strengthening its relationships with countries committed to cultural preservation. Italy has developed solid diplomatic ties with governments and organizations that preserve the world's cultural and environmental legacy through heritage restoration programs and sustainable tourism practices (Colavitti & Usai, 2015; Debarbieux et al., 2023). This strategic emphasis on heritage-driven tourism diplomacy enhances Italy's reputation as a cultural leader and advocate for international cooperation. By highlighting its

UNESCO sites, Italy secures economic benefits from increased tourism. It reinforces its diplomatic influence, solidifying its identity as a custodian of world heritage and a hub for cultural diplomacy.

Morocco's Collaboration With UNWTO for Sustainable Tourism: Morocco has used tourism diplomacy to enhance its international profile, primarily through its partnership with the UNWTO to promote sustainable tourism. Morocco has established itself as a progressive nation dedicated to preserving its cultural heritage while fostering economic development by focusing on rural and cultural tourism that respects and celebrates local traditions (Kagermeier et al., 2019; Seyfi & Hall, 2020). This approach not only attracts global visitors but also strengthens Morocco's reputation as a leader in sustainable tourism, aligning with increasing international values regarding responsible travel. Through its collaboration with UNWTO, Morocco has launched initiatives that showcase its rich cultural and natural environments, from the lively souks and historic medinas of Marrakech and Fes to the beautiful Atlas Mountains and the Sahara Desert. By promoting eco-friendly tourism practices and supporting rural communities, Morocco aims to create authentic and sustainable travel experiences that benefit both local populations and the environment. This strategy resonates strongly with European tourists and environmental advocates who prioritize destinations committed to sustainability. Morocco's efforts in sustainable tourism have strengthened its diplomatic relationships with both European and African countries (Lamnadi, 2010; Seyfi & Hall, 2020). By showcasing its commitment to responsible tourism, Morocco not only attracts visitors but also reinforces its standing as a reliable partner in international sustainability efforts. This approach enhances Morocco's soft power, projecting an image of a nation that respects its heritage and environment while actively contributing to global conservation efforts (Kagermeier et al., 2019). Morocco's tourism diplomacy, grounded in sustainable and culturally sensitive practices, has advanced its economic goals and strengthened its diplomatic ties. Through these initiatives, Morocco builds goodwill and promotes a progressive, culturally rich identity on the global stage.

3.8 Enhancing National Image Through Tourism

Colombia's "Colombia: The Only Risk is Wanting to Stay" Campaign: Colombia's tourism diplomacy has effectively transformed its international image. Previously associated mainly with violence and instability, Colombia has rebranded itself as a vibrant, culturally rich, and welcoming destination. Central to this transformation was the campaign "Colombia: The Only Risk is Wanting to Stay," which highlighted Colombia's diverse attractions – from the colorful streets of Cartagena to the lush coffee regions and the Amazon rainforest. This campaign aimed to dispel outdated stereotypes, inviting the world to experience Colombia's beauty and warmth firsthand (Fletcher, 2011). The campaign's success in attracting tourists has created a ripple effect on Colombia's international relations. Colombia has actively changed perceptions by welcoming visitors to experience its culture, music, cuisine, and natural environments, fostering a more positive and nuanced understanding of the country (Guilland, 2012). This shift supports Colombia's diplomatic goals by positioning it as a stable and attractive partner for cultural exchange, investment, and collaboration. Tourism growth has bolstered Colombia's local economies and promoted peacebuilding efforts by providing alternative livelihoods in former conflict zones. Colombia's tourism rebranding aligns with its broader diplomatic objectives, helping to cultivate goodwill, trust, and international respect. By showcasing its progress and cultural richness, Colombia not only boosts its economy through tourism but also strengthens diplomatic ties and builds lasting partnerships. The transformation of Colombia's image into that of a safe, inviting, and dynamic nation illustrates the significant role that tourism diplomacy can play in enhancing a country's global standing.

South Africa's "Rainbow Nation" Campaign: After the end of apartheid, South Africa turned to tourism diplomacy to reshape its global image and promote itself as a "Rainbow Nation" that celebrates diversity and unity (Irlam, 2004; Turner, 2019). This rebranding effort, which included campaigns like "Meet South Africa," highlighted the country's natural wonders, cultural richness, and openness to visitors from all backgrounds. By positioning itself as a welcoming and inclusive destination, South Africa has not only boosted its tourism sector but also strengthened its diplomatic ties, particularly with Western nations. "Meet South Africa" emphasizes the country's remarkable environments, from the iconic Table Mountain and Kruger National Park to its stunning coastlines and vineyards, alongside its vibrant cities and diverse communities. These campaigns invite tourists to experience South Africa's unique blend of cultures, cuisine, art, and history, creating a platform for cultural exchange that promotes understanding and goodwill. The message of a united, multicultural South Africa has resonated well internationally, helping to shift perceptions from the nation's turbulent past to its modern identity as a harmonious and progressive society. This approach has had a significant impact on South Africa's diplomatic relationships. South Africa has enhanced its soft power by engaging Western nations through tourism and cultural experiences and building partnerships based on mutual respect and shared interests (Cornelissen, 2017; Muresan, 2019). Moreover, tourism has supported economic growth and community development across South Africa, further reinforcing stability and unity within the country. Through tourism diplomacy, South Africa has succeeded in showcasing its transformation. Using its diverse identity as a bridge to foster diplomatic goodwill and position itself as a model for inclusivity and resilience, this strategy has not only boosted tourism revenue but also strengthened South Africa's global image as a dynamic and inclusive nation (Muresan, 2019; Turner, 2019).

3.9 Tourism Diplomacy and Environmental Conservation

Costa Rica's Eco-tourism Initiatives: Costa Rica has effectively utilized tourism diplomacy to enhance its global reputation as an eco-tourism and environmental conservation leader (Vargas Madrigal, 2021). Known for its rich biodiversity,

Costa Rica capitalizes on its unique natural resources, positioning itself as a premier destination for eco-conscious travelers. The country's efforts to preserve its rainforests, protect wildlife, and promote sustainable tourism practices attract a global audience that values environmental responsibility. Costa Rica's tourism strategy has highlighted its national parks, wildlife reserves, and pristine beaches, drawing tourists seeking adventure and relaxation in an environmentally sustainable setting (Miller, 2016). By promoting eco-tourism, Costa Rica boosts its economy while reinforcing its commitment to preserving natural ecosystems for future generations. The country's environmental policies, such as ambitious goals to become carbon neutral, demonstrate its leadership in sustainable tourism, resonating with nations and organizations that prioritize environmental conservation. Costa Rica's commitment to sustainability has strengthened its diplomatic ties, particularly with environmentally focused nations. By aligning with global environmental standards, Costa Rica has established itself as a reliable partner in international climate change and conservation discussions. The country's proactive approach to eco-tourism and sustainability enhances its influence, fostering goodwill and diplomatic relationships with countries with similar environmental priorities. Costa Rica's tourism diplomacy, based on its biodiversity and dedication to sustainability, has not only attracted eco-tourists but also enhanced its global reputation as a leader in environmental preservation (Owens, 2006; Vargas Madrigal, 2021). This strategy has enabled Costa Rica to cultivate meaningful diplomatic relationships and reinforce its image as a progressive, environmentally responsible nation.

Norway's Visit Norway" Initiatives: Norway has effectively utilized tourism diplomacy to showcase its commitment to sustainability through initiatives like "Visit Norway," which emphasizes eco-friendly practices, particularly in its iconic fjord tourism (Sverdrup-Thygeson, 2017). By highlighting the stunning natural beauty of its fjords, mountains, and northern lights, Norway attracts tourists interested not only in adventure but also in responsible travel experiences. This emphasis on sustainable tourism helps preserve the country's natural environments for future generations while also supporting the local economy. The "Visit Norway" initiative promotes environmentally conscious tourism by encouraging low-impact travel, carbon offsetting, and sustainable accommodations (Edlom, 2019). This strategy aligns with Norway's broader environmental goals, such as reducing carbon emissions and preserving biodiversity. By focusing on these eco-friendly practices, Norway has established itself as a global leader in sustainable tourism, drawing an increasing number of tourists who prioritize environmental responsibility. Norway's commitment to sustainability in tourism strengthens its diplomatic relations with other environmentally focused nations. As global discussions about climate change and conservation intensify, Norway's tourism diplomacy enhances its reputation as a country that leads by example in environmental stewardship. This alignment with other eco-friendly countries, particularly in the Nordic region, solidifies Norway's position as a trusted partner in international efforts to promote sustainability and environmental conservation. Through its "Visit Norway" initiative, the country effectively uses tourism as a diplomatic tool to highlight its environmental achievements, attract like-minded travelers, and strengthen its relationships with nations that share similar values of sustainability and conservation (Leiren, 2000; Sverdrup-Thygeson, 2017).

3.10 Campaign Challenges in Tourism Diplomacy

United Arab Emirates's Tourism Diplomacy Campaigns: The United Arab Emirates (UAE) has become a global tourism hub by leveraging innovative projects and strategic initiatives to lead the tourism industry (King, 2016). Although it faces challenges in balancing rapid tourism development with sustainability, the UAE has made significant progress in overcoming these issues, mainly through events like Expo 2020 Dubai and its increasing involvement in space tourism. Expo 2020, hosted in Dubai, was a landmark event that showcased the UAE's modern infrastructure and cultural diversity while serving as a platform for international collaboration (Chadli, 2024; Issac, 2024). It attracted millions of visitors, fostering diplomatic relations by connecting nations through shared innovation and sustainability goals. The event highlighted the UAE's commitment to tackling global challenges such as climate change and sustainable development while also reflecting its unique cultural heritage and futuristic vision. In addition to Expo 2020, the UAE has taken bold steps in the emerging field of space tourism, partnering with private companies to explore the potential for leisure travel in space (Issac, 2024). This forward-thinking initiative highlights the UAE's ambition to be at the forefront of cutting-edge tourism experiences, attracting global investors and reinforcing its reputation as a hub for innovation and technological advancement. Through these initiatives, the UAE employs tourism diplomacy not only to enhance its international image but also to attract foreign investment, foster global partnerships, and promote its long-term sustainability goals.

Iceland's "Inspired by Iceland" Campaign: Iceland has seen rapid tourism growth in recent years. While this benefits its economy, it has put significant pressure on the natural environment and infrastructure. In response to these challenges, Iceland launched the "Inspired by Iceland" campaign, which promotes responsible tourism practices (Erlingsdóttir, 2021). This initiative is crucial to Iceland's tourism diplomacy, showcasing the country's unique environments and emphasizing the need to preserve these natural wonders for future generations. The "Inspired by Iceland" campaign encourages visitors to respect Iceland's fragile environment by promoting sustainable travel practices, including minimizing waste, reducing carbon footprints, and respecting wildlife and local communities (Ornston, 2024; Pálsdóttir, 2016). This approach highlights Iceland's proactive strategy to balance tourism growth with environmental preservation. By emphasizing responsible tourism, the campaign attracts eco-conscious travelers who share the country's sustainability and environmental stewardship values. Iceland's focus on responsible tourism fosters international partnerships with nations prioritizing environmental protection. This approach strengthens diplomatic relations, especially with countries sharing similar sustainability goals. It also positions Iceland as a leader in sustainable tourism, demonstrating its commitment to long-term growth without compromising natural resources. The "Inspired by Iceland" campaign has reflected the country's dedication to balancing tourism growth with environmental preservation (Erlingsdóttir, 2021; Ornston, 2024). Iceland has attracted eco-conscious tourists through this tourism diplomacy and enhanced its global reputation as a sustainable destination, fostering international collaboration.

4. Conclusions

Tourism diplomacy has become a crucial tool for nations worldwide to strengthen international relations, promote economic growth, and position themselves as global leaders in sustainability, cultural exchange, and innovation. Through strategic tourism initiatives, countries such as China, South Korea, Thailand, Turkey, Rwanda, Israel, Jordan, India, Australia, New Zealand, Greece, Italy, Morocco, Colombia, South Africa, Costa Rica, Norway, the United Arab Emirates, Iceland, and others have successfully used tourism to foster positive international perceptions, create economic opportunities, and address global challenges.

Tourism diplomacy is multifaceted, involving the promotion of tourism and the cultural, economic, and diplomatic efforts supporting it. A key theme from the cases of these countries is the critical connection between tourism and international relations. Nations recognize that tourism can transcend borders, act as a bridge between cultures, and create opportunities for cooperation. For instance, China's Belt and Road Initiative, which focuses on tourism to improve relationships with countries across Asia and Africa, exemplifies how tourism can be a tool for geopolitical influence and cultural exchange.

Similarly, South Korea's "Korean Wave" (Hallyu) has successfully transformed K-pop, K-dramas, and Korean cuisine into cultural exports, attracting millions of international visitors and deepening the country's diplomatic ties, especially in the Asia-Pacific region. South Korea has shown that tourism diplomacy can be closely linked with global soft power, utilizing its popular culture to influence perceptions and strengthen international relationships. Likewise, the UAE's strategic position in the global tourism market, primarily through events like Expo 2020 and its emphasis on space tourism, has demonstrated how innovative tourism initiatives can enhance a nation's diplomatic influence and attract global collaboration and investment.

Tourism diplomacy has played a crucial role in rebuilding national identity and changing international perceptions of countries like Rwanda. After the 1994 genocide, Rwanda rebranded itself through eco-tourism initiatives, such as gorilla trekking in Volcanoes National Park. This not only generated economic growth but also transformed its image into a peaceful, conservation-minded nation. Similarly, Morocco's dedication to sustainable tourism, in collaboration with the UNWTO, has spurred tourism and established the country as a regional leader in sustainability, strengthening diplomatic ties with Europe and Africa.

Tourism diplomacy is critical in promoting regional cooperation and economic interdependence in Southeast Asia. Thailand's collaboration with ASEAN countries to enhance tourism is particularly evident. Such initiatives strengthen regional diplomatic relations, leading to a more cohesive and economically integrated Southeast Asia. Thailand's focus on regional tourism cooperation highlights tourism's potential as a tool for economic development and diplomatic engagement.

Countries such as Greece and Italy have utilized their rich cultural heritage and UNESCO World Heritage sites to enhance their tourism diplomacy efforts. By participating in UNESCO initiatives, Italy has strengthened its diplomatic position by aligning with global cultural preservation efforts. Meanwhile, Greece's emphasis on attracting tourists to stabilize its economy during the economic crisis shows how tourism diplomacy can address domestic challenges. These examples highlight how cultural heritage and historical significance can be valuable assets in diplomatic relations, promoting cross-border collaborations in conservation, education, and cultural exchange.

In the context of sustainability, countries like Costa Rica and Norway have set global standards for eco-tourism. Costa Rica's commitment to biodiversity and environmental conservation has attracted eco-conscious tourists and strengthened its international reputation as a leader in sustainable tourism. Similarly, Norway's "Visit Norway" initiative, which focuses on eco-friendly practices in its fjord tourism, demonstrates how responsible tourism can align with national environmental goals while enhancing diplomatic ties with other environmentally focused nations. Both nations have utilized tourism diplomacy to promote sustainability, attract like-minded partners, and establish themselves as leaders in environmental conservation.

Meanwhile, countries like South Africa and Colombia have used tourism diplomacy as a tool for national rebranding. South Africa's postapartheid transformation into a "Rainbow Nation" has been supported by initiatives like "Meet South Africa," which highlight the country's diversity and natural beauty. Through tourism, South Africa aims to strengthen ties with Western nations while promoting its multicultural society and inclusive image. Similarly, Colombia's rebranding efforts, showcased in the campaign "Colombia: The Only Risk is Wanting to Stay," have successfully changed international perceptions of the country from one of violence to a vibrant cultural destination. These initiatives not only boost tourism but also align with broader diplomatic efforts to improve the national image and attract international support.

Iceland's proactive approach to addressing the environmental challenges posed by tourism growth emphasizes the need to balance tourism development with sustainability. The "Inspired by Iceland" campaign promotes responsible tourism, establishing Iceland as a leader in sustainable tourism practices and strengthening diplomatic relations with eco-conscious nations. This balance between growth and environmental preservation resonates with many countries, especially in regions where tourism is vital to the economy but also presents considerable environmental risks.

Tourism diplomacy is a powerful tool that countries use to promote their culture, values, and economic interests worldwide. Through cultural exchange, regional cooperation, environmental sustainability, and innovation, tourism diplomacy shapes international perceptions, fosters partnerships, and supports diplomatic goals. The countries analyzed in this report illustrate how tourism strengthens global relationships and addresses both domestic and international challenges. Tourism diplomacy will play a crucial role in promoting international cooperation, cultural understanding, and economic development as the world becomes more interconnected.

References

Arieli, T. (2012). Borders of peace in policy and practice: National and local perspectives of Israel-Jordan border management. *Geopolitics*, *17*(3), 658–680.

Bae, E. S., Chang, M., Park, E. S., & Kim, D. C. (2017). The effect of Hallyu on tourism in Korea. *Journal of Open Innovation: Technology, Market, and Complexity*, *3*(4), 1–12.

Beirman, D. (2018). Thailand's approach to destination resilience: An historical perspective of tourism resilience from 2002 to 2018. *Tourism Review International*, *22*(3–4), 277–292.

Byrne, A. (2013). A gentlemanly tour on the fringes of Europe: William Hartigan Barrington in Scandinavia and Russia, 1837. *Irish Economic and Social History*, *40*(1), 31–47.

Chadli, L. (2024). Expo 2020 Dubai's impact on the United Arab Emirates' brand: A quantitative analysis about American and European media companies. *Journalism*, *14*(1), 11–22.

Chitty, N. (2008). Australian public diplomacy. In N. Snow, N. Snow, & P. M. Taylor (Eds.), *Routledge handbook of public diplomacy* (pp. 334–342). Routledge.

Clarke, D., Bull, A. C., & Deganutti, M. (2020). Soft power and dark heritage: multiple potentialities. In O. Bennett (Ed.), *Cultural diplomacy and international cultural relations* (Vol. I, pp. 2–16). Routledge.

Colavitti, A. M., & Usai, A. (2015). Partnership building strategy in place branding as a tool to improve cultural heritage district's design. The experience of UNESCO's mining heritage district in Sardinia, Italy. *Journal of Cultural Heritage Management and Sustainable Development*, *5*(2), 151–175.

Cornelissen, S. (2017). National meaning-making in complex societies: Political legitimation and branding dynamics in post-apartheid South Africa. *Geopolitics*, *22*(3), 525–548.

Cropanzano, R., & Mitchell, M. S. (2005). Social exchange theory: An interdisciplinary review. *Journal of Management*, *31*(6), 874–900.

Debarbieux, B., Bortolotto, C., Munz, H., & Raziano, C. (2023). Sharing heritage? Politics and territoriality in UNESCO's heritage lists. *Territory, Politics, Governance*, *11*(3), 608–624.

Demir, M., & Dalgıç, A. (2022). Examining gastronomy festivals as the attractiveness factor for tourism destinations: The case of Turkey. *Journal of Convention & Event Tourism*, *23*, 412–434. https://doi.org/10.1080/15470148.2022.2089797

Demir, M., Demir, Ş. Ş., & Aktürk, O. (2023). The effects of distance education capabilities and competencies on learning outcomes during COVID-19 in higher education institutions. *Journal of Hospitality and Tourism Education*, 1–12.
Demir, M., Demir, Ş. Ş., Dalgıç, A., & Ergen, F. D. (2021). Impact of COVID-19 pandemic on the tourism industry: An evaluation from the hotel managers' perspective. *Journal of Tourism Theory and Research*, *7*(1), 44–57. https://doi.org/10.24288/jttr.857610
Demir, M., Günaydın, Y., & Demir, Ş. Ş. (2020). Koronavirüs (Covid-19) salgınının Türkiye'de turizm üzerindeki öncülleri, etkileri ve sonuçlarının değerlendirilmesi. *International Journal of Social Sciences and Education Research*, *6*(1), 80–107.
Di Giovine, M. A. (2008). *The heritage-scape: UNESCO, world heritage, and tourism*. Lexington Books.
Draper, S., & To, J. (2020). Driving New Zealand's economic relationship with Asia: The importance of growing connections, capacity and confidence. *Policy Quarterly*, *16*(4), 1–10.
Edlom, J. (2019). Sparking the Nordic music brand. In C. Cassinger, A. Lucarelli, & S. Gyimóthy (Eds.), *The Nordic wave in place branding* (pp. 39–53). Edward Elgar Publishing.
Erlingsdóttir, I. (2021). Trouble in paradise?: Icelandic gender-equality imaginaries, national rebranding and international reification. In E. Larsen, S. M. Moss, & I. Skjelsbaek (Eds.), *Gender equality and nation branding in the Nordic region* (pp. 90–112). Routledge.
Fletcher, R. (2011). "The only risk is wanting to stay": Mediating risk in Colombian tourism development. *Recreation and Society in Africa, Asia and Latin America*, *1*(2), 1–13.
Fullerton, J. A., & Kendrick, A. (2011). Australia tourism advertising: A test of the bleed-over effect among US travelers. *Place Branding and Public Diplomacy*, *7*, 244–256.
Fusté-Forné, F., & Michael, N. (2023). Limited tourism: Travel bubbles for a sustainable future. *Journal of Sustainable Tourism*, *31*(1), 73–90.
Gelbman, A., & Maoz, D. (2012). Island of peace or island of war: Tourist guiding. *Annals of Tourism Research*, *39*(1), 108–133.
Guilland, M. L. (2012). "Colombia, the only risk is wanting to stay". From national tourism promotions to travelling in the Sierra Nevada: Uses and refutations of risk. *Tourism Review*, *1*, 1–26.
Hazbun, W. (2012). Itineraries of peace through tourism: Excavating territorial attachments across the Arab/Israeli frontier. *Peace and Change*, *37*(1), 3–36.
Irlam, S. (2004). Unraveling the rainbow: The remission of nation in post-apartheid literature. *South Atlantic Quarterly*, *103*(4), 695–718.
Isar, Y. R. (2020). Cultural diplomacy: India does it differently. *Cultural Diplomacy and International Cultural Relations*, *I*, 47–58.
Issac, A. L. (2024). Sustainability at the crossroads of global showcases: Balancing economic progress and environmental conservation in Expo 2020 Dubai. In D. Sharma, H. Abdullah, & P. Singh (Eds.), *Sustainable tourism, Part B: A comprehensive multidimensional perspective* (pp. 1–18). Emerald Publishing Limited.
Kagermeier, A., Amzil, L., & Elfasskaoui, B. (2019). The transition of governance approaches to rural tourism in Southern Morocco. *European Journal of Tourism Research*, *23*, 40–62.

Kim, H. S. (2018). When public diplomacy faces trade barriers and diplomatic frictions: The case of the Korean Wave. *Place Branding and Public Diplomacy*, *14*(4), 234–244.

King, J. M. (2016). Dubai wins: A content analysis of global media coverage of the 2020 world exposition bidding process using nation branding theory. *International Journal of Business and Administrative Studies*, *2*(6), 202.

Kokkinidis, T. (2022). *Greece's new tourism campaign based on visitor's true story by Tasos Kokkinidis*. https://greekreporter.com/2022/05/31/greece-tourism-campaign-visitor-true-story/. Accessed 11 10, 2024.

Krinis, N. (2022). *Greece invites tourists to live "A life-changing experience"*. https://news.gtp.gr/2023/05/11/greece-invites-tourists-to-live-a-life-changing-experience/. Accessed 11 10, 2024.

Lamnadi, Y. (2010). The evaluation of tourism marketing model within Moroccan public policy management. *Athens Journal of Tourism*, *6*(1), 15–38.

Leiren, T. I. (2000). Pilgrimage and propaganda: The American newspapermen's tour of Norway in 1927. *Norwegian American Studies*, *35*(1), 197–216.

Li, T., Shi, H., Yang, Z., & Ren, Y. (2020). Does the belt and road initiative boost tourism economy? *Asia Pacific Journal of Tourism Research*, *25*(3), 311–322.

Marijnen, E. (2022). Eco-war tourism: Affective geographies, colonial durabilities and the militarization of conservation. *Security Dialogue*, *53*(6), 550–566.

Maydell, E. (2020). The visual representation of indigenous cultural identities in Australian and New Zealand tourism campaigns. *Visual Communication Quarterly*, *27*(4), 183–195.

Merkelsen, H., & Rasmussen, R. K. (2016). Nation branding as an emerging field–An institutionalist perspective. *Place Branding and Public Diplomacy*, *12*, 99–109.

Miller, A. P. (2016). *Sustainable ecotourism in Central America: Comparative advantage in a globalized world*. Lexington Books.

Minardi, A., Afriantari, R., & Hasanah, N. U. (2021). Indonesian tourism diplomacy to India. *Indonesian Tourism Diplomacy to India*, *1*(1), 1–13.

Muresan, A. (2019). South Africa's image in Africa and the impact on its BRICS-Africa relationships. *Africa Insight*, *48*(4), 56–72.

Nair, B. B. (2021). Gastrodiplomacy in tourism: 'Capturing hearts and minds through stomachs'. *International Journal of Hospitality & Tourism Systems*, *14*(1), 30–40.

Nakamura, T. (2013). Japan's new public diplomacy: Coolness in foreign policy objectives. *Media and Society*, *5*(1), 1–23.

Negassa, S. B. (2024). Tourism diplomacy: Fostering economic development through global connectivity. In A. B. Basnur (Ed.), *Tourism: For global connectivity and economic development* (pp. 68–75). Paramedia Komunikatama.

Nye, J. S. (1990). Soft power. *Foreign Policy*, (80), 153–171.

Ornston, D. (2024). Success story or tall tale? Discursive cooperation and economic restructuring in Iceland. *Review of International Political Economy*, 1–23.

Owens, D. M. (2006). *Costa rican sovereignty and development in the shadow of the central American-dominican republic free trade agreement (CAFTA): Strategic adoptions of technology in a globalizing economy*. Drexel University.

Pálsdóttir, I. H. (2016). Promoting Iceland: The shift from nature to people's power. *Place Branding and Public Diplomacy*, *12*, 210–217.

Putri, M. Y., & Purnawarman, A. (2024). ASEAN tourism forum efforts to increase tourist visits in Southeast Asia. *Research Horizon*, *4*(3), 137–148.

Quer, D., & Andreu, R. (2023). International strategies of Chinese tourism MNEs: The impact of the belt and road initiative and state ownership. *International Journal of Emerging Markets*, *18*(9), 2934–2953.

Saha, R., & Raghuvanshi, L. (2025). Intercultural communication in tourism during COVID-19 pandemic: Analyzing audience appeal of Indian tourism campaign through social media. In S. S. Ghosh, D. Roy, T. Putatunda, & N. Ray (Eds.), *Language and cross-cultural communication in travel and tourism* (pp. 49–67). Apple Academic Press.

Seyfi, S., & Hall, C. M. (2020). *Cultural and heritage tourism in the Middle East and North Africa: Complexities, management and practices*. Routledge.

Soyez, P. (2019). Economic diplomacy, an innovative force of the French–Australian relationship. In P. Soyez (Ed.), *Australia and France's mutual empowerment: Middle powers' strategies for pacific and global challenges* (pp. 55–100). Palgrave Macmillan.

Stewart, S., Warburton, F., & Smith, J. D. (2016). *Cambridge international AS and A level travel and tourism coursebook*. Cambridge University Press.

Sverdrup-Thygeson, B. (2017). The Norway-China relationship: For better, for worse, for richer, for poorer. In B. Sverdrup-Thygeson, W. Y. Lindgren, & M. Lanteigne (Eds.), *China and Nordic diplomacy* (pp. 77–100). Routledge.

Talozi, S. A., & Westheimer, N. (2020). Water diplomacy in the absence of a river basin organization: A case study in Jordan, Israel, and Palestine. In A. Kittikhoun & S. Schmeier (Eds.), *River basin organizations in water diplomacy* (pp. 179–200). Routledge.

Tamaki, T. (2019). Repackaging national identity: Cool Japan and the resilience of Japanese identity narratives. *Asian Journal of Political Science*, *27*(1), 108–126.

Timothy, D. J. (2022). Tourism mobility and transport: Issues and developments in Pacific Island states. In M. L. Stephenson (Ed.), *Routledge handbook on tourism and small Island States in the Pacific* (pp. 56–74). Routledge.

Turner, I. (2019). Axing the rainbow: Does fallism reconfigure post-apartheid nationhood in South Africa? *Modern Africa: Politics, History and Society*, *7*(1), 81–110.

Vargas Madrigal, J. (2021). The belt and road initiative enhances cooperation opportunities for costa rica and brings development strategies for SMEs. In Y. Li & A. C. Zottele (Eds.), *A new blue ocean: Prospects for Latin American SMEs in the belt and road initiative, A New Blue Ocean* (pp. 159–185). Palgrave Macmillan.

Yeoman, I., Kim, S., & Park, E. (2019). Emerging research themes of food tourism in Asia: A cognitive mapping perspective. *Food tourism in Asia*, 187–216.

Zhu, J., Siriphon, A., Airey, D., & Mei-Lan, J. (2022). Chinese tourism diplomacy: A Chinese–Style modernity review. *Anatolia*, *33*(4), 550–563.

Printed and bound by CPI Group (UK) Ltd, Croydon, CR0 4YY

15/09/2026

14962486-0001